# Canadian Culture IN A Globalized World

## The impact of trade deals on Canada's cultural life

D1445302

# Canadian Culture IN A Globalized World

## The impact of trade deals on Canada's cultural life

GARRY NEIL

James Lorimer & Company Ltd., Publishers
Toronto

James Lorimer & Company Ltd., Publishers acknowledges funding support from the Ontario Arts Council (OAC), an agency of the Government of Ontario. We acknowledge the support of the Canada Council for the Arts, which last year invested $153 million to bring the arts to Canadians throughout the country. This project has been made possible in part by the Government of Canada and with the support of Ontario Creates.

  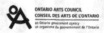 

Cover design: Tyler Cleroux
Cover images: iStock, Shutterstock

Library and Archives Canada Cataloguing in Publication

Title: Canadian culture in a globalized world : the impact of trade deals on Canada's cultural life / Garry Neil.
Names: Neil, Garry, author.
Description: Includes bibliographical references and index.
Identifiers: Canadiana (print) 20190049669 | Canadiana (ebook) 20190049685 | ISBN 9781459413313 (softcover) | ISBN 9781459413320 (EPUB)
Subjects: LCSH: Popular culture—Canada. | LCSH: Cultural industries—Canada. | LCSH: Globalization Canada. | LCSH: Canada—Commerce. | LCSH: Canada—Cultural policy.
Classification: LCC FC95.5 .N45 2019 | DDC 306.0971—dc23

James Lorimer & Company Ltd., Publishers
117 Peter Street, Suite 304
Toronto, ON, Canada
M5V 0M3
www.lorimer.ca

Printed and bound in Canada.

# Contents

# Contents

# Preface

This book weaves together three parts of my career.

For more than forty years, I have been involved in cultural poli-cymaking, working in Canada and globally for artists' and industry associations, publishers, broadcasters and producers and governments. Cultural policies are the essential foundation for the development of Canadian storytellers, musicians, visual artists, filmmakers, other art-ists and for those who produce and distribute their works. In the last half of this time, my work has often focused on the policies needed to ensure Canadian voices and cultural content are available and acces-sible in the digital era.

As head of ACTRA in the late 1980s, I helped raise awareness of how the proposed free trade agreement with the United States, and then NAFTA, threatened our ability to implement cultural policies. As a consultant, I helped ACTRA and others respond to our most recent trade agreements, and participated in consultations with Canadian negotiators.

As Executive Director of an international NGO, I was at the forefront of the campaign that led to the adoption in 2005 of a ground-breaking UNESCO Convention on cultural diversity.

In this book, I explore how these issues intersect in a way that will continue to profoundly affect the cultural life of Canadians.

The population of Canada is relatively small and widely dispersed across the second largest landmass in the world. Most Canadians share a language and cultural references with our southern neighbour. U.S. cultural producers have enjoyed a tremendous competitive advantage over their Canadian counterparts, since their primary market is more than ten times larger. Yet, like the Niagara River, this music, literature, radio, television and cinema flows freely north across our border.

Since the earliest days, Canadians have sought to ensure we can find our stories, music, dance and art among this free-flowing cascade of content. To ensure we can see our lives, and those of our fellow inhabitants from coast-to-coast-to-coast, reflected in the media of the day. From the 1849 preferential postal rate for publishers in the Province of Canada, through the 1932 launch of the Canadian Radio Broadcasting Corporation (now CBC), to the 2016 federal budget commitment to double the funding of the Canada Council for the Arts, Canada has developed the most comprehensive cultural policies in the world. Direct and indirect funding, content quotas, public cultural institutions, tax and copyright measures and a wide array of other regulations and supportive policies have been implemented by governments of every political stripe.

In the past 20 years, digital technologies have revolutionized how cultural expressions are produced and distributed. In the digital era, the consensus that existed around our cultural policymaking is wavering. Some argue we should not, others argue we cannot, regulate these technologies. I am among those who believe we can and must regulate to ensure the continuing availability and accessibility of Canadian content, irrespective of the technologies.

Canada's cultural policies have increasingly come into conflict with trade agreements, since *prima facie* many of these policies violate the "principles" of "free" trade. The pressure has grown as the world has moved from agreements that cover trade in goods, to those that, since the mid-1980s, cover trade in services. While this book you are reading is a "good," the writing, editing, design and illustrations it contains are "services." This pressure grows as the work of the artist is increasingly digital and thus strictly a service in trade terms.

In 1987, 1988 and again in 2018, successive federal ministers of culture, both Conservative and Liberal, proclaimed that Canada successfully negotiated a cultural exemption in a trade agreement. The reality is far more complicated than those simple proclamations suggest.

In the Trade Agreement, we agreed explicitly to implement several cultural policies and informally to forego others. More importantly, we erected a box around our cultural industries and our policies. While that box was pretty large and there were few sectors or policies outside it, with each successive trade agreement the box has shrunk. And more policies have been altered or shelved. NAFTA 2019 is stronger than its predecessor, but even it requires Canada to amend various cultural policies. More importantly, were it not for the last second deal we made with our remaining partners after the U.S. withdrew from the Trans-Pacific Partnership Agreement, the box would have been shattered.

For more than 30 years, we have been fighting a rearguard action to protect Canadian culture in the globalized world; to preserve our cultural policies. Particularly in the dynamic digital era, this is no longer an effective strategy. It is time for a new and innovative approach. The UNESCO *Convention on the Protection and Promotion of the Diversity of Cultural Expressions* can be the foundation of that new approach.

The UNESCO Convention was negotiated and implemented remarkably quickly. The original concept emerged in Canada in 1999 and the Convention was negotiated, approved and came into effect only eight years later, because a powerful alliance of civil society groups and key governments worked together in response to the growing threats of cultural homogenization. The Convention did not succeed in carving out cultural expressions from the trade agreements as its leading proponents, including me, had hoped. But, since it does confirm the right of Member States to implement policies and measures which support their domestic artists and cultural industries, and commits them to work together to promote more balanced exchanges between cultures, it can be a powerful tool. By looking at Canada's relationship with China, we will see what this could mean in practice.

If we have the courage to respond to the digital shift with appropriate cultural policies and measures, and to take a bold new approach in trade negotiations, our artists and cultural producers will continue to flourish. If we fail to confront these challenges, our cultural life will stagnate in the coming decades.

Garry Neil
Toronto, January 2019

# Chapter 1
# Roots of Canadian Cultural Policies

Before discussing cultural policy, we need to define some basic terms. Definitions of "culture" can be controversial, but the United Nations Educational, Scientific and Cultural Organization (UNESCO) defines it this way: "that complex whole which includes knowledge, beliefs, arts, morals, laws, customs, and any other capabilities and habits acquired by [a person] as a member of society."[1] Canadian literary scholar Northrop Frye wrote that there are three aspects to a society's culture:

**Lifestyle** — the way that a society lives, organizes itself, eats, dresses and carries on its daily social rituals

**A shared sense of historical experiences** — a society's knowledge and memory, real and mythologized, passed along from generation to generation through a common language

**Intellectual output** — including a society's visual arts, crafts, literature, music, dance, architecture, scholarship, films and television.

While these three aspects of culture are intertwined, our concern in this work is Frye's third aspect, a society's intellectual output. As UNESCO's name implies, the intellectual output can be divided into education, science and culture. Culture then can be defined as a society's creative output, at the heart of which is the artist. UNESCO defines the artist as any person who creates or gives creative expression to, or recreates, works of art, in any discipline, including visual arts and sculpture, music, dance, performing arts, literature, film, television and all other interdisciplinary and multimedia forms that can combine together text, music, movement, images and/or sounds.

The work of an artist may be individual and ephemeral, such as a musician who writes and performs his or her own works live. But more often artistic works are collaborative efforts fixed in a material form. Books offer the simplest example of the artistic process — the author writes the work alone, and then the editor, illustrator and designer each add value to the project before it is published as a book. That book will then be distributed and made available to audiences in a variety of ways.

More complicated artistic works will involve a vast array of specialists who will all contribute their own artistic vision. Let us consider a feature film. The script may be based on a novel, but in the process of adaptation, it may be written and rewritten by several scriptwriters. The director will interpret the script and bring it to life using performers, sets and locations, lighting, wardrobe and special effects. Each actor brings his or her unique perspective and skills to the role. The director of photography will put a personal stamp on the look and feel of the movie. The composer and musicians who lay down the soundtrack, or the pre-recorded musical works, provide the mood. Even after all the scenes are finished, the computer-generated imagery (CGI) specialists, the editor and sound mixer will all play important roles in determining the final product audiences will see and hear. Each of the individuals in this collaborative process is an artist, as each one is "creating or giving creative expression to, a work of art." There are also many others beyond these creative people involved in bringing the movie to our screens.

There are all the other technicians, labourers and hair and makeup specialists. The producer is the one who finances the film, organizes the distribution and hires the key players; the distributors promote and sell it in many different markets, nationally and globally; the cinemas and broadcasters make it available to audiences. Today, Internet service providers (ISPs) must be considered yet another key player in this mix because they can make these works available to audiences around the world.

We should also consider the cycle of artistic activity. This begins with artists' education, with most attending specialized institutions to learn their respective crafts or receiving specialized training or mentorship. It then moves to the creation of the artistic work, its production in a material form, and its distribution and exhibition to the public. The cycle ends with the artistic work's preservation.

The term *cultural industries* refers to all the individuals and firms involved in the entire process of creating, producing, distributing, exhibiting and preserving the creative expression. This process may take place on a for-profit or not-for-profit basis, or as a public service.

Cultural policies then, in the words of UNESCO's 2005 *Convention on the Protection and Promotion of the Diversity of Cultural Expressions*, constitute:

> those policies and measures relating to culture, whether at the
> local, national, regional or international level that are either
> focused on culture as such or are designed to have a direct
> effect on cultural expressions of individuals, groups or societies,
> including on the creation, production, dissemination, distribution
> of and access to cultural activities, goods and services.[2]

## Public Support for Arts and Culture

Stretching back centuries, there has been a long history of patronage and sponsorship of the arts. It existed not just in Renaissance Europe, but in ancient China and Japan and in virtually every human society, on every continent. The patrons were sometimes rulers, nobles, wealthy merchants or the church. They may also simply have been family, friends or neighbours.

With new discoveries of ancient art, we continue to refine our understanding of how far back art history extends. For many years, the stunning animal cave paintings in the Chauvet Cave in France and the paintings in El Castillo in Spain were believed to be the oldest examples of representational art made by *Homo sapiens*, dating to roughly 32,000 years ago. However, examples found in 2014 in Sulawesi, Indonesia have been dated to 35,400 years ago.[3] In November 2018, scientists reported the discovery of the oldest known figurative art painting, estimated to be between 40,000 and 52,000 years old. It was an unknown animal painted in a cave on the island of Borneo. Recently uncovered wall paintings that are 64,800 years old have been found in three caves in Spain. Since this is generally considered to be before the arrival of *Homo sapiens* from Africa, these paintings have been linked to Neanderthals who populated Europe at that time. "If [the researchers'] results hold," reported *National Geographic* in February 2018, "the finds imply that the smarts underpinning symbolic art may date back to the common ancestor of Homo sapiens and Neanderthals, some 500,000 years ago."[4] It is fascinating to contemplate the work of these very earliest artists and to see their interpretation of the world they knew and inhabited. We must also recognize that while these artists were toiling away in dark and damp caves to create these paintings, other members of their societies were busy hunting and gathering, cooking meals or minding children. They represent the earliest examples of art patronage.

Before Johannes Gutenberg developed movable type in 1439, all art was either ephemeral or available in only a single copy, like the cave paintings. Music and stories were passed along orally, or were available in one handwritten copy that was made by someone with what was, at the time, a very special skill. The paintings of Jan van Eyck and the sculptures of Donatello stand as individual works of art. With the development of the printing press, some works of art could now be copied and made available to more people. While the history of publishing can be traced to 1439, it took another 400 years before photography was invented. The pace of technological change accelerated, and by the end of the nineteenth century, we also had the earliest beginnings of sound recording and films.

The works of the early painters were bought and sold, and audiences paid money to see and hear music, dance and stories, for example in the English Renaissance theatres in the beginning of the 1560s. But commercialization of artistic expressions did not really begin until the industrial age. As artistic media developed, the nature of public support for the arts also developed and changed, from the simple patronage model to the complex system of cultural policies that continue today, in Canada and around the world.

## Canada's Cultural Predicament

Since Canada's very foundation, public policies have been put in place to support our own artists and cultural producers. In large measure this is because other cultural producers have enjoyed a competitive advantage over Canadian producers. For some, the advantage arises because they have a substantially larger domestic market; others are protected by language and still others are protected by physical distance.

In 1849, Canada was a work in progress. Following the 1837–38 rebellions in both Lower Canada (Quebec) and Upper Canada (Ontario), the British Parliament passed the *Act of Union*, creating the Province of Canada in February 1841. While efforts were underway to establish responsible government, political turmoil continued. In early 1849, a large mob of British loyalists stormed the parliament building in Montreal and burned it to the ground in response to an act providing amnesty to the rebels and financial compensation for those whose property had been damaged in the fighting.

At some time during these tumultuous events in the early months of 1849, the Province of Canada's parliament passed a law establishing the territory's postal rates. That legislation included a special lower rate for mailing newspapers, periodicals and journals — publications that offered news, information and entertainment for residents. This constituted Canada's first cultural policy; the preferential postal rate has continued in one form or another for 170 years.

At the time, the population of the Province of Canada was roughly 1.5 million, stretched out over an enormous geographical area, from the Gulf of St. Lawrence to Sandwich (now Windsor), and north to isolated communities. There may have been another one million people in the other provinces and regions that now make up Canada. At the same time, the population of the United States was more than twenty-three million. Since the unit cost of producing newspapers, periodicals and journals was greater for a Canadian publisher producing for a market less than 10 per cent the size of our neighbour (and competitor), and the population's low density made distribution more expensive, publishers needed support to help level the playing field.

This highlights what I call Canada's cultural predicament. In 2019, Canada is a nation of thirty-seven million people. We are spread over the second largest land mass in the world, and while most natural geographic flows run north-south, Canada's orientation is east-west. Thus a relatively open 8,900-kilometre-long border is all that separates us from the world's largest producer of cultural materials, and up to 30 million of us share a language and idiom with that southern neighbour, whose population is 326 million. We have always enjoyed virtually unrestricted and immediate access to U.S. books, magazines, music, radio, television, films and other cultural goods and services, which U.S. producers are creating for a primary market that is more than ten times larger than Anglophone Canada.

The film industry offers one clear example of how this challenge plays out. Despite exponential growth in China's theatrical feature film market in the past decade, and the shift to electronic on-demand distribution, which is most pronounced in the United States, total receipts in the U.S. domestic market in 2017 were $11.1 billion USD, according to statistics compiled by the Motion Picture Association of America.

China was next at $7.9 billion USD, and the next ten nations in total had receipts in 2017 of $13.2 billion USD.[5] Until 2003, with the exception of one year, the U.S. domestic market was greater than all foreign markets combined.[6] While we will return to this later, it is important to note that Canada is considered to be part of the U.S. domestic market in this calculation of theatrical box office receipts, as our film industry has been fully integrated into the U.S. system since the early twentieth century. Canada's theatrical box office revenues in 2016 were only $993 million, down from a high of $1,094 million in 2012. Our market also has a significant French-language component. Thus, anyone producing a Canadian English-language feature film is chasing a primary market worth only $874 million.[7]

In part as a consequence of this market imbalance, the budget for the average English-language feature film produced in Canada in 2016–17 was $3.2 million. The average budget for a Hollywood feature film was in the $70–90 million USD range, with the blockbusters coming in at $150 million USD or more. Canadian director James Cameron's *Avatar* was produced in 2009 for $237 million USD, while the entire Canadian box office that year was $800 million.

This imbalance primarily manifests as a concern for those producing material for the English-language market. Quebec has a distinct language and culture. Its domestic and foreign cultural reference points are generally not the same as those of the rest of Canada. It does not share a language and idiom with our southern neighbour. For example, the early television series about working-class families portrayed in the *Beachcombers* and *Les Plouffe* were worlds apart. While Canada's French-language cultural producers share many concerns with their Anglophone colleagues, and they also significantly have to contend with erosion of the language protection that has been critical to their development, they have historically not faced the same degree of competitive disadvantage. Their primary competitors are in France, Belgium, Switzerland, Francophone Africa and other French-speaking countries, all of whose domestic markets are far smaller than the United States. In addition, for much of the last century, Canada's physical distance from Francophone competitors played a significant role. For example, the cost of shipping books from Europe to Canada has always been significant, thus creating an advantage for French publishers in Canada relative to their foreign counterparts. Put simply, with respect to cultural industries in Canada, the "two solitudes" prevail.

While digital technologies and globalization are breaking down these natural competitive advantages around the world, cultural industries in other countries have grown and developed based on these historical advantages.

## A Brief Survey of Canada's Cultural Policies

In 1917, Ontario established the first state film agency in the world, the Ontario Motion Picture Bureau. The following year the federal government launched the Canadian Government Motion Picture Bureau to promote Canadian agriculture and industry, attract tourists and encourage immigration through films. It produced a series of short documentary-style films that it distributed theatrically. By 1920, the bureau operated the largest studio in Canada and distributed its movies in many countries. In May 1939, the government launched the National Film Board (NFB) with the broader mandate of creating and distributing films of all kinds that would tell Canadians about each other and tell the world about Canada. The NFB absorbed the Bureau in 1941.

Radio first came to Canada in 1919 when Montreal's Marconi Company launched an experimental station, which became CFCF in 1922. CFCF was on the air for ninety years. Even as radio was being rolled out however, concerns were being expressed about how Canada's radio waves were already being dominated by U.S. stations. In 1929, the government appointed the *Royal Commission on Radio Broadcasting* (the Aird Commission), which recommended creating a national public broadcasting system. Aird also recommended that provinces have the authority to broadcast within their own borders. As this recommendation was being promoted by the Conservative government of the day,

Prime Minister R.B. Bennett famously said:

> *This country must be assured of complete Canadian control of broadcasting from Canadian sources. Without such control, broadcasting can never be the agency by which national consciousness may be fostered and sustained and national unity still further strengthened.*[8]

The Canadian Radio Broadcasting Commission was launched under the Conservative government in 1932, not only as Canada's public service broadcaster, but also as the broadcasting regulatory and licensing authority. It became the Canadian Broadcasting Corporation (CBC) four years later.

The postal subsidy, the Canadian Government Motion Picture Bureau and the Canadian Radio Broadcasting Commission were each implemented to address a specific challenge or opportunity at a moment in time. Canadian cultural policymaking really began in earnest, however, after World War II.

As Canada emerged from the war, serious concerns emerged about Canada's trade imbalance with the United States and the anemic state of Canadian arts and culture. There were few Canadian books, our music sector was moribund — often just informal performances in schools and churches — and our cinemas showed Hollywood movies. In addition, Canada's visual arts scene was diminished from earlier years. Several important developments occurred in the next few years to address the situation.

First, politicians turned their attention to the film business. By 1947, two foreign-owned chains — Famous Players and Odeon — controlled two-thirds of the Canadian cinema market. The Hollywood studios had adopted a vertically integrated model of production, distribution and exhibition in the 1920s. Canadian distribution rights were indivisible from U.S. rights for any movie made or distributed by the major studios. Through this model, the studios controlled virtually all theatrical revenues.

A nascent Canadian film industry that had existed in the early part of the century had all but disappeared by the early 1930s. In 1946–47, the federal government began to discuss ways to promote the Canadian industry. Specifically, it considered introducing cinema screen quotas or applying tariffs to capture some of the box office revenues to support Canadian films. *The Canadian Encyclopedia* tells us what happened:

> *Instead, the president of the Motion Picture Association of America (MPAA), Eric Johnston, intervened and proposed what became known as the Canadian Cooperation Project, which was approved by the Liberal government of Louis St-Laurent in 1948. The Hollywood film lobby agreed to shoot some of their films on location in Canada, include favourable references to Canada in Hollywood movies in order to promote tourism, and encourage the distribution and exhibition of NFB films in the U.S., all in exchange for the uninterrupted flow of dollars out of Canada . . . The nationalistic lobby . . . was successfully defeated. Famous Players' profits were not restricted, the idea of an exhibition quota for Canadian-produced films was dropped and a multi-million-dollar film studio under development in Vancouver was shuttered.*[9]

It is important to note that the distribution of NFB films in the United States did not increase and U.S. tourism in Canada actually declined. As the balance of payments issue subsided, the Canadian Cooperation Project was quietly shelved in 1958. Famous Players appointed Prime Minister St-Laurent to its Board of Directors shortly after he left office.

More positively, in 1949, the government appointed the Royal Commission on National Development in the Arts, Letters and Sciences. Like the Aird Commission before it, one of the principal preoccupations of the Massey-Lévesque Commission was the pervasive influence of U.S. culture in every artistic sector. After two years of research, hearings across the country and presentations from thousands of Canadians, the Commission released its report in June 1951.

The report argued forcefully in favour of state support for the arts on the grounds that

> *it is in the national interest to give encouragement to institutions which express national feeling, promote common understanding and add to the variety and richness of Canadian life, rural as well as urban.*

The report recommended creating new institutions and providing direct funding for artists and cultural producers, stating, "Good will alone can do little for a starving plant; if the cultural life of Canada is anaemic, it must be nourished, and this will cost money. This is a task for shared effort in all fields of government, federal, provincial and local."[10]

Since that landmark report was tabled in 1951, successive Canadian governments of all political stripes, at every level, have embraced that premise. Indeed, Canada has developed among the most comprehensive cultural policies in the world.

From the beginning, the objective of our cultural policymaking has been to support Canadian artists and cultural producers to tell our stories and bring our perspectives to audiences. In pursuit of this objective, the policies also respect certain key principles:

**Freedom of expression** — Canadians live in a free and democratic society where freedom of artistic expression is viewed as both necessary and desirable.

**Freedom of choice** — Canadians can choose from a broad range of domestic and foreign cultural goods and services. Canada has always been one of the most open markets in the world for cultural works from abroad.

**Pride of place for Canadian stories** — The government uses policy tools to maintain a place for Canadian cultural products in the Canadian market and to give Canadians ready access to their culture.

**Cultural diversity** — Canada is a diverse, multiracial and multicultural nation, and its artistic expressions need to reflect that rich diversity. Various programs and measures support the two linguistic markets, First Nations and the country's many regional and cultural differences.

To explore how Canada's cultural policies intersect with trade and investment agreements, it is useful to group them into three different categories:

## 1. Grants and funding support

The Massey Commission report led directly to the creation of the Canada Council for the Arts in 1957, as Canada's primary arts funding body. Because of concerns about propaganda from totalitarian regimes during World War II, it was established as an arm's-length agency. Over the years, every province and many municipalities have established funding programs, many modelled on the Canada Council. Collectively, these agencies provide hundreds of millions of dollars annually to artists, arts organizations and other cultural producers. Some of these programs are particularly important for young and emerging artists and for artists from marginalized, diverse and racialized communities.

Over the past sixty years, all levels of government have also developed other programs to support artists, communities and cultural producers. The Department of Canadian Heritage currently lists sixteen funding programs as varied as the Arts Training Program, Book Fund, Periodicals Fund and the Travelling Exhibitions Indemnification Program, to the Building Communities through Arts and Heritage program. Both the National Film Board and Telefilm Canada host a variety of programs to support filmmakers.

Some of the most important current programs, particularly in film and television, provide indirect funding support through a tax credit system. Cultural producers can receive a tax credit based on some or all of their expenditures made to produce a movie, television program or book. The credit is applied when filing their tax returns after completion of the production. This method of supporting film and television production has become popular in many countries, including many states in the United States, in part because it rewards what is considered to be socially beneficial conduct by a private company, and unlike a grant, is given only after production is fully completed and the work is being circulated.

## 2. Structural measures

These are government legislative mechanisms and regulatory agency policies that provide an advantage or protection for Canadian artists or producers.

Probably the single most important Canadian cultural policy is the broadcasting Canadian content quotas (Cancon) that obligate broadcasters to devote a certain percentage of their schedule to Canadian music and programs.

The first television quotas were introduced in 1958 when a new *Broadcasting Act* was adopted. The new *Act* transferred the broadcasting regulatory role of the CBC to a new Board of Broadcast Governors, which established core requirements. After the Fowler Committee on Broadcasting reported in 1965 that Canada needed a stronger broadcasting authority to ensure Canadian programs could be seen on our television screens, the Canadian Radio-television Commission (CRTC) was established in 1968. It immediately implemented minimum Canadian content requirements on all television broadcasters.

The textbook success for content requirements is best demonstrated by the Canadian music industry. Nicholas Jennings wrote in *Before the Gold Rush* about the formative years of Canadian rock, pop and folk music, from the 1960s through the early 1970s. While musicians from Leonard Cohen, Joni Mitchell, Gordon Lightfoot and Buffy Sainte-Marie to Neil Young were developing creatively, their works were ignored by Canadian radio and they were little known beyond their bohemian community. That changed radically in 1971 when the CRTC implemented a Canadian content rule for radio broadcasters, despite their vociferous protests. Creative success rapidly became market success, and the Canadian music industry has never looked back. Our musicians now enjoy unprecedented success globally and often dominate charts, a positive legacy of the Cancon rules.

The success of content rules is also highlighted by our failure to develop a film industry. Financial subsidies, in one form or another, have been available to film producers and television producers for more than a half-century. These producers use the same infrastructure and the same talent pool. Canadians in large numbers watch and enjoy Canadian television programs, some of these programs are sold into the U.S. market, and we are witnessing impressive foreign sales overall. Nevertheless, the market share in Canada for our own English-language movies struggles to reach 2 per cent. The difference in marketplace success between these fields relates directly to the fact that while Canadian content quotas for television have existed for fifty years, there are none for our cinemas.

As we shall see later, despite the changes that have resulted from the CRTC's "Let's Talk TV" process, the Commission has had and continues to maintain a number of robust structural measures that have been essential for our successes in television.[11] Various rules for cable and satellite services have given priority carriage and placement to Canadian channels. Our highly successful media companies, which have grown under the protection of these and other preferential measures, are required to produce and broadcast Cancon, or to make a reasonable financial contribution to Canadian content production, typically 5 per cent of their gross revenues from relevant activities. The simultaneous substitution rule, which requires Canadian cable companies to substitute a Canadian broadcaster's signal for a U.S. signal when each is broadcasting the same program at the same time, protects the integrity of the Canadian market for a broadcaster that has acquired rights to the U.S. program, ensuring that every Canadian watching the U.S. program will see the commercials sold by the Canadian broadcaster. Some of these additional revenues earned by the broadcaster are returned to Cancon production.

Other important structural measures include:

Limits or prohibition of foreign ownership of Canadian cultural industry firms in broadcasting, film distribution and book publishing.

Copyright provisions that give preferential treatment for Canadian rights holders, such as the 1999 parallel importation rules that ensure Canadian booksellers obtain imported works from the Canadian company that holds Canadian distribution rights. This preserves the integrity of the distribution agreement, and some of the profits from this distribution activity are invested into new Canadian works.

Section 19.1 of the *Income Tax Act*, which provides a disincentive for Canadians to advertise on U.S. border television stations or in U.S. magazines by disallowing such spending as a business expense for tax purposes.

Coproduction treaties with fifty-six countries that permit the film or television show created by the partners to qualify, in each country, as domestic content for purposes of financial support and content quotas.

### 3. Government agencies
Finally, there are a large number of federal government agencies and institutions, including the Canadian Broadcasting Corporation, Telefilm Canada, the Canadian Radio-television and Telecommunications Commission, the public-private Canada Media Fund, the National Arts Centre, the Canadian Museum of History, Library and Archives Canada and the National Gallery of Canada. There are equivalent agencies and institutions at other levels of government in Canada, and an array of publicly owned or supported venues and facilities.

## Case Study: How Cultural Policies Help Develop and Sustain an Industry
In his 2017 work *Arrival,* literature professor Nick Mount has documented the rise of Canadian literature (CanLit) from the 1950s to the early 1970s. He theorized that Canada's growing affluence meant that Canadians had more time to read and greater disposable income to

spend on the new generation of Canadian authors. Writers such as Margaret Atwood, Alice Munro, Leonard Cohen, Michael Ondaatje and others were coming of age in an era where nationalism was growing, as Canadians rejected both British colonialism and U.S. cultural hegemony.

All of this is true, of course, and can be applied equally to the rise of Canadian music, television, theatre and visual arts in the postwar years. However, all of these industries were also supported by government policies and actions, beginning with the Canada Council, which has, since its launch in 1957, provided grants to artists of all kinds, including many of the writers highlighted in Mount's book.

The story of CanLit is also the story of the Canadian book publishing industry, whose most famous character and influential publisher was Jack McClelland. His firm, McClelland & Stewart, emerged as the leading publisher of Canadian works by the mid-1960s. By 1971, the company was drowning in debt incurred by publishing too many books for Canada's 1967 centennial celebrations. At the same time, Ontario's government had established a Royal Commission on Book Publishing arising from concerns about the lack of Canadian textbooks in Ontario schools and the sale of The Ryerson Press and Gage to foreign interests. The Ontario government accepted an interim recommendation in March 1971 to back a million-dollar debenture issued by McClelland & Stewart to keep the company afloat. "The Commissioners described the M&S publishing program as 'a national asset worthy of all reasonable public encouragement and support.'"[12]

In 1972, the Ontario government established a program, which continues to this day, to support Canadian publishers. The Ontario Media Development Corporation also operates a tax credit program for Ontario publishers. The same year, the Federal Book Publishing Policy provided funding for the Canada Council to support the production and distribution of books. In 1979, the Canadian Book Publishing Industry Development Program (now the Canada Book Fund) was created in the Department of the Secretary of State to fund publishers and the industry's organizations. The Foreign Investment Review Agency was created in 1973, and its rules for publishing required special permission before a Canadian-owned firm could be directly or indirectly acquired by a foreign firm.

One of the most remarkable policies that briefly supported Canadian publishing was Wintario's Half Back program. A ticket for Wintario, which was Ontario's first lottery, cost one dollar. In early 1978, the government implemented a plan whereby consumers could receive a fifty-cent credit for each non-winning ticket, which could be redeemed toward the purchase of a book by a Canadian author, or a Canadian magazine. The program was extended later to music and films and was wildly popular. People began searching in bookstores for the "Eligible for Half Back" sticker on book spines or magazine covers. Schools organized students to collect non-winning tickets from family, friends and neighbours so they could add Canadian works to their library collections. The program was a victim of its own success; the government discontinued it because it was diverting funds from the central purpose of the lottery, which was to raise money for community recreation facilities.

While affluence and time may have been important factors in the rise of CanLit as documented by Mount, perhaps more vital are the many cultural policies that have supported Canadian authors and the Canadian book publishing industry for fifty years.

# Chapter 2
# Global Free Trade – From Goods to Services

The economic theories underpinning free trade were developed more than 240 years ago, in works by two British economists. Adam Smith (1723–1790) argued that positive social benefits flow as an unintended consequence of actions that individuals take in their own self-interest, and thus free markets improve everyone's circumstances. David Ricardo (1772–1823) developed the theory of comparative advantage to explain how nations can gain by specializing in the production and export of particular goods. Both Smith and Ricardo argued that import tariffs were counterproductive. A few countries embraced these economic ideas and reduced or eliminated some tariffs over the next century, particularly on agricultural products. However, most developed countries continued to use high import tariffs to protect fledgling and sensitive industries until the middle of the twentieth century.

The fundamental reasoning behind free trade can be summarized like this: For many traditional goods and services, economies of scale can benefit consumers. In theory, large-scale production of goods offers manufacturers and producers the potential to create a higher-quality product at a lower price. While they benefit from capturing a larger share of the market, consumers benefit by obtaining better value for money. Growing profits allow these manufacturers and producers to become even more efficient and innovative, benefiting everyone from shareholders to consumers. Free traders argue that removing barriers to the free movement of goods and services will extend these benefits globally. When you permit the most efficient producers to dominate global markets, consumers everywhere benefit. While this may force inefficient producers in some countries out of business, free traders argue these countries will either have an advantage in another economic sector or will be able to specialize in a sector where their disadvantage is the smallest. On balance, they too will gain from free trade because incomes everywhere will rise.

At the end of World War I, the Western world entered a period of economic growth and expansion that came to a crashing end in 1929 with the Great Depression. In the 1920s, the U.S. average import tax was roughly 40 per cent. While the Depression was most severe in the United States, where the peak-to-trough decline in industrial production was almost 47 per cent, its effects were global. Production declined in Canada and Germany by 42 per cent, in France by 31 per cent and in the United Kingdom by 16 per cent.[1]

The Great Depression created widespread unemployment as consumer spending plummeted and industrial investment stopped. The price of agricultural products fell for a variety of reasons. Protectionist sentiments grew around the world. In the United States, the 1930 *Smoot-Hawley Tariff Act* raised the already high tariffs on over 20,000 imported goods.

Economists still debate the causes of the Great Depression, but most agree it was exacerbated when the United States introduced these super high tariffs. Other countries retaliated by increasing their own tariffs, effectively choking off international trade. All of this economic uncertainty contributed as well to the outbreak of war. As World War II approached, the Great Depression finally ended as countries began investing millions in the production of military equipment, supplies and personnel.

As the world emerged from the devastation of World War II, there was considerable support for new forms of international cooperation and governance, highlighted by the launch of the United Nations in October 1945. The victorious Allies believed that economy and commerce comprised an essential element of this new system, and that one arm of the new governance model should involve a multilateral framework for world trade. The prevailing view held that this would create economic growth and interdependency, foster global partnerships and thus reduce the risk of conflict. While the original goal of creating an International Trade Organization to take its place alongside the International Monetary Fund and the World Bank was not achieved, twenty-three countries did successfully negotiate the General Agreement on Tariffs and Trade (GATT).

The GATT was signed in Geneva in October 1947 and came into effect on January 1, 1948. The twenty-three original GATT members were Australia, Belgium, Brazil, Burma, Canada, Ceylon, Chile, China, Cuba, Czechoslovakia, France, India, Lebanon, Luxembourg, The Netherlands, New Zealand, Norway, Pakistan, Southern Rhodesia, Syria, South Africa, United Kingdom and the United States.

## General Agreement on Tariffs and Trade (GATT) Takes the Stage

A short preamble establishes the fundamental purpose of the GATT:

> *Recognizing that their relations in the field of trade and economic
> endeavour should be conducted with a view to raising standards
> of living, ensuring full employment and a large and steadily
> growing volume of real income and effective demand, developing
> the full use of the resources of the world and expanding the
> production and exchange of goods,*

*Being desirous of contributing to these objectives by entering into reciprocal and mutually advantageous arrangements directed to the substantial reduction of tariffs and other barriers to trade and to the elimination of discriminatory treatment in international commerce.*[2]

The 1947 GATT contains the core principles that underpin all successive trade agreements, whether global, regional or bilateral:

**Most-Favoured-Nation (MFN)** — This provision obligates each contracting party to give to all other contracting parties the most favourable provision it offers to any other party.

**National Treatment (NT)** — This provides that, where a party imports goods from any other party, these goods shall be accorded treatment no less favourable than domestic goods "in respect of all laws, regulations and requirements affecting their internal sale, offering for sale, purchase, transportation, distribution or use." In other words, imported goods cannot be treated less favourably than domestic goods.

The GATT also includes important exceptions. Provided they do not constitute "a disguised restriction on international trade," parties may take measures to achieve certain objectives, including "protection of public morals, protection of human, animal or plant life or health, and conservation of exhaustible natural resources." A party is also free to take "any action which it considers necessary for the protection of its essential security interests."

Based on these and other core principles, the substantive work of the GATT was carried out in successive rounds of negotiations in which the parties negotiated with each other, individually or in groups, on reducing tariffs and removing barriers to trade. The Geneva Round introduced the initial GATT, and the Annecy Round started shortly afterward, in April 1949. The Tokyo Round, the seventh, concluded in November 1979, by which time the agreement had 102 contracting parties.

## GATT and Cultural Policies[3]

From the very beginning, the negotiating process that ultimately led to the GATT involved discussions about how cultural policy issues intersect with "free trade."

Non-controversially, the General Exceptions clause XX(f) provides that parties may impose measures "for the protection of national treasures of artistic, historic or archaeological value." In other words, parties may control the import and export of important cultural artifacts without worrying about MFN and NT obligations.

Theoretically, Article XIX could also be used to sustain cultural policy measures. The so-called Safeguard Article provides that, if a product is:

> imported into the territory of that contracting party in such
> increased quantities and under such conditions as being to cause
> or threaten serious injury to domestic producers in that territory
> of like or directly competitive products, the contracting party
> shall be free, in respect of such product, and to the extent and for
> such time as may be necessary to prevent or remedy such injury,
> to suspend the obligation in whole or in part or to withdraw or
> modify the concession.

To date, no party has cited this provision to support a cultural policy that is designed to build a national cultural industry in the face of imports from a dominant foreign market. Canada could easily make such a case in respect of its film industry.

Most importantly, GATT Article IV details special provisions relating to films:

> If any contracting party establishes or maintains internal
> quantitative regulations relating to exposed cinematograph films,

*such regulations shall take the form of screen quotas, which shall conform to the following requirements:*

a)  *Screen quotas may require the exhibition of cinematograph films of national origin during a specified minimum proportion of the total screen time actually utilized, over a specified period of not less than one year, in the commercial exhibition of all films of whatever origin, and shall be computed on the basis of screen time per theatre per year or the equivalent thereof*

b)  *With the exception of screen time reserved for films of national origin under a screen quota, screen time including that released by administrative action from screen time reserved for films of national origin, shall not be allocated formally or in effect among sources of supply*

c)  *Notwithstanding the provisions of subparagraph (b) of this Article, any contracting party may maintain screen quotas conforming to the requirements of subparagraph (a) of this Article, which reserve a minimum proportion of screen time for films of a specified origin other than that of the contracting party imposing such screen quotas; Provided that no such minimum proportion of screen time shall be increased above the level in effect on April 10, 1947*

d)  *Screen quotas shall be subject to negotiation for their limitation, liberalization or elimination.*

The structure of the exception for cinema screen quotas is interesting because it established principles that continue to apply in relation to a variety of exceptions from, or limitations to, liberalization commitments. Most importantly, paragraph (d) explicitly states that parties are obligated in future to negotiate ways to limit the quotas or to eliminate them entirely. Paragraph (b) effectively provides that, while a party can establish a quota for domestic content, they cannot discriminate amongst foreign films — all must compete equally for the remaining screen time. Paragraph (c) says that, if there are existing quotas for some foreign movies but not others (for example, those from Francophonie or Commonwealth member countries), these may be maintained or decreased, but they can never be increased. Given all its elements, the screen quota exception is seen as a temporary anomaly from the agreed-upon principles behind free trade.

There is little in the historical record concerning how and why this provision came about. Of the twenty-three original GATT members, only four had screen quotas at the time of its negotiation. France and the United Kingdom established quotas in 1928, Brazil in 1932 and Australia in 1935.[4] Most likely the primary pressure to include such an exception came from the U.K. and its former colonies.

In the early twentieth century, the European film industry led the world. European film companies had pioneered important technological innovations, such as projection, colour and talking pictures. They also developed the weekly newsreel, the cartoon, the serial and the feature film. According to one study, European films held a large share of the U.S. market, at times reaching 60 per cent.[5]

This changed with the devastation suffered by Europe during World War I. Hollywood became a centre for film production in the United States in the early twentieth century and expanded rapidly in the immediate postwar period when European filmmakers were in recovery mode. Between the two wars, Hollywood studios established their dominance in both production and distribution to theatres, many of which they owned. They attracted global talent. Hollywood studios owned or controlled most Canadian cinemas and fully incorporated them into the domestic release model and timetable. It was just as easy to transport the film to Vancouver as it was to Seattle, and this was less expensive than transporting the film to New York and Toronto. Hollywood studios also colluded with respect to export markets. The studios formed an export cartel that essentially forced cinema owners around the world to program Hollywood movies. Whenever foreign governments or companies created problems, the studios acted as one. All of this was allowed under U.S. law at the time, and the studios were fully supported by U.S. diplomacy.

A discussion paper entitled *Exhibition within the Empire of Empire Cinematographic Films* was circulated in preparation for the 1926 Imperial Conference in London, where the British Commonwealth of Nations was launched. The paper noted the importance of cinema as an "instrument of education in the widest sense of that term" and decried the lack of Empire content in Great Britain, Northern Ireland, Canada, Australia and New Zealand. The Committee recommended that all member states take action. This led to the U.K.'s *Cinematograph Films Act* in 1927, which established a 15 per cent quota for British and Commonwealth films in U.K. cinemas for the year ending September 30, 1929. It would slowly rise each year afterward.

Of interest to Canadians, that same Imperial Conference brought the creation of the Empire Marketing Board (EMB), which sought to promote intra-Empire trade and encourage citizens to "Buy Empire." One of the most famous parts of the advertising campaign was the EMB film unit, led by John Grierson, the father of the documentary film genre. In 1938, Grierson was invited by the Canadian government to study the country's film industry. His report led to the creation of the National Film Commission in 1939, which later became the National Film Board. Grierson was appointed as the first Commissioner.

Following introduction of the U.K.'s *Cinematograph Films Act,* an industry emerged to produce "quota quickies," so called because they were made very quickly and with low budgets. Paramount, Warner Bros. and other U.S. studios created branch plant operations around London, England for this purpose. Some also worked with production companies that set up in Montreal, Toronto, Calgary and elsewhere in Canada soon after the legislation was adopted. The most active Canadian producer of quota quickies was Kenneth Bishop of Victoria, who produced four-teen films in five years. While some of his movies were set in Canada, all were essentially generic Hollywood B movies. Since Bishop had a financing and distribution arrangement with Columbia Pictures, he did postproduction and editing in Hollywood, and Columbia Pictures had final approval over the films.

Another centre of film production during that period was Trenton, Ontario, where a movie studio had opened in 1917. In the early years, it produced several commercial silent films. The Ontario government purchased it in 1923 as a hub for the Ontario Motion Picture Bureau, which used it to produce travelogues and films about the province. They also rented it to other filmmakers, especially during the quota quickie era. The government closed the studio in 1934 because it could not be easily converted for the production of sound. Over 1,500 silent films were produced during the seventeen years the studio operated in Trenton.

The U.K. film quota rose to 20 per cent in 1938, but the *Act* was amended to restrict the quota to British films. This brought an end to the quota quickies industry, including in Canada. While some dismiss this period of Canadian filmmaking, George Melnyk argues in his 2004 book *One Hundred Years of Canadian Cinema* that quota quickies "played their own historical role in marking Canada's transition from its British colonial past to its new imperial master, the United States."[6]

Given this history of Empire and British cinema quotas, as well as those France introduced in 1928, it is easy to speculate that these countries drove the GATT exemption for cinema screen quotas when it was negotiated after World War II.

## Uruguay Round of Trade Negotiations and Cultural Policies

From the perspective of cultural policies, the next significant development related to global trade emerged during the eighth round of multilateral trade negotiations launched under the GATT, which opened in

Montevideo, Uruguay in 1986. The Uruguay Round involved the 123 countries that were parties to GATT at the time.

The most significant development of the Uruguay Round was that negotiations went far beyond the traditional agenda of mutually agreeing on tariff reductions for goods flowing across borders. Negotiators were given a broad mandate, both to expand GATT to sectors previously considered too challenging, such as agricultural goods and textiles, and to include new areas.

The Round concluded in 1994 with the agreement to launch the World Trade Organization (WTO) as the mechanism to administer a wider array of agreements, including:

- GATT 1994
- The General Agreement on Trade in Services (GATS)
- The Agreement on Trade-Related Investment Measures (TRIMs)
- Agreement on Trade-Related Aspects of Intellectual Property Rights (TRIPS), and
- Agreements on a new dispute settlement mechanism and the collective monitoring of governments' trade policies and practices.

For cultural policies, these developments represented a seismic shift.

Until the digital age, the celluloid film was wound around a reel. This constituted the physical form of the movie. Studios transported these movie reels to cinemas and broadcasters so the movie could be shown to audiences. When they crossed borders, they could be taxed, charged fees or subjected to regulatory requirements. Thus, the provisions of the General Agreement on Tariffs and Trade apply in all respects to movies, with the exception of the content quotas (and other exceptions, such as "public morals") negotiated into the text. While the script, set, wardrobe and other elements of a movie may also constitute "goods," these were typically not transported across borders and thus fell outside GATT rules.

However, as we have seen, movies are made by artists and others who are providing services to the producer, and the creative nature of the work is protected by copyright laws. By including services and intellectual property rights, the agreements negotiated in the Uruguay Round thus had far broader scope to affect cultural policymaking. In the case of the movie now crossing a border electronically, provisions of GATS and TRIPS cover the services embodied in that movie and the underlying copyright works.

A movement to acknowledge "l'exception culturelle" developed during the Uruguay Round. Led by France, this movement argued that cultural goods and services have a dual nature. The preamble of the 2005 UNESCO *Convention on the Protection and Promotion of the Diversity of Cultural Expressions* states it succinctly:

> *Cultural activities, goods and services have both an economic*
> *and a cultural nature, because they convey identities, values and*
> *meanings, and must therefore not be treated as solely having*
> *commercial value.*[7]

In this process, some began to argue that the fundamental theory behind free trade does not apply to the cultural field. Cultural goods and services embody cultural traditions, mores and values. Unlike traditional goods, where consumers gain when there are fewer, more efficient manufacturers, with cultural expressions consumers benefit most from having a wider range of choices from a wider variety of suppliers. Cultural diversity is about ensuring that local arts and culture flourish, and about more balanced exchanges between cultures around the world. This increased trade will be in "like" products and services as ever more music, films, books and other cultural expressions move back and forth across all borders. This runs directly counter to the free trade ideology of Adam Smith and David Ricardo.

The economics of cultural production are also different from other sectors in a number of ways, the most significant of which relates to the cost of each individual unit produced. The cost of the first copy of a work can be substantial. For example, the average production budget of a major Hollywood movie has been more than $60 million USD for many years; with promotion and advertising added to the equation, the total cost exceeds $100 million USD. However, each subsequent copy of the movie can be produced for pennies.

This is unlike virtually all other goods. While there may be considerable research and development costs before production begins, there is little difference between the still significant cost of the first and each subsequent unit that flows off an assembly line.

For the movie, this also means that when it is distributed into foreign markets, it can be sold at substantially different prices depending on the circumstances of each market. In most cases, it is sold for less than the cost of producing a domestic alternative. A broadcast license fee for a U.S. television drama series in Canada is typically hundreds of thousands of dollars, whereas a broadcast license fee in Nigeria will be much less, typically only a few thousand dollars, despite the larger potential audience in Nigeria. This type of disparity in price simply cannot exist for traditional goods, where the cost of each additional product will be much closer to the first one produced.

As an important aside, the practice of exporting products at a price that is lower in the foreign importing market than the price in the exporter's domestic market constitutes "dumping" in the context of international trade. Dumping is prohibited by GATT rules. Since this practice applies to many U.S. cultural exports, it may be the reason that Hollywood studios have not been tempted to challenge expansion of GATT's cinema screen quotas into television and radio.

## General Agreement on Trade in Services (GATS)[8]

Comprehensive trade negotiations that have taken place since the late 1980s now include consideration of trade in services and have often included intellectual property issues.

As we shall see, the most important issues when it comes to cultural policies and trade agreements revolve around cultural expressions as "services." Thus we must start with an understanding of GATS.

The GATS contains the same basic principles as GATT, including MFN and NT. It also has requirements for transparency of government rules and regulations that may affect service providers. The agreement commits signatories to negotiate issues of government procurement of services and mechanisms to prevent government subsidies from distorting trade.

GATS Part IV highlights the notion that liberalization of trade is a fundamental objective in itself:

> In pursuance of the objectives of this Agreement, Members shall enter into successive rounds of negotiations, beginning not later than five years from the date of entry into force of the WTO Agreement and periodically thereafter, with a view to achieving a progressively higher level of liberalization. Such negotiations shall be directed to the reduction or elimination of the adverse effects on trade in services of measures as a means of providing effective market access.

GATS also contains exceptions as found in the GATT that go even further. For example, the "security" exception is broader, and the public morals exception now adds "public order." There are also exceptions for economic integration areas (free trade zones) and for agreements that provide for labour market integration (like the European Union).

GATS contains no exceptions, however, for the cultural sector. Significantly, the commitments that provide market access for foreign service providers on a National Treatment basis apply only to those sectors that contracting parties agree to list. GATS is the first significant trade agreement negotiated on a bottom-up, or positive list, basis. This means that sectors for which trade commitments are made have been selected individually by each contracting party. Previously, the agreements considered that every sector was included unless it had been exempted either by the terms of the agreement, or by a reservation that an individual party would express regarding a certain sector or policy (i.e., a top-down or negative list approach).

In addition to the National Treatment obligation, where a party agrees to commit a certain sector, other provisions apply. These include a requirement that regulations must be "administered in a reasonable, objective and impartial manner," and subject to agreed limits, including that they be "not more burdensome than necessary." Significantly, if a country has listed a certain sector it can withdraw this commitment only by compensating all foreign service providers affected by such a decision.

Finally, for purposes of the cultural sector, it is important to note that the obligation to provide Most-Favoured-Nation treatment to all other parties applies to all sectors, whether or not the party has committed the sector fully under GATS. In the trade world, this is known as a "horizontal commitment." A party can provide preferential treatment to any other party (for example, by means of a cultural exchange or coproduction treaty) only if it has recorded this as a reservation or limitation on that party's MFN obligation.

Before we look at how cultural policies have been affected by these global trade agreements, we will consider the trade agreements Canada has concluded with the United States, since these have the most significant impact on our cultural policymaking.

# Chapter 3
# Canada and Free Trade with the United States

Every human society has arts and artists. Music, dance, design, storytelling, painting, sculpting and more are ubiquitous. Artists not only reflect a society to itself and to others, but can also be our conscience when they challenge us to think about what we can become. When we consider the value of arts and culture, we usually start with the intrinsic value — it can enrich our lives and our emotional state. Arts and culture have an important impact on many facets of our lives and societies, including improving health and wellbeing, promoting positive educational outcomes, reducing social isolation, fostering social cohesion and integrating new citizens.

The production, distribution, exhibition and preservation of cultural expressions, in every medium, also constitutes a sustainable industry. These activities are based on creativity and intellectual property, rather than on finite natural resources. They are generally labour-intensive rather than capital-intensive, high-wage and more gender-equal in their use of human resources than most other economic sectors. As cultural expressions are increasingly produced and distributed electronically, they are environmentally sustainable.

While the work of one artist may be ephemeral and be seen or heard by only a few friends and family, cultural industries are increasingly big business. In announcing her Creative Canada initiative in September 2017, Canadian Heritage Minister Mélanie Joly said, "The arts and culture sector is a $54.6-billion industry and a cornerstone of Canada's economy." Indeed, this sector provides jobs to more than 650,000 Canadians and contributes 2.8 per cent to Canada's GDP.[1]

The Conference Board of Canada report *Valuing Culture: Measuring and Understanding Canada's Creative Economy* was perhaps the most authoritative examination of the sector's economic impact. While now more than ten years old, the report concluded that the sector generated $46 billion of activity in 2007, or 3.8 per cent of Canada's gross domestic product that year. When you include all direct, indirect and induced contributions by the culture sector, it represented over one million jobs, with an economic impact of $84.6 billion in 2007, or 7.4 per cent of total real GDP. In its report, the Conference Board started with the Statistics Canada framework for culture statistics, encompassing written media, the film and television industry, broadcasting, sound recording and music publishing, performing arts, visual arts, architecture, photography, crafts, design, advertising, museums, art galleries, archives, libraries and arts-culture education. It also included the creative elements of video games.[2]

However large Canada's cultural sector is, it pales in comparison to the industry in the United States. According to a report from the Bureau of Economic Analysis and the National Endowment for the Arts, U.S. cultural industries contributed $698 billion USD or 4.3 per cent to the country's GDP in 2014. The sectors covered in the U.S. report were narrower than in the Conference Board report, including movie and television production, broadcasting, publishing, performing arts and individual artists, advertising and retail sales of cultural products. The U.S. cultural industry is also a very significant player in U.S. trade.[3]

The U.S. Copyright Alliance is an association representing more than 13,000 organizations across all of the copyright disciplines. According to the 2016 *Copyright Industries in the U.S. Economy* report, copyright industries contribute significantly to the U.S. trade balance, particularly the surplus in U.S. services trade:

> *From a global perspective, sales of U.S. recorded music, television,*
> *video and motion pictures, software, newspapers, books and*
> *periodicals in foreign markets amounted to $177 billion, which*
> *exceeds exports of major U.S. industries such as chemicals,*
> *aerospace, agricultural, electrical, and pharmaceuticals.*[4]

The Recording Industry Association of America added that the trade surplus for the copyright-based industries in 2014 was $88.2 billion USD, the largest of any service sector. Given these statistics, it is easy to understand the U.S. preoccupation with global trade issues that affect cultural industries.

From the Canadian side of the border, this powerful U.S. cultural industry is a juggernaut, which has historically dominated both the English-language and French-language cultural markets. Canadians (except those in the Atlantic provinces) live in the same time zones as our American neighbours, and most of us live closer to the United States than we do to our fellow Canadians in the next province or territory. On the English side, we have grown up watching the same television shows and movies, enjoying the same music, reading the same novels and sharing many of the same cultural reference points. Before the tragic events of September 11, 2001, one could move freely back and forth across the border, in many places even without a passport. On a trip to Quebec's Eastern Townships in the early 1980s, we inadvertently crossed the border while bicycling on rural roads, with only a few dollars in our pockets and little identification. We dutifully reported to the U.S. and Canadian border stations, explained our mistake and were waved through with a smile and best wishes for the rest of our holiday.

Canadians have always felt uneasy about the closeness of our relationship with the United States. Writing in the Winter 2005 issue of

*Canada World View,* Carleton University professor Norman Hillmer put it this way:

> *Seventy-five per cent of Canada's population resides in a narrow
> 150-kilometre band pushing up against the U.S., with close
> ties south of the line. We are a border people. The border is our
> livelihood. The border is our identity.*
>
> *Canadians take the border seriously. From the country's
> beginnings, [we] emphasized the contrasts with [our] neighbours
> and nation-built with a vengeance. That was the point of
> the Canadian Pacific Railway, the Canadian Broadcasting
> Corporation and the Canada Council. The boundary, writes
> journalist Peter Newman, "is the most important fact about this
> country. It defines not only our citizenship but how we behave
> collectively and what we think individually. It determines who we
> are." And what we are, many Canadians insist, is an un-America
> of the spirit — stable, pacific and compassionate, utterly unlike the
> extreme and unruly Yanks.*[5]

While Professor Hillmer points to two cultural examples of nation-building, he could have just as easily added content quotas, preferential copyright laws and funding programs in film and television, music and publishing. Clearly, the Canada–U.S. trade relationship is vital for the Canadian cultural sector.

## Canada-U.S. Trade Agreements Before World War II

In January 1847, Lord Elgin assumed his post as Governor General of the Province of Canada. He arrived at a time when tensions were high; provincial political leaders were grappling with the aftermath of the 1837–38 rebellion and with the challenges of integrating the two parts of Canada and transitioning to responsible government. Despite personal misgivings, in 1849 Lord Elgin gave royal assent to the *Rebellion*

*Losses Bill*, which resulted in the parliament building of the Province of Canada being razed to the ground by angry citizens.

He also arrived at a time of economic uncertainty in the North American British Colonies. Britain had the most dominant economy in the world, and the government in London determined that free trade as espoused by Smith and Ricardo, rather than tariffs, would better serve the economy's interests. In 1846, Britain repealed the *Importation Act 1815*, the so-called Corn Laws, that imposed tariffs and restrictions on the importation of food and grains. The laws had considered products from the British colonies to be domestic and thus had given Canadian producers privileged access to what was then the world's largest market. Local merchants had prospered from this British monopoly control, and Canada's economy suffered when the preferential access was eliminated.

In order to secure new export markets, Lord Elgin and provincial leaders launched negotiations with the United States and concluded the Elgin-Marcy Treaty (Reciprocity Treaty) in 1854. Under the treaty, the 21 per cent tariff the United States applied on resources and agricultural produce from the Province of Canada, New Brunswick, Nova Scotia, Prince Edward Island and Newfoundland was eliminated. In return, U.S. fishers were allowed to enter the northeastern Atlantic fishing zones, a major irritant in U.S.–British relations at the time. The next ten years became a boom time for the Canadian economy. Exports to the U.S. grew, particularly as states acquired supplies to prepare for and fight the Civil War from 1861 to 1865. The year after the war ended, the United States abrogated the Reciprocity Treaty because of Canada's positive trade balance and a belief that Britain had favoured the Confederate side in the conflict. Abrogation of the Treaty was one factor in the decision that led to Canadian Confederation in 1867 — clearly issues of free trade with our southern neighbour make up part of Canada's very DNA.

Over the next century, there were divisive and sometimes heated debates about free trade with the United States, and Canada's policies vacillated. During this period, Canada's Liberal party supported free trade, while the Conservative party was opposed.

After Confederation, Prime Minister John A. Macdonald set the position of the Conservative party when he implemented the National Policy in 1879. The Policy set high tariffs to protect Canada's nascent manufacturing industry. It also called for building a transcontinental railway to unite the far-flung provinces, and immigration to populate the west. After implementing the Policy, Macdonald's government was elected three more times.

While tariffs had been in place during the 1873–78 term of Liberal Prime Minister Alexander Mackenzie, these were used strictly as a revenue tool. Tariffs and import duties were the primary source of federal revenues before Canada introduced corporate and income taxes in the World War I era. The Liberal party position on free trade was set by Wilfrid Laurier. After he became prime minister in the 1896 election, Laurier launched negotiations for an elaborate new reciprocity agreement with the United States. In January 1911, Laurier and U.S. President Howard Taft announced that the protracted negotiations had resulted in an agreement.

The reciprocity agreement negotiated by the Liberal government became the central issue in the September 1911 Canadian election. The Conservative party under Robert Borden opposed it on the grounds it would weaken ties with Britain and risked submerging the Canadian economy and identity into the United States. With the election slogan of "No Truck nor Trade with the Yankees," Borden won 49 per cent of the vote and a comfortable majority government; Laurier won 46 per cent of the popular vote.

In 1879 Canada had become a country with relatively high tariffs under the National Policy and these were confirmed after the 1911 election. Tariffs on the importation of most finished products were high, while lower rates were levied on selected raw materials and sophisticated production equipment used in manufacturing. Until the end of World War II, the only significant tariff change came in 1930–35 when Canada hiked tariffs overall in response to the U.S. *Smoot-Hawley Tarrif*

*Act* and the protectionist sentiment that swept the world during the Great Depression.

In 1932, Franklin D. Roosevelt was elected president of the United States on the promise to launch his "New Deal" to respond to the continuing Great Depression. As part of this plan, legislation adopted the following year gave the president power to negotiate bilateral, reciprocal trade agreements with other countries. The U.S. approached Canada, which agreed to start talks, despite the reluctance of Conservative Prime Minister R.B. Bennett, who had inherited the traditional party position that protective tariffs were necessary to develop Canadian industry.

Bennett was defeated in the election of 1935 by the Liberal party under the leadership of William Lyon Mackenzie King. One of Prime Minister King's first acts was to enthusiastically sign the trade agreement with the United States. It provided that each party would give Most-Favoured-Nation treatment to the other, with the exception of the British Empire preferential tariffs and the preferential treatment the U.S. accorded to its overseas territories and Cuba. Perhaps as a precursor to future developments, Canada agreed in 1935 to significantly reduce its tariff rate on U.S. magazines imported into Canada. This was the first time in seventy years that the Canada–United States trade relationship was governed by a negotiated agreement.

## Post-World War II Free Trade Initiatives

The next significant step in the trading relationship was the signing in 1965 of the Canada–United States Automotive Products Agreement, under Liberal Prime Minister Lester B. Pearson. In return for agreement by General Motors, Ford and Chrysler to produce in Canada at least as many cars as they sell in Canada, the Auto Pact allowed car parts and the finished vehicles to be shipped freely back and forth across the border with no tariffs. Over the next decades, Canada experienced an exponential growth in car manufacturing, particularly as the Big Three far exceeded their commitments. While the elimination of automotive tariffs was largely superseded by subsequent trade agreements, the

Auto Pact officially continued until 2001 when a World Trade Organization decision against the Pact was implemented.

The 1960s and 1970s were marked by relatively strong economic growth in Canada and the emergence of a strong sense of Canadian nationalism. As we have seen, Canadian arts and culture flourished in every artistic sector, from visual arts, music, dance, theatre, literature and television, to museums and galleries.

In 1967, the government of Liberal Prime Minister Pearson appointed a *Task Force on Foreign Ownership and the Structure of Canadian Investment*, chaired by economist Mel Watkins. The Watkins Report, tabled in 1968, documented the high level of foreign ownership in Canada, argued this high level was unacceptable for a sovereign nation, and recommended interventionist policies. The new Liberal prime minister, Pierre Trudeau, accepted the key recommendations of the Report and created the Foreign Investment Review Agency (FIRA) in 1973. FIRA established special restrictions on foreign investments in Canadian firms dealing with publishing and film distribution. Trudeau also introduced other significant interventionist policies such as Wage and Price Controls in 1975 and the National Energy Program in 1980.

A large number of studies about Canada's economic future were commissioned in the 1970s and 1980s. The most seminal was the Royal Commission on the Economic Union and Development Prospects for Canada. While the commission was appointed by prime Minister Trudeau and chaired by former Liberal Finance Minister Donald Macdonald, the newly elected Conservative prime minister, Brian Mulroney, had just taken office when it reported in 1984. Despite being chaired by a former Liberal minister, the Macdonald Royal Commission, in its report, generally reflected the conservative ideology of the day as practised by British Prime Minister Margaret Thatcher and U.S. President Ronald Reagan, and embraced by Canada's new prime minister. This ideology included open markets, privatization of public services and deregulation and reform of the welfare state. One of the report's central recommendations was that Canada should pursue a free trade agreement with the United States. Just as Pierre Trudeau had set aside 100 years of Liberal party policy by supporting market interventionist policies, Mulroney's embrace of the recommendation to negotiate a free trade agreement with the United States set aside 100 years of Conservative party policy.

The general view in Canada holds that the proposal for a Canada–United States Free Trade Agreement was a Canadian initiative that Prime Minister Mulroney famously pitched to U.S. President Ronald Reagan at the March 1985 Shamrock Summit in Quebec City. According to this narrative, the U.S. president embraced the idea because of his friendship with Mulroney and their shared values and vision. The small-c conservatism of Reagan and Mulroney was of a very different sort from the Conservative principles of John A. Macdonald and his successors.

However, the U.S. had its own strong interest in negotiating with Canada. In announcing his candidacy in 1979, Ronald Reagan put forward the idea of a free-trade zone stretching from "the Yukon to the Yucatan," where people and commerce could flow more freely across borders. He believed free trade and free enterprise would unleash an economic potential far greater than the component parts could manage on their own.[6] In 1985, the United States was a major proponent of expanding GATT into new areas, particularly to trade in services, investment measures and intellectual property rights. A top priority for the United States was the entertainment industry, or what is referred to in Canada as the cultural industries.

In 1983 the Office of the United States Trade Representative appointed a high-level industry panel to look at trade barriers experienced by U.S. entertainment industries. The panel, chaired by Thomas H. Wyman, Chairman and CEO of CBS, conducted a survey of leading executives and trade associations. Its September 1984 report, *Trade Barriers to U.S. Motion Picture, Pre-recorded Entertainment, Publishing and Advertising Industries,* identified these issues as the leading barriers:

- copyright infringement (identified by 100 per cent of respondents)
- cultural restrictions, including content quotas on programs and television advertising (81 per cent)
- restrictions on repatriating profits (74 per cent)
- unfair competition from government-owned or government-subsidized production or distribution (53 per cent) and
- foreign ownership restrictions (32 per cent).[7]

The report was primarily written to inform the position of the United States in the Uruguay Round of GATT negotiations. Canada featured heavily in the Wyman Report, however, with Canadian cultural policy measures front-and-centre in virtually every area of the survey. In 1985, GATT was still trying to establish the parameters of the Uruguay Round of negotiations, and the U.S. was unhappy with the reluctance of some GATT parties to negotiate new areas that were particularly important to the U.S. entertainment industry. Thus, when Prime Minister Mulroney pitched the idea of a free trade agreement with Canada, President Reagan welcomed the initiative and the United States Congress gave him authority to negotiate. It established October 5, 1987 as the date by which the proposed agreement had to be tabled in Congress.

## Canada and the United States Negotiate a Free Trade Agreement

Canadian and American negotiators began their work in May 1986. The deal was not concluded, however, until October 4, 1987, after Mulroney personally intervened. His role involved convincing Reagan to accept a dispute settlement system that would allow Canada to challenge, and take to arbitration, U.S. trade remedy decisions it considered to be unfair.

It is hard to overstate the degree of controversy that existed about the proposed Free Trade Agreement with the United States. When the Canadian Senate blocked ratification, Prime Minister Mulroney called an election for November 1988; the election was all about free trade.

The Council of Canadians was launched in 1985 as a broad-based cit-izen's organization concerned about maintaining "control of our econ-omy, our culture and our sovereignty." Founding members included well-known writers Margaret Atwood, Pierre Berton, Graeme Gibson, Margaret Laurence, Farley Mowat, Peter C. Newman and Heather Rob-ertson; Publishers Mel Hurtig and James Lorimer; labour leaders Robert White and Grace Hartman; academics and activists Doris Anderson, Maude Barlow, Gerry Caplan, Stephen Clarkson, Gordon Laxer, David Suzuki and Mel Watkins; as well as a number of politicians including Sheila Copps, Marion Dewar, Hon. T.C. Douglas, Hon. Walter Gordon, Hon. Herb Gray, Pauline Jewett, Hon. Eric Kierans and Paul Martin, Jr.

In announcing its formation, Council of Canadians Chair Hurtig said:

> *The new organization is very concerned about the dangers of a*
> *possible comprehensive bilateral trade agreement with the U.S.*
> *and the potential harmful effects to the Canadian economy of*
> *such an agreement. The C.O.C. will devote much effort towards*
> *studying the economic and political ramifications of the soon-to-*
> *be-released report of the Macdonald Royal Commission, which is*
> *widely thought to be on the verge of recommending a free trade*
> *agreement with the U.S.*[8]

In 1987, the grassroots resistance to the agreement coalesced around the Pro-Canada Network, a broad coalition of labour unions, farm groups, women's groups, environmentalists, church and social activ-ists, as well as most of the cultural community. There were marches, public meetings and demonstrations across Canada. Debates about the (de)merits of the agreement took place at home, at parties, in restau-rants and bars, and even on public transit.

In October 1988, *The Journal*, CBC's flagship current affairs program, staged a high-profile debate, which it broadcast over two days. Robert White, President of the Canadian Labour Congress, and Maude Barlow,

Chair of the Council of Canadians, debated the proposed agreement with Alberta Premier Peter Lougheed and Thomas D'Aquino, CEO of the Business Council on National Issues (now the Canadian Business Council).

The overwhelming majority of the cultural community was concerned about how the proposed Free Trade Agreement could negatively affect Canadian culture, and the policies and programs so critical to its successes in the 1970s and '80s. The community mounted a significant campaign to have culture excluded from its terms. Virtually every association of artists and cultural producers was involved in one way or another, and leading artists stepped forward to voice their concerns.

In 1986, the Alliance of Canadian Cinema, Television and Radio Artists (ACTRA) brought together a speakers' bureau of leading members to raise the cultural dimension of free trade in editorials, media interviews and public speeches. Leading writers did the same. In 1988, ACTRA President Dale Goldhawk penned an article in *ACTRAScope*, the union's newsletter, calling on members to engage in the debate because the Free Trade Agreement "jeopardized the economic and social interests of artists who work in Canada's cultural industries."

At the time, Goldhawk was host of CBC Radio's weekly call-in show, *Cross Country Checkup*. CBC called Goldhawk to the office and gave him an ultimatum — either resign as ACTRA president or resign as a CBC host. While he stepped down as president, ACTRA disputed the CBC action before the Canada Labour Relations Board (CLRB). It won there, and again in 1994 when the Supreme Court concurred with the CLRB and the lower court, ruling that the ultimatum constituted an inappropriate interference in internal union affairs and thus represented an unfair labour practice.[9]

In response to the cultural sector's concerns, in 1986 the government appointed the Cultural Industries Sectoral Advisory Group on International Trade (SAGIT) to advise it and Canada's negotiators regarding cultural issues. SAGIT was comprised of business and industry leaders as well as some artists and representatives of their associations. This advisory committee played a key role in convincing the government to seek a cultural exemption in the agreement and continued to play an important role in influencing government policies over the next fourteen years.

In one of the more colourful moments of the culture sector's campaign, Margaret Atwood, testifying before a parliamentary committee in 1987, offered this metaphor:

> *Our national animal is the beaver, noted for its industriousness*
> *and cooperative spirit. In medieval bestiaries it is also noted for its*
> *habit, when frightened, of biting off its own testicles and offering*
> *them to its pursuer. I hope we are not succumbing to some form of*
> *that impulse.*[10]

Cultural issues stood front and centre in the negotiations, where they also proved very contentious. This arises from the simple reality that what Canadians view as culture, the Americans view as entertainment, and what we view as promoting choice, the Americans view as erecting barriers.

In the November 1988 election, focused almost exclusively on the Free Trade Agreement, the government of Conservative Prime Minister Brian Mulroney was returned to power with a reduced majority government — still sufficient for him to proceed with implementation.

Interestingly, the Conservative party received only 43 per cent of the popular vote. Both the Liberal party and the New Democratic party opposed the Free Trade Agreement vigorously during the campaign. In the 1911 "reciprocity" election, 49 per cent of Canadians, a plurality at the time, had voted *against* free trade with the United States. Seventy-seven years later, in the "free trade" election of 1988, at least 52 per cent of Canadians did the same thing.

## Culture and the Canada-United States Free Trade Agreement (CUSFTA)

When the final agreement was released, the Conservative Minister of Communications, Flora Macdonald, announced that Canada's right to determine our own culture was unchanged. The centrepiece of this argument is the cultural exemption provision:

*Article 2005: Cultural Industries*

*Cultural industries are exempt from the provisions of this Agreement, except as specifically provided for in Article 401 (Tariff Elimination), paragraph 4 of Article 1607 (divestiture of an indirect acquisition) and Articles 2006 and 2007 of this Chapter.*

*Notwithstanding any other provision of this Agreement, a party may take measures of equivalent commercial effect in response to actions that would be inconsistent with this Agreement but for paragraph 1.*

However, one can see from even a cursory reading of this text, as well as other relevant clauses, that numerous provisions in the Agreement touch on cultural policies:

Article 4 eliminates tariffs imposed on various cultural goods imported into Canada.

Article 16, paragraph 4 states:

*In the event that Canada requires the divestiture of a business enterprise located in Canada in a cultural industry pursuant to its review of an indirect acquisition of such business enterprise by an investor of the United States of America, Canada shall offer to purchase the business enterprise from the investor of the United States of America at fair open market value, as determined by an independent, impartial assessment.*

Article 14 covers Services, Investment and Temporary Entry. These are some of the new issues that were embraced later in the Uruguay Round of GATT negotiations. The covered Commercial Services detailed in Annex 1408 include "Advertising and Promotional Services." The annex also specifically covers "telecommunications-network-based enhanced services."

Article 2004 provides that the parties will work to improve intellectual property protections in the Uruguay Round of GATT talks and other international fora.

Article 2006 obligates Canada to amend its *Copyright Act* by January 1, 1990 to provide the right of remuneration for the retransmission of a copyright holder's television program by Canadian cable companies and satellite service providers. This addressed the concerns of U.S. TV broadcasters located near the border whose signals were being redistributed widely by cable companies in Canada without payment.

Article 2007 calls for the repeal of the print-in-Canada requirement for Canadian newspapers or periodicals as defined in the *Income Tax Act* (S. 19.1) for purposes of allowing deductions from income of expenses incurred by a taxpayer for advertising space in these publications.

CUSFTA defines cultural industries in Article 2012:

> *Cultural industry means an enterprise engaged in any of the following activities:*
>
> a)  *the publication, distribution, or sale of books, magazines, periodicals, or newspapers in print or machine readable form but not including the sole activity of printing or typesetting any of the foregoing*

b)  *the production, distribution, sale or exhibition of film or video recordings*

c)  *the production, distribution, sale or exhibition of audio or video music recordings*

d)  *the publication, distribution, or sale of music in print or machine readable form*

e)  *radio communication in which the transmissions are intended for direct reception by the general public, and all radio, television and cable television broadcasting undertakings and all satellite programming and broadcast network services . . .*

In the next chapter, we will analyze what all these provisions mean and how the Canada–United States Free Trade Agreement has affected Canada's cultural policymaking. But, before heading in that direction, we will consider how CUSFTA was transformed into the North American Free Trade Agreement (NAFTA). The two agreements are inextricably linked, including in relation to culture.

## North American Free Trade Agreement

George H.W. Bush succeeded Ronald Reagan as president in 1988, around the same time Prime Minister Mulroney was victorious in Canada's free trade election. Shortly after he took office, President Bush launched free trade negotiations with Mexico. Before NAFTA, Mexican tariffs on U.S. imports were 250 per cent higher than U.S. tariffs on Mexican imports, so the United States had a powerful incentive to seek an agreement.

Canada's government and businesses had little interest in the Mexican market because of the low level of Canada-Mexico trade. However, Prime Minister Mulroney decided it would be better to join the negotiations and help shape the outcome, fearing that a deal without

Canada might divert trade and investment away from the country. In 1991, Canada joined the negotiations and NAFTA was signed by the three countries in 1992.

From the beginning, NAFTA was controversial in all three countries. When Bill Clinton was elected as U.S. president in 1992, he successfully pressed for the inclusion of two side deals, one designed to protect the environment and the other to promote labour rights. This delayed the ratification process.

In Canada, free trade once again became an election issue, although this time it was not the central focus of the campaign. In the early 1990s, support for Prime Minister Mulroney and his Conservative government was falling to record lows, and Mulroney resigned in February 1993. In that year's election campaign, under the leadership of Jean Chrétien, the Liberal party introduced its Red Book, which contained a detailed list of election promises and the cost for each. Promises included everything from establishing a national childcare policy, eliminating the unpopular Goods and Services Tax and reforming the unemployment insurance program, to cancelling privatization of Toronto's Pearson Airport. In the Red Book, Chrétien also promised to renegotiate NAFTA.

The Liberal party won a majority government in the October 1993 election, although it took only a minority (41 per cent) of the popular vote. The New Democratic party had also promised to tear up NAFTA, and it received 7 per cent of the popular vote. While the position of the newly formed Bloc Québécois had been ambivalent with regard to NAFTA, at least some of the 14 per cent of Canadians who voted for the Bloc were likely in the anti-NAFTA camp. Thus, it can be argued that for the third time in the twentieth century, i.e., at every opportunity, Canadians had voted against a free trade agreement with our southern neighbour.

After his election, Prime Minister Chrétien quickly retreated from his commitment to renegotiate NAFTA and Reagan's vision of a free trade area from "the Yukon to the Yucatan" was realized on January 1, 1994.

CUSFTA contains rights for business people and professionals to move freely across the Canada–U.S. border. NAFTA does not extend any such rights to Mexican business people or professionals. Otherwise, NAFTA is a far more comprehensive agreement than the Canada–United States Free Trade Agreement. In negotiating NAFTA, the Parties fully embraced the new trade issues being discussed in the Uruguay Round of GATT negotiations.

In place of the minimal CUSFTA provision for Canada and the United States to work together in other fora to improve the protection of intellectual property rights and the retransmission right for U.S. border broadcasters, NAFTA's Chapter 17 establishes minimum standards the Parties must meet in copyright, patent, trademark and other intellectual property laws.

NAFTA's Chapter 11 establishes extensive rights for foreign investors, including the right of private investors to challenge government policies that interfere with their operations. Under the Investor-State Dispute Settlement (ISDS) system of Chapter 11, Canada became the most sued developed country in the world. The United States has never lost a Chapter 11 challenge, and by the end of 2017 the challenges launched by private investors against Canadian federal and provincial policies had cost the government $314 million, with billions of dollars of claims outstanding at that time. Of the forty-one cases filed against Canada, over 60 per cent involved environmental protections and resource management.[11]

Significantly, NAFTA is a top-down or negative list agreement, meaning that every relevant sector is covered, except if it is subject to an exception or reservation. This is particularly relevant for NAFTA's Chapter 12 regarding services. Remember that the FTA is a bottom-up or positive list agreement, meaning that the CUSFTA Chapter on services includes only those specifically listed. NAFTA on the other hand includes every existing service sector, and any new sector that develops in the future, unless a party has listed it as an exception and/or taken a "reservation" for existing policies that would otherwise violate the core rules of National Treatment and Most-Favoured-Nation treatment.

What then becomes relevant are the rules concerning such reservations — now common in trade agreements, but which were relatively new when NAFTA was concluded.

### Article 1206: Reservations

1. *Articles 1202 (National Treatment), 1203 (Most-Favoured-Nation Treatment) and 1205 (Prohibition of government measures to require a foreign service provider to have a Local Presence) do not apply to:*

   a) *any existing non-conforming measure that is maintained by (any level of government)*

   b) *the continuation or prompt renewal of any non-conforming measure . . .*

   c) *an amendment to any non-conforming measure . . . to the extent that the amendment does not decrease the conformity of the measure, as it existed immediately before the amendment, with Articles 1202, 1203 and 1205.*

In non-legalese, this provision means that where a party has a measure or policy that supports or gives preference to local service providers, or discriminates between foreign service providers, that policy can be maintained or made weaker, but it can never be strengthened.

Cultural industries are then exempted from NAFTA in a very curious way:

### Annex 2106: Cultural industries

*Notwithstanding any other provision of this Agreement, as between Canada and the United States, any measure adopted or maintained with respect to cultural industries, except as specifically provided in Article 302 (Market Access – Tariff Elimination), and any measure of equivalent commercial effect taken in response, shall be governed under this Agreement exclusively in accordance with the provisions of the Canada–United States Free Trade Agreement. The rights and obligations between Canada and any other party with respect to such measures shall be identical to those applying between Canada and the United States.*

Thus, the NAFTA "cultural exemption" does not exist. It is included in NAFTA only by reference to the Canada–United States Free Trade Agreement. The CUSFTA definition of Cultural Industries ("any enterprise engaged in any of the following activities . . .") was changed in NAFTA to "any person engaged in any of the following activities . . ." Otherwise, the definition is identical to that found in CUSFTA.

The use of the imprecise words *industry* and *enterprise* in CUSFTA may reflect the fact that the cultural exemption was agreed to only at the last minute in the 1987 negotiating process. The term *cultural industries* is more typically used since there are different media of production. *Person* is a more precise legal term because it includes all businesses, whether incorporated or not, and whether operating for profit or not, as well as natural persons.

In 1989–92, I was a member of the Cultural Industries SAGIT and participated in discussions with government officials, ministers and those who were negotiating NAFTA. Unsuccessfully, I argued that the definition of cultural industries needed to be updated and expanded. It includes only some of the media ("activities") that existed in 1987 and leaves out visual arts, performing arts, design and crafts. This was an important issue for NAFTA because of the top-down nature of the agreement. With the implementation of NAFTA, visual arts, performing arts, design and crafts would now be considered covered services, since they are not exempted or reserved in any way. I also pointed out that we cannot possibly know what new media artists will use in the coming decades to create their works. The static nature of the definition is problematic since any such new medium may fall outside the 1987 definition.

Most SAGIT members agreed to some extent with my analysis. Some felt that, since Canada would never want to "regulate" visual arts or performing arts, their inclusion was irrelevant. The majority felt it would be impossible for Canada to renegotiate the definition in any case.

So, let us now turn to understanding how trade agreements are affecting cultural policymaking.

# A Digression
# Elsewhere in the World

Before we look at how trade agreements have affected Canadian cultural policies and policymaking, we consider two straightforward international examples that illustrate clearly how trade negotiations and agreements can have a profound and negative impact on cultural policies.

## New Zealand Broadcasting

In 1989, the government of New Zealand deregulated its broadcasting system when it began to allow competition to the state-owned Television New Zealand. When GATS came into force on January 1, 1995, New Zealand was one of few countries to commit its audiovisual services. In running for election in 1999, the Labour party under Helen Clark pledged to introduce format-specific domestic content quotas for radio and television since New Zealand shows, particularly in culturally significant areas such as scripted content and music, were in short supply. The Labour party took office in December 1999. That year, over the whole television system, New Zealand programs were shown for 38.5 per cent of the evening hours (6–10 p.m.).

Only after assuming office did the government discover that it would be extremely difficult, and very expensive, for it to fulfill its pledge to introduce local content quotas. Having already committed the audio-visual sector under GATS, any new content quotas — which would constitute restrictions on access to New Zealand by foreign television programs and sound recordings — would directly violate the National Treatment provision of the agreement and could thus be challenged at the WTO. As we have seen, under GATS rules, New Zealand was free to withdraw the audiovisual sector from its commitments, but only if it "compensated" all foreign service providers that could be affected by the decision. It would have been virtually impossible to identify all those that could potentially be affected, let alone to provide the required financial compensation.

Instead, the government brought the industries together and, after several years of negotiations, reached agreements to introduce voluntary quotas for radio in 2002 and for television in 2003. Perhaps needless to say, the voluntary quotas have had mixed results.

The radio quota required relevant formats to achieve 20 per cent New Zealand music content by 2006. *The Spinoff*, a site covering New Zealand pop culture, reported in May 2018 on an informal survey of radio stations it conducted during New Zealand Music Month.[1] While the results were mixed, only five of the fourteen stations achieved the required standard in the survey period. Nine fell far short of the 20 per cent domestic content requirement, and five of these did not broadcast *any* New Zealand music during the survey period.

Canadian radio stations must ensure that at least 35 per cent of their popular music content is Canadian music. Australia has a tiered system that varies depending on genre, although the highest level is 25 per cent. In the Australia–United States Free Trade Agreement, which came into effect in 2005, the radio content quotas were capped at this 25 per cent level. Once again, the quota can be lowered, but it can never be raised.

On the television side, New Zealand content in prime time rose to a high of 43.3 per cent in 2006, it fell to 36 per cent in 2015 and 31 per cent in 2016, lower than when Prime Minister Clark took office.[2] In this same period, the conventional Canadian broadcasters were required to show Cancon for 60 per cent over the entire broadcast day and 50 per cent in evening hours; Australian broadcasters had to meet a 55 per cent Australian content requirement.

## South Korea Cinema Screen Quotas

In 1966, the government of South Korea enacted a movie promotion law that required each theatre to show Korean movies 40 per cent of the time (146 days per year). The law was not implemented however because the government also had import quotas at the time. The import quotas were abandoned in 1986, and the market share of Hollywood movies rose quickly once they were able to enter the country freely.

After years of mobilization and pressure from the Korean film industry, the government agreed in 1993 to enforce the quota, which it informally reduced to 106 days per year. After a period of adjustment to having guaranteed market, the Korean film industry grew explosively. The domestic market share for Korean films increased from 16 per cent in 1992 to more than 60 per cent in 2006. Korean movies were exported, and the leading directors and actors became global stars. In 2002, Im Kwon-Taek was the first Korean director to win the best director award at Cannes.

But the screen quotas represented a major impediment to free trade talks with the United States. American opposition to the quotas became one of the primary issues preventing talks from getting underway. In January 2006, the Korean government announced that the screen quota would be slashed in half — to 73 days per screen per year.[3] Negotiations leading to a free trade agreement began the next month and concluded successfully in 2007.

Not surprisingly, the share of box office revenues earned by Korean films dropped dramatically in the next five years to well below 40 per cent, before beginning a recovery in 2011. Some believe this shows a negative impact on the Korean film industry from the screen quota reduction, while others argue it became irrelevant given the subsequent upturn.[4]

Additional factors should be considered in this analysis. First, there is a strong Korean-owned distribution and exhibition industry, which favours domestic content. Second, beginning in 2007, government subsidies and tax breaks for the Korean industry began to increase. Finally, the reduced quota of 73 days per year still creates a floor of 20 per cent local content measured by time, which is far greater than the domestic market share in many other major markets, including Canada. Taken together, these additional factors have successfully overcome the significant quota reduction, although the 60 per cent market share reached in 2006 is unlikely ever to be achieved again. We must remember that the quota reduction came about because of U.S. insistence and represented the price Korea had to pay to enter free trade talks.

# Chapter 4
# "Free Trade" Limits Cultural Policymaking

## Film Policy is the First Victim

When CBC television was launched in 1952, it quickly began to hire producers, directors and technicians. They studied television techniques in the classroom and gained hands-on experience in the studios. CBC began to produce and broadcast high quality Canadian content programming of all kinds. With the emergence of stars such as Wayne and Shuster, Juliette, Tommy Hunter and Don Messer, some have dubbed the decade after CBC's launch "the Golden Age" of Canadian television. Directors, including Arthur Hiller, Norman Jewison and Ted Kotcheff learned and refined their craft in this process.

Except for the National Film Board, support for Canadian filmmakers was modest. The Canadian Cooperation Project did nothing to generate production activity, and a 50 per cent capital cost allowance introduced in 1954 to encourage investment in films had only a minor impact. Some serious emerging filmmakers felt their opportunities in Canada were limited. Hiller, Jewison and Kotcheff all left the country and established distinguished and award-winning careers in Hollywood and England. They were joined by some of the foremost early performers, including Leslie Nielsen, Lorne Greene and William Shatner.

In the early 1960s, film production began to blossom in Canada as mobile 16mm cameras made production easier, and the European auteur-driven movies created a new aesthetic. Responding to this emerging sector, the government created the Canadian Film Development Corporation (CFDC, now Telefilm Canada) in 1967. With financial support from CFDC, Canadian moviemakers began to bring unmistakably Canadian stories to life. Examples include Don Shebib's *Goin' Down the Road,* Claude Jutra's *Mon oncle Antoine,* which succeeded in both French and English, Peter Carter's *The Rowdyman,* and the first feature-length drama made by a Canadian woman, Sylvia Spring's *Madeleine Is . . .* While these movies were critically acclaimed, audiences were hard to find.

In 1974, the capital cost allowance was increased to 100 per cent, meaning investors could deduct the full cost of their investment in a Canadian movie from their income, regardless of the source of that income, in one tax year. It became trendy for doctors, lawyers, engineers, bankers and other professionals to invest in movies. This unleashed a tremendous boom in film that lasted for eight years until the allowance was returned to the 50 per cent level. While many of the movies from the tax shelter era were of questionable artistic quality, the production activity helped to create a world-class film infrastructure in Canada.

The 1981 film *Porky's,* which until 2002 was the highest grossing Canadian movie in history, highlighted many of the concerns that led to the end of the tax shelter era. Produced by Canada's Astral Media, the film was written and directed by Bob Clark, an American who worked in Canada between 1973 and 1983. It was a teenage coming-of-age story, set and filmed in Florida, with a largely American cast. Nevertheless, it technically qualified as a Canadian film, and once again, it enabled Canadian artists and craftspeople to work and gain valuable experience. Prominent producers Harold Greenberg, Robert Lantos and Garth Drabinsky emerged from this period as movie heavyweights. Directors such as David Cronenberg were able to work with much larger budgets than in their formative years, and Ivan Reitman's first commercial film productions were two Cronenberg films. Others were encouraged to enter the industry as well.

Throughout this period, the primary problem for Canadian movies was distribution and exhibition. For Hollywood, Canada has always been part of the domestic market. The practice was so pervasive that when the Screen Actors' Guild, under the leadership of its president Ronald Reagan, first negotiated residuals for film performers in 1960, foreign release rights did not become payable until after the movie was released beyond the United States and Canada. This remains the case today. At that time, Hollywood dominated distribution of films everywhere, including in Canada, and Canadian movies had little access, even to our own screens. *Porky's* succeeded in the market because it was essentially an American movie and part of the Hollywood system. It was first released in Colorado.

After creation of the CFDC and the capital cost allowance tax shelter boom of the 1970s, successive governments searched for ways to provide space in cinemas for Canadian movies and to reinvest into our films some of the substantial amounts Canadians spend on movie admissions. Hugh Faulkner, Secretary of State for Canada (the portfolio included culture at the time), negotiated voluntary quotas with Famous Players and Odeon Theatres in 1973 to guarantee a minimum of four weeks per theatre per year for Canadian movies, and a commitment to invest in those films. By 1976 it was clear the voluntary quota had failed yet again, and Minister Faulkner's successor, John Roberts, announced that the government intended to impose a 10 per cent tax on distribution revenues to fund Canadian film production.

Jack Valenti led the Hollywood pushback. Valenti was a powerful political operative in the United States before he became president of the Motion Picture Association of America (MPAA) in 1966. Following the 1963 assassination of U.S. President John F. Kennedy, Valenti can be seen in the famous photograph of Lyndon Johnson's swearing-in ceremony aboard Air Force One. His campaign against the proposed

Canadian measures was supported by the U.S. State Department. Together they forced the government to back down. When yet another "new" film policy was announced in May 1978, it did not include any tax on distribution revenues, only an increase in government funding to the CFDC and NFB.

Over the decades, there has been considerable discussion about implementing cinema screen quotas to provide access for Canadian movies, since these have worked exceptionally well in television and radio. In 1973, an Ontario Conservative government task force on film headed by broadcast executive John Bassett concluded: "a basic film industry exists. It's the audiences that need to be nurtured through theatrical exposure. The optimum method of accomplishing this is to establish a quota system for theatres."[1]

The federal government cannot directly introduce cinema screen quotas since the regulation of movie theatres falls under provincial jurisdiction according to Canada's constitution. While the federal government has authority to regulate broadcasting and productions made by the broadcasters, movie theatres fall outside direct federal authority, as do television programs and films produced independently. Thus, federal support for independent producers must be attached to the federal government's authority to:

1.  tax and spend (tax credits and direct grants)
2.  create federal institutions (Telefilm Canada, CBC and NFB), or
3.  control international trade.

Creative ideas being floated at the time included using the *Income Tax Act* to provide preferential tax treatment for tickets sales by movie theatres that showed a certain percentage of Canadian films.

In 1984, Hollywood movies accounted for 96.5 per cent of North American box office receipts. However, the business of moviemaking had changed from the 1930s when studios not only produced and distributed their own movies, they also owned the cinemas. By 1984, many Hollywood movies were being made by a growing number of independent production companies. The major studios could be the primary investor in the movie or could acquire exclusive release rights, but some independent distributors had also emerged. While the major studios began to move out of direct ownership of theatres, they still controlled scheduling by making the most popular movies available to theatres only in packages with their other films. Concurrently, some small Canadian distributors had gained a foothold. They survived by acquiring the rights to Canadian movies or Canadian release rights to some films produced independently in the United States or outside North America.

## Efforts to Regulate Film Distribution Become an Issue in Trade Talks

The first serious effort to legislate the film distribution system in Canada took place in Quebec. In 1981, the Parti Québécois came to power with strong backing from the powerful cultural community. The government quickly commissioned a study of the film industry, *Le cinéma: une question de survie et d'excellence*, which led to the tabling of Bill 109 in December 1982. The bill required distribution companies in Quebec to be at least 80 per cent Canadian-owned, and distributors and exhibitors to contribute a percentage of profits to a production fund. Valenti was livid and threatened that Hollywood would boycott Quebec theatres. Negotiations began, and the Bill was weakened before being unanimously adopted by the National Assembly in June 1983. As we will see shortly, this did not settle the dispute.

At the federal level, Marcel Masse, a moderately nationalist Quebec MP, was appointed federal Minister of Communications (which had assumed responsibility for culture) in September 1984. He served twice in that position until June 1986. Minister Masse appointed a committee to examine Canada's film industry. The report of the Film Industry Task Force: *Canadian Cinema – a Solid Base* was tabled in February 1986. It recommended a feature film fund and a requirement that, through a film importation licensing system, Canadian distribution rights for all films be acquired separately from U.S. rights. Many in the Canadian industry were lobbying hard for cinema screen quotas. Minister of Communications Flora Macdonald announced on February 13, 1987 that the government would table a bill on film distribution that would create such a licensing system.

Valenti kept up his campaign against these efforts to create a separate Canadian distribution market, and he was concerned that cinema screen quotas could emerge as a serious policy option. As before, the MPAA was fully supported by the U.S. government. The film sector issues were thus put on the table by the United States when negotiations for a free trade agreement began in 1986.

Ten days after the conclusion of negotiations for the Canada–United States Free Trade Agreement, the opposition parties tabled a briefing paper in the House of Commons. The paper, which was addressed to James Baker, U.S. Secretary of the Treasury, and Clayton Yeutter, the U.S. Trade Representative, reported on various Canadian positions on the FTA. On October 15, 1987, this exchange took place in the House of Commons between NDP leader Ed Broadbent and the Minister of Finance, Michael Wilson:

> *Mr. Broadbent (Oshawa): I want to go to another area in
> the same document concerning the so-called protection the
> government obtained in the cultural domain. Mr. Jack Valenti, a
> Hollywood film mogul, said recently before Canadian audiences
> on television that he objected to the proposed new film legislation
> that was to be brought in by the Government of Canada.
> Subsequently that was denied by the Minister involved, but I want
> to read what it says in this document about what was agreed on
> that subject. It says, and I quote: "They (with reference to the
> Government of Canada) have also promised to solve Jack Valenti's
> problem on film distribution within the next two weeks." Could
> the Government tell us what that means?*

*Mr. Wilson (Etobicoke Centre):* That was never even discussed. On the question of Mr. Valenti's problem, there was no commitment, no understanding to solve Mr. Valenti's problem. The Minister of Communications has stated quite clearly that *the government has a commitment to ensure that Canada is treated as a separate market for film distribution. That commitment still stands.*

*Mr. Broadbent (Oshawa): Mr. Speaker, some of us are inclined to believe something, let me put it this way, other than that. We are going to look with interest at the Bill the Minister has promised to introduce.*[2] *(emphasis added)*

The events that surrounded the free trade negotiations and this exchange in Parliament should be of little surprise.

In October 1986, the new Quebec Liberal government announced it had reached an agreement with the MPAA. The Hollywood majors would be grandfathered under its laws and would be allowed to continue to release in Quebec those movies for which they had "proprietary rights," based on having worldwide release rights or a substantial (majority) investment. The Hollywood majors also agreed to make French-language versions of their movies available in Quebec. At the federal level, the Conservative government reneged on its promise to ensure that Canada was treated as an entirely separate market when it tabled a revised *Film Products Importation Act* in June 1988 containing the same grandfathering provision as in Quebec. Even that modest approach did not proceed when the proposed act died quietly on the Order Paper.

Finally, Investment Canada (previously known as FIRA) issued a directive concerning the film distribution industry. The directive provides that:

- takeovers of Canadian-owned and -controlled distribution businesses would not be allowed

- investments to establish new distribution businesses in Canada would only be allowed for importation and distribution activities related to proprietary products (where the importer owns world rights or is a major investor), and
- indirect and direct takeovers of foreign distribution businesses operating in Canada would be allowed only if the investor undertakes to reinvest a portion of Canadian earnings in Canadian content production.

Importantly, it also provided that the policy would apply to *applications* made after February 13, 1987 (the date of Minister Macdonald's announcement).[3] Since the Hollywood majors were already established in Canada at that date, they would not need to apply to Investment Canada and could effectively distribute any movie they wanted.

The 1987 film distribution policy remains in place today. It has perhaps been one reason there is a small space for Canadian companies to distribute some U.S. indie films, Canadian films and some of those independently produced outside North America. But its effect has been limited, and the cracks in the policy have been revealed, as we will see below and later in the PolyGram case.

Appearing before the House of Commons Heritage Committee in March 2015, Richard Rapkowsky of the Canadian Association of Film Distributors and Exporters (CAFDE) called for a more vigorous implementation of the policy. He argued that several recent cases were eroding the "intent of the policy" by permitting U.S. companies Warner Bros. Entertainment Inc. and Paramount Pictures to acquire Canadian distribution rights as an add-on to their U.S. rights. Worse still, Sony Pictures was allowed to acquire Canadian rights to a suite of movies for which they did not even own U.S. rights. According to Rapkowsky, these examples signal:

> *a disturbing erosion of the policy and its intent, an erosion that*
> *will inevitably lead to a decline in the success that the sector*

*and the government have worked so hard to achieve for close to three decades . . . (and demonstrate) clearly the slippery slope of allowing the U.S. studios to fly in the face of the spirit and intent of the policy. The erosion of the policy's protections puts the gains that the sector and Heritage Canada have made to date in jeopardy. I can assure you that, if left unchecked, these activities will decimate the Canadian distribution sector.*[4]

Any thought of introducing Canadian cinema screen quotas also appears to have disappeared with the Conservative Government's 1987 commitment to "solve Jack Valenti's problem on film distribution."

In 2016, American movies accounted for 87.7 per cent of Canadian box office receipts. Those imported from markets other than the United States accounted for 10.5 per cent. Further, CMPA's *Profile 2017* reports that, in the English-language market, Canadian films' share of the box office "increased" to 0.8 per cent. In the French-language market, Canadian films' share of the box office declined to 8.7 per cent.[5]

While it may have taken more than the two weeks to which the Canadian government agreed, Mr. Valenti must surely now be fully satisfied since his problem has been solved.

## Canadian Ownership Rules Eroded in Trade Talks

Canadians are more likely to tell our stories and to reflect our worldview. In every cultural industry, Canadian-owned firms are responsible for the overwhelming preponderance of production by Canadian artists. In every year for more than four decades, 80 per cent of Canadian books and virtually all movies and television programs that are Canadian in content, and use Canadian artists, are produced by Canadian-owned firms. Thus, from early days, Canada has mandated Canadian ownership and/or restricted foreign investment in Canadian companies.

As we have seen, the Foreign Investment Review Agency (FIRA) was set up in 1973 and given power to review all proposed acquisitions of

Canadian firms by foreign interests. It could approve only those that were of "net benefit to Canada." Though FIRA was designed primarily to review takeovers in manufacturing and natural resources, acquisitions of firms dealing with book and magazine publishing and film distribution were also covered.

In book publishing, special regulations were announced in 1974. These prohibited direct foreign takeovers of Canadian firms or the establishment of new operations by foreign companies. FIRA would permit a foreign investor to acquire an existing foreign-controlled subsidiary, typically as part of a larger international acquisition, providing there was a "net benefit" to Canada, in both cultural as well as economic terms.

While FIRA's implementation of the policy was inconsistent, it achieved substantial gains for Canadian ownership in two early cases.

In 1976, American company Gulf + Western Industries bought U.S. publisher Simon & Schuster, including its mass-market paperback imprint Pocket Books, and announced its intention to distribute directly into Canada. At the time, Canadian-owned General Publishing Corporation was the distributor for both Simon & Schuster and Pocket Books in Canada. As a result of FIRA's intervention, General Publishing acquired Pocket Books Canada and also retained distribution rights to the Simon & Schuster list. Jack Stoddard's General Publishing Corporation was one of Canada's big three publishing companies at that time.

The following year, FIRA reviewed the change of ownership of Bantam Books Canada. FIRA allowed the acquisition to proceed, but only when Bantam's new owners entered a joint venture with another of Canada's three largest publishers, McClelland & Stewart, to create a new imprint, Seal Books. Jack McClelland owned 51 per cent of the new company, which went on to publish a significant number of Canadian-authored mass-market paperbacks in the following years.[6]

When the Conservative government of Prime Minister Brian Mulroney was elected in September 1984, it moved quickly to change FIRA's name to Investment Canada and its mandate to one that would facilitate foreign investment into Canada. It retained the requirement that any acquisition should be of "net benefit" to Canada.

In November 1984, Gulf + Western Industries announced its latest acquisition, the takeover of Prentice Hall Inc., one of the largest textbook publishers in the world. The acquisition would have included the indirect acquisition of two small Canadian textbook publishers, Ginn and Company, and General Learning Corporation (GLC).

The new Minister of Communications, Marcel Masse, was thus confronted with a number of challenges relating to foreign ownership, film distribution and the debate around the cultural implications of the proposed Canada–United States Free Trade Agreement. In 1985, Minister Masse convinced his cabinet colleagues to implement the Baie Comeau foreign ownership policy. This policy prohibited the sale of a Canadian-owned publisher to a non-Canadian. It also stipulated that, if a foreign firm indirectly acquired a Canadian subsidiary as part of a takeover of another foreign firm, it would have to divest its interest in the Canadian subsidiary. The policy was expanded later to cover record producers as well as film and video distributors.

As a result of the Baie Comeau policy, the government announced in March 1986 that it had approved Gulf + Western's acquisition of Prentice Hall Canada, but as part of the deal the company had agreed to sell 51 per cent of both Ginn and Company and GLC to Canadian buyers within two years. In reporting on this development on March 16, 1986, the New York Times noted:

> In a meeting last October in Calgary, Alberta, Secretary of State
> George P. Shultz put pressure on Canada's Secretary of State for
> External Affairs, Joe Clark, to get the controversy over Prentice
> Hall resolved . . . The accord, announced five days before Prime
> Minister Brian Mulroney flies to Washington for an annual
> meeting with President Reagan, defuses, at least temporarily,
> one dispute that clouded the negotiations on freer trade planned
> between the world's two largest trading partners.[7]

As we have seen, the Canada–United States Free Trade Agreement's Article 1607, paragraph 4, regarding divestiture of an indirect acquisition, is *excluded* from the cultural exemption and hence subject to the Free Trade Agreement. This provision states:

> In the event that Canada requires the divestiture of a business
> enterprise . . . in a cultural industry pursuant to its review of an
> indirect acquisition of such business . . . Canada shall offer to
> purchase the business enterprise . . . at fair open market value, as
> determined by an independent, impartial assessment.

There was no successful Canadian private sector bidder for the companies because Gulf + Western was seeking far too much for them. As a result, in 1988 the Canada Development and Investment Corporation (CDIC), established by the government in 1982 to manage investments the government assigned to it, purchased a 51 per cent interest in Ginn and Company and GLC. Gulf + Western not only remained in charge, they also had a veto over disposition of the CDIC shares. In 1994, in a move that received a great deal of publicity at the time, the firm was sold back to the new U.S. parent of Prentice Hall. It was revealed that CDIC had paid *three times more* than the highest private-sector offer for the company in 1988 and had sold it back for the same amount six years later.

The resolve of successive federal governments to maintain Canadian ownership in cultural industries has weakened gradually over the years. In 1992, the latest iteration of the book publishing policies was developed. Investment Canada moved away from forced divestment of cultural industry firms and instead stipulated that any new foreign investment should be compatible with national cultural policies and be "of net benefit to Canada and to the Canadian-controlled sector."

Author and book industry expert Roy MacSkimming has analyzed the thirteen cases reviewed by Investment Canada from 1992 to 2017 and reached this conclusion:

*The findings show broad disparities and inconsistencies in
the policy's implementation, depending on the nature of the
transaction, the government in power, and the political and
economic context of the day. In several cases, rulings favoured
expansion of the foreign investment in stages, beyond limits
previously approved — a process that the (Association of
Canadian Publishers) has likened to the "camel ('s nose) in the
tent" analogy. Only two rulings — Indigo / Borders (1996) and
Prentice Hall / Addison-Wesley (1999) — provided significant
net benefit to Canada and the Canadian-controlled sector. A
partial case could also be made for rulings in a third transaction.
The remaining ten rulings strengthened, primarily or exclusively,
the interests of the foreign investors. They accomplished little or
nothing for Canada or the Canadian-controlled sector, sometimes
doing the sector demonstrable harm.*

*The unavoidable conclusion is that the policy has been effective
in achieving its objectives only rarely. In more recent years its
implementation has been largely ineffective and, indeed, counterproductive — the result of successive rulings that circumvented
the policy's core purpose by providing foreign investors with
unjustified "exceptions" to its guidelines.*[8]

While the terms of the agreements reached under the net benefit
negotiations are generally confidential, in several cultural sectors they
appear to have generated significant negative consequences for Canadian firms in one respect. That is where there has been a requirement that foreign firms working in Canada publish Canadian authors
or sign Canadian musicians. This obligation has increased the value
of leading Canadian artists as they became sought after by the large
multinational firms, to the benefit of the individual artists who signed
lucrative deals. Overall, however, the policy hurt the Canadian firms
as they have been generally too small to compete with these contracts

and could not offer the same degree of foreign distribution. As a result, Canadian firms lost an important revenue stream that had previously been used to reinvest in the development of up-and-coming Canadian talent.

The ownership rules governing telecommunications companies, cable television firms, and broadcasters were standardized in 1996 as part of the federal government's Convergence Policy Statement, which recognized that there would be increasing competition between them. At the same time, the foreign ownership limits in the broadcasting and cable sectors were increased. As of 2004, foreign interests could acquire a 20 per cent direct interest in a television broadcaster or cable company, and up to one-third of a holding company, effectively permitting foreign ownership of 46.7 per cent.

## Specific Canadian Policy Changes Mandated or Affected by FTA and NAFTA

In addition to the deals made specifically relating to the film and publishing sectors during the negotiations and despite the cultural exemption, cultural measures were included in the Free Trade Agreement and NAFTA.

Some of these were of little concern to the cultural sector:

- Elimination of the print-in-Canada requirement did not materially affect our capacity to create and produce Canadian books, magazines, periodicals or newspapers.
- The tariff on books was already set at zero by 1987.
- The tariff on records and tapes was being phased out over ten years, and
- The tariff on motion pictures and commercials was scheduled to be eliminated in 1994.

While the inclusion of "telecommunications-network-based enhanced services" potentially could have affected music, audio or television programs distributed via the telephone copper wire, technological advances have rendered this section moot. These advances include the rollout of coaxial and fibre optic cables and subsequently wireless technologies, which have far greater capacity than the old copper wire technology used to provide telecommunications services in 1987.

But other provisions of CUSFTA and NAFTA were more significant.

## The Decline in Canadian Television Commercials

"Advertising and promotional services" are included under the Commercial Services covered in CUSFTA Annex 1408. In a brief submitted on July 19, 1988, to the House of Commons Legislative Committee regarding Bill C-130, *An Act to Implement the Free Trade Agreement between Canada and the United States*, ACTRA raised concerns that this inclusion would have negative consequences for the production and broadcast of Canadian television commercials. The union pointed out that many who work in the film and television industry rely on their earnings from commercials and emphasized that more than one-third of performers' earnings in 1987 came from commercial work.[9]

When Canada first introduced television content quotas, there was discussion of implementing quotas for television commercials. With the industry's voluntary agreement to maintain the existing level of Canadian content, roughly 80 per cent at the time, quotas were not introduced. In the decade after CUSFTA came into force, the production and use of Canadian commercials fell. In an August 2001 submission to the House of Commons Standing Committee on Canadian Heritage, an informal coalition, the Alliance for Canadian Advertising Tax Credits (ACATC), reported that fewer than 50 per cent of the commercials broadcast by Canadian television services in 1997 were created in Canada. The ACATC recommended that a tax credit incentive be devised to encourage commercial production. No action was taken however, and the slow decline has continued. ACTRA reports that in 2017 less than 14 per cent of performer earnings came from commercial work.[10]

The globalization of the advertising business has clearly played a role in the diminished use of Canadian commercials and the loss of important work opportunities for Canadian artists. But the inclusion of advertising services in CUSFTA is also implicated.

Some might suggest that television commercials should not be considered part of our cultural industries, but I would argue their content can be profoundly cultural. One need only consider the famous Bell Canada *Dieppe,* Canadian Tire *Bicycle,* or Molson Brewery *I am Canadian* commercials. Commercials constitute a powerful cultural medium, a means of transmitting the mores, values, traditions and lifestyle of a society to future generations and new citizens. The nuance of social ritual is perhaps reflected more fully in commercials than in any other medium, since commercials are about everyday goods and services. As ACTRA and the ACATC pointed out many years ago, work on television commercials comprised an important part of the way that performers, technicians and directors could earn a living in their profession; yet work in the sector has plummeted since 1987.

When the ACATC raised the issue of declining levels of Canadian television commercials in the early 2000s, senior government officials argued that imposing television commercial content quotas may well violate CUSFTA. They also felt that a tax incentive as proposed by the ACATC could likely be challenged by the United States based on the sector's inclusion in the original agreement. We will see this issue again when we consider the WTO *Canadian Periodicals Case.*

## Canada-United States Free Trade Agreement Brings Changes to Copyright Law

The CUSFTA had several provisions that obligated Canada to amend the *Copyright Act* in January 1989.

U.S. stations near the border and their program suppliers had sought, in Canadian law, the right to authorize any retransmission of their signal in Canada. This would have enabled them to negotiate a fee from the cable and satellite companies. The compromise agreement reached in the CUSFTA did not establish such a right. Instead, it provided that Canadian cable and satellite companies could retransmit signals that were within the footprint of the traditional microwave television transmission towers without seeking permission or making any payment. Thus, Buffalo television stations, which I watched in east-end Toronto in the 1950s with a regular TV antenna, could be provided freely in Toronto by cable companies. Cable and satellite companies were also free to retransmit distant signals (for example, Boston or Detroit television stations into Toronto) without authorization, however, they would be required to pay a royalty, established by Canada's Copyright Board, to the copyright owners of the programs broadcast. While the Canadian royalty applies equally to U.S. and Canadian distant signals, it inevitably favours the U.S. services since they are the most likely to be retransmitted.

The amendments also expanded the concept of "communication to the public" from broadcasting to include all forms of telecommunication. While this was designed primarily to ensure programs carried by cable and satellite transmissions were covered under the appropriate laws, it was a fortuitous decision in light of the digital technologies that were to emerge in the next decade.

As required by the North American Free Trade Agreement, Canada's *Copyright Act* was further amended in January 1994 to introduce a rental right for sound recordings and computer programs (copyright owners could authorize or prohibit the rental of works). The amendment also increased protections against the importation into Canada of copyright works that were not authorized to be imported.

While the 1989 and 1994 amendments generated little controversy in Canada (one does not often "rent" a computer program or a sound recording today), the fact is they represent significant policy changes made not because of domestic policy considerations but because the United States insisted on them in trade negotiations.

## United States Threatens Retaliation under CUSFTA/NAFTA Notwithstanding Clause

The CUSFTA cultural exemption, and its NAFTA extension, is accompanied by a clause that authorizes retaliation against measures taken under the exemption. This provision comes into effect if the measure in question would have violated the agreements if not for the exemption. The retaliation is supposed to be limited to measures of equivalent commercial effect to the initial measure.

In 1984, the CRTC authorized cable and satellite companies to make the U.S. Country Music Television (CMT) channel available to Canadian subscribers. The rules at the time provided that if the CRTC subsequently licensed a Canadian service in the same genre, this authorization could be revoked. This was explicitly stated in the CMT licensing decision. In June 1994, the CRTC licensed the Canadian-owned New Country Network, and removed the authorization for carriage of CMT, effective the following January.

CMT first challenged this decision in the Canadian courts. When the challenge failed, it turned to the U.S. government for help. That investigation quickly escalated to threats of retaliation under the CUSFTA/NAFTA notwithstanding clause. Washington's list of retaliation targets included Canadian media companies operating in the United States, sound recordings, as well as seemingly random products likely chosen for greatest political effect, including maple syrup, bacon and fur coats. It also included imposition of a mirror Federal Communications Commission regulation against Canadian services.

As part of its case, CMT submitted a detailed legal brief prepared by a leading U.S. law firm. The brief argued that the CRTC's order to remove CMT from carriage constituted expropriation of CMT's Canadian assets, in violation of the National Treatment (and other) provisions of NAFTA Chapters 11 and 12, which cover investment and trade in services, as well as relevant international law.

The brief made two arguments that would have made for an interesting case had it proceeded to a dispute resolution panel.

1. The cultural industries exemption did not apply because there was no cultural purpose served by requiring the service to be Canadian-owned rather than American-owned, and the effect of the CRTC's decision was purely economic, and

2. The exemption did not cover derogations from new obligations in NAFTA that did not exist in the CUSFTA.

In other words, the brief argued that the CUSFTA exemption had a cultural purpose and that its incorporation by reference into NAFTA meant that its effect was limited to the scope of the older agreement and did not extend to new sectors and new obligations included for the first time in NAFTA.

The dispute was resolved when CMT and New Country Network reached a commercial agreement, under which they launched CMT (Canada), with the Canadian partner holding a sufficiently large ownership stake to permit licensing as a Canadian service.[11]

Since the implementation of the Canada–United States Free Trade Agreement, this is the only case where the United States seriously considered retaliating against Canadian cultural measures "that would have been inconsistent with" CUSFTA or NAFTA obligations were it not for the cultural exemption.

This also raises the question of whether or not Canada would have the right to seek adjudication of any U.S. decision to implement retaliatory measures or the quantum of such measures. The notwithstanding clause "limits" the amount of the measures to "equivalent commercial effect." While CMT estimated its loss at $63 million USD (including future earnings), the cost of the retaliatory measures under consideration in 1995 by the United States far exceeded that amount. Most believe Canada would not have been able to challenge retaliatory measures.

# The Threat of Retaliation Limits Canada's Cultural Policymakers

When the terms of CUSFTA were first released, differing interpretations of the notwithstanding clause emerged. In its July 19, 1988 brief to the House of Commons Legislative Committee regarding Bill C-130, ACTRA said this:

> *This paragraph is interpreted very differently by the two parties to the Agreement. The United States says that Canada has agreed that future measures in the cultural area will be limited and in accord with the principles of the Agreement. Canada says that it has defended our right to introduce cultural measures. The United States has reserved its right to retaliate against those measures, but it agrees to limit its reaction to equivalent commercial effect.*[12]

Canadian cultural policymakers have changed their thinking as a direct result of this clause and the threat of retaliation. In discussions with senior officials on several policy files, I have been told directly that they needed to consider whether a particular policy measure being considered would risk retaliation. Not surprisingly, policymakers began to show a clear preference for solutions that would not permit retaliation and that thus needed to be consistent with CUSFTA/ NAFTA obligations, as the U.S. analysis anticipates. Concretely, this often means that they would recommend funding programs, rather than structural measures, since subsidy of domestic producers and artists is generally trade-compliant.

Furthermore, in 1997 the CRTC quietly and indirectly eliminated its policy that a competitive service would be removed when a similar Canadian service is licensed.

## Canada's Coproduction Treaties at Risk

In 1963, Canada and France negotiated the world's first coproduction treaty. Canada currently maintains the largest number of such treaties — with fifty-seven other countries.[13] Some partners have an established production capacity. Others, like Luxembourg and Macedonia are not production powerhouses, and the treaties were signed either because one producer had a script related to that country or because, as I was once told by a senior official, the government needed "something for the minister to sign" on a visit.

The story behind our coproduction treaty with China illustrates how such a treaty can come about. Canada and China have historically enjoyed a positive relationship. Norman Bethune, a doctor from Gravenhurst, is a hero in China. After fighting for the Republican side in the Spanish Civil War, Dr. Bethune joined Mao Zedong's Eighth Route Army in 1938 and worked selflessly as a battlefield surgeon, while also bringing modern medicine to nearby Chinese villages. He died in China of blood poisoning in 1939. Mao's eulogy of Dr. Bethune was for many years required reading in China. In 1970, Canada became one of the first Western counties to recognize the government of the People's Republic of China, and Prime Minister Pierre Trudeau travelled there in 1973, among the first major Western leaders to visit.

Canada director Phillip Borsos, whose 1982 film *The Grey Fox* is widely regarded as one of the best Canadian films of all time, was keen to bring Dr. Bethune's story to the big screen. He had eager, and highly successful, collaborators. Actor Donald Sutherland, who had been involved in the U.S. anti–Vietnam war movement alongside Jane Fonda, was keen to play the part of Dr. Bethune (and has done so on three occasions). Ted Allan was a Montreal author who befriended Dr. Bethune in 1934. He wrote the story and screenplay for the film, *Lies My Father Told Me* which won the 1975 Golden Globe Award for Best Foreign Film. His 1952 book (co-authored with Sydney Gordon) *The Scalpel, The Sword,* is the definitive biography of Dr. Bethune and one of the most globally widely read Canadian books in history. By 1987, the three had agreed to make *Bethune: The making of a hero.*

Not surprisingly and given the background, Canada and China entered into a film coproduction treaty that year. The treaty facilitated the production of what was at that time the most expensive Canadian movie ever made and one of the first major Western movies to be shot in China. It was released in 1990. Unfortunately, creative differences led to problems on set, the movie did not receive strong reviews from critics and it obtained only limited release. Allan had known Dr. Bethune as a human being with flaws and challenges, while Sutherland wanted to portray him strictly as a hero. Borsos, and no doubt Dr. Bethune, were caught in the middle.

When Prime Minister Justin Trudeau visited China in 2016, the countries signed a "refreshed" coproduction treaty that came into effect May 1, 2017. After all, the Prime Minister apparently needed "something to sign" on the visit.

The treaties offer Canadian and foreign producers a benefit if they combine their financial resources as well as creative and technical talent. An official treaty coproduction is granted national status in each of the partnering countries. Thus, the Canadian producers have access to grants and the incentives available for eligible Canadian expenses, and the movie or television program qualifies as Cancon, regardless of the mix of creative talent used. *Bethune: The making of a hero*, received an investment from Telefilm Canada, support from China's film agency and was exempted from China's strict film importation rules since it was considered a domestic film.

According to Profile 2017, Canada's leading coproduction partners over the decade ending in 2017 were France (185 projects), the United Kingdom (174 projects), followed by Germany, Australia, Ireland and Brazil (101 combined projects).

Since they offer special treatment to nationals of specific other countries, coproduction treaties violate the GATS Most-Favoured-Nation provisions. MFN applies whether or not a country has committed a particular economic sector under GATS. Thus, Canada and its treaty partners were required to list these treaties as nonconforming measures when the GATS came into effect in January 1995. Canada's listing is open-ended: "differential treatment is accorded to works coproduced with persons of countries with which Canada may have agreements . . ."[14] While this would enable Canada to enter into a future coproduction treaty with any other country, the other country may be prohibited from doing so, unless it also has a similar open-ended listing.

## *Canada Periodicals Case* – WTO Forces Canada to Change Magazine Policies

The economics of Canada's magazine industry historically have fully reflected the larger problem for Canadian cultural producers. The average print run of a U.S. magazine is many times greater than a similar Canadian magazine. Because it is published for a domestic market more than ten times the size of the market for the Canadian magazine, the U.S. magazine publisher amortizes editorial costs across a much larger potential circulation. The cost to the U.S. publisher of printing additional copies for export to Canada is marginal. Given that the Canadian markets for U.S. magazines mostly fall within a few hundred kilometres of the U.S. border, the additional transportation costs are negligible.

From the earliest days, Canadian magazines had a related competitive problem. Many popular U.S. magazines would sell space to Canadian advertisers and the print run of the magazine would be split, so that those exported to Canada would contain the Canadian advertisements. These became known as split-run magazines. As early as the mid-1950s, Canadian magazines lobbied for support, and the Liberal government introduced a tax on advertising in split-run editions in 1957. The tax was repealed the following year by Conservative Prime Minister John Diefenbaker, and the new government appointed a Royal Commission on Publications, chaired by Grattan O'Leary, a respected Conservative journalist.

The Royal Commission studied the complaints of the Canadian industry that U.S. split-run magazines enjoyed a huge competitive advantage. The two magazines that were the focus of the debate were *Reader's Digest*, which made only a few small editorial changes in the magazine sold to Canadians, and *Time*, which had a Canadian editorial office and offered numerous pages of Canadian editorial content in the Canadian edition it had launched in 1944. When the O'Leary Commission reported in 1961, it found that, of the seventy-six U.S. magazines offering split-run editions, six had Canadian "regional" editions.

The commission made two recommendations. The first was that advertisers should not be allowed to deduct their advertising expenditures in split-run magazines when filing their business tax returns. The second was that foreign periodicals containing more than 5 per cent advertising that was primarily directed to the Canadian market and was not contained in all editions of the publication released in the home country (the United States), would be prevented from entering Canada by Tariff Item 9958. While the recommendations were implemented, *Time* and *Reader's Digest* were exempted following their successful lobby campaign.[15]

Over the next decade, the situation of Canadian magazine producers did not improve dramatically. In 1970, a Senate committee chaired by Senator Keith Davey found that 70 per cent of all magazines distributed in Canada came from the United States, and that *Time* and *Reader's Digest* had actually increased their share of periodical advertising revenues from 43 per cent in 1958 to 56 per cent in 1969. While Canadian magazines were world leaders in developing strategies to maximize subscriptions, revenues from advertising remained essential to their survival and the diversion of advertising to split-run editions was significant. It concluded that exempting *Time* and *Reader's Digest* from the legislation had been a mistake.

While the tariff item prohibiting the importation of split-run magazines remained unchanged, the *Income Tax Act* was amended. Under the amendment, eligibility to deduct advertising expenses would be limited to magazines that were at least 75 per cent Canadian-owned and contained not more than 20 per cent content identical to the foreign publication. *Time* closed its Canadian editorial office in 1976 but continued to have a Canadian edition with some specific editorial content, which it sold at a discount to Canadian advertisers for many years. Interestingly, it avoided the tariff item by bringing its Canadian edition into Canada for printing via microfilm. *Reader's Digest* established a Canadian foundation in which 75 per cent of the shares were owned by Canadians.

Thus, as we entered the 1980s, the Canadian government supported Canadian magazines by prohibiting the importation of U.S. split-run magazines, by preventing Canadian businesses from deducting as an expense the costs of advertising placed in a split-run magazine, and by the preferential postal rate for Canadian magazines shipped across the country, which then came in the form of a financial subsidy provided to Canada Post.

In January 1993, Time Warner announced that *Sports Illustrated* would begin to publish a new Canadian edition of its very popular magazine. Well aware of the tariff item and the approach taken by *Time*, the publishers stated they would be transmitting the copy electronically to be printed in Canada.

There was initially some uncertainty on the part of the government about how to respond. To a certain extent, this was because Time Warner had approached Investment Canada about its *Sports Illustrated Canada* plans in 1990 and the agency had approved the application on the grounds that it was an expansion of *Time* magazine's existing business. In March 1993, just weeks before the first Canadian edition of *Sports Illustrated* appeared on newsstands, the government created a task force to examine the Canadian magazine industry. In March 1994, *A Question of Balance: Report of the Task Force on the Canadian Magazine Industry* recommended that the government apply a new excise tax of 80 per cent on each edition of a split-run magazine. The calculation was that this would be equal to the savings for advertisers placing their ads in split-run magazines. The legislation received royal assent in December 1995. The bill grandfathered all periodicals published in the twelve-month period prior to the launch of the task force in March 1993.

The United States objected strenuously to the new measure, but Canada refused to back down. After considering retaliation under the notwithstanding clause, the United States ultimately decided to pursue a formal appeal to the World Trade Organization in 1996.[16]

Before the WTO dispute settlement panel, Canada argued that

its measures were targeted at advertising and thus should be judged against its obligations under the General Agreement on Trade in Services (GATS). Canada noted that it had made no GATS commitments respecting advertising or publishing services. However, the dispute settlement panel (and subsequently the Appellate Body) found that magazines are a "good" and the content qualifies as "services," and they ruled that the obligations of both the GATT and GATS apply. The panel further found that since the excise tax was calculated on a "per issue" basis and thus applied to the whole magazine (the good) rather than to the advertising (a service) it contained, the measure was connected to the good. It also noted that the tax applied only to periodicals and not to advertising contained in other media. The panel concluded that these Canadian advertising measures violated the National Treatment commitment under GATT. On the other hand, the panel ruled in favour of Canada with respect to the postal subsidy, finding that such a subsidy for domestic producers was permitted under GATT.

Unwisely in the end, Canada appealed the panel's ruling. The Appellate Body upheld the core decision and further ruled that the postal subsidy did not constitute a direct subsidy of domestic producers, permitted under GATT, but was rather a subsidy of Canada's postal service. Canada was ordered to bring all of the measures found to be "inconsistent with the GATT 1994" into conformity with its obligations under the agreement.

An important element of the decision concerned the issue of whether Canadian and split-run U.S. magazines were "like products." The panel decided that indeed they were like products, however, the appellate body overturned this finding on the grounds the panel had based its decision on an unrealistic hypothetical comparison. However, the appellate body did rule that "newsmagazines like *Time*, *Time Canada* and *Maclean's* are directly competitive and substitutable in spite of the 'Canadian' content of *Maclean's*."

*Maclean's* is Canada's leading newsmagazine and *Time Canada* is a split-run magazine. In research I conducted around the time the case was finally concluded in 1998, that week's sixty-page *Maclean's* contained thirty pages of articles about Canadian society, politics, business, media, sports and entertainment, written by Canadian authors. It also featured fourteen pages of articles about international developments, all of which were written from a Canadian perspective. In that same week, the fifty-eight-page *Time Canada* magazine had only three pages devoted to Canadian items, two of which were authored by U.S. writers and the third by an expatriate Canadian working in the United States. The other pages dealt with U.S. society, politics, business, media, sports and entertainment, or were international stories written from a U.S. perspective.

The Appellate Body rejected Canada's argument that the editorial content of a magazine is culturally specific and is crucial to the consumers. It found that, under the trade agreements, it does not matter if the magazine is covering U.S. or Canadian news, or if it is covering international stories from a Canadian or U.S. perspective — all magazines dealing with news and current affairs are goods which are "directly competitive and substitutable" for one another.

Canada responded to the decision by rescinding the tariff item and the excise tax and reorganizing the postal subsidy so that it is paid into individual producer accounts. The government also introduced a measure to prohibit the sale of advertising services directed solely to Canadians, except by Canadian publishers. The United States threatened retaliation against this measure, and the parties ultimately negotiated a settlement bilaterally in 1999.

As a consequence of these developments, Canada now permits foreign magazines to sell advertising to Canadian businesses up to certain limits, which increase to the extent that the editorial content in the Canadian edition is original and not recycled from the U.S. edition. The United States agreed that it would not challenge Canadian magazine subsidies and Canada agreed to increase its limit on foreign ownership of Canadian magazine publishers to 49 per cent.[17]

As an important footnote, when the government was considering its response to the WTO ruling and possible policy measures it could use to support Canadian magazines in future, government officials realized that advertising services are included explicitly in CUSFTA. Thus, any strong measures to prohibit advertising in U.S. split-run magazines or other media would not be covered by the cultural exemption and would likely be prohibited under that agreement.

As a result of the final settlement of the dispute, the Canadian government was effectively limited to a direct funding strategy. In addition to the producer accounts at Canada Post, the government established the Canada Magazine Fund (now the Canada Periodical Fund) in 2000 to subsidize publishers of Canadian magazines.

## Film Distribution Policy at Risk under WTO Rules

The WTO was almost called upon to rule on the legitimacy of Investment Canada's 1987 film distribution policy that sought to ensure Canadian companies distribute all nonproprietary foreign films in Canada.

When PolyGram, a European company, established PolyGram Filmed Entertainment Canada (PFEC) in 1997, it applied to Investment Canada for permission to distribute nonproprietary films in Canada. The application was denied under the 1987 policy. The European Union requested formal consultations at the WTO, the first step in the dispute settlement process. Canada defended its policy on the grounds that it had not committed audiovisual services under GATS.

The EU argued that the problem was not with the cultural policy *per se*, but rather with the fact that the Hollywood studios were grandfathered. Since they do not need to apply to Investment Canada under the policy, they have always been free to distribute nonproprietary films. Any voluntary agreement they may have reached to limit their activities to proprietary films is irrelevant (and, as we have seen, has been breached in recent years). Since Canadian and American companies could distribute nonproprietary films in Canada, and only PFEC could not, this clearly violated the Most-Favoured-Nation (MFN) obligation. If you treat foreign investors from one foreign country in an advantageous manner, this same treatment must be provided to investors from all other countries that are

WTO members. The EU correctly pointed out that the MFN obligation applies to all services, whether committed by the country or not, except where the party has taken a reservation for a specific policy. Since Canada had not listed the federal film distribution policy as a reservation (only the coproduction treaties and Quebec's distribution policy were listed), the obligation remained, even though Canada had not included the audiovisual sector in its GATS commitments.

Particularly given the WTO decision in the Canada Periodicals Case, the case would have been extremely problematic for Canada. Once again, a commercial transaction resolved the problem. In 1998, the Canadian company Seagram acquired PolyGram as part of its adventure into the entertainment industry. While Seagram CEO Edgar Bronfman Jr. was most interested in the music assets of the company, PFEC had suddenly become a Canadian company that could distribute whatever films it wanted. The final installment in this tale began when the Seagram's empire collapsed in 1999 and PolyGram Filmed Entertainment was folded in 2000.

## Takeaways

Canada's right to design, implement and modify cultural policies was virtually unhindered by international agreements before the Canada–United States Free Trade Agreement. In the CUSFTA negotiations and in the final agreement, Canada agreed to modify certain cultural policies — the first time this had happened in the context of trade negotiations. More significantly, in 1987 Canada agreed to put a box around our cultural industries and cultural policies and agreed that certain sectors and policy instruments fall outside that box. Taken as a whole, the cultural exemption, the definition of cultural industries, the notwithstanding clause and the various agreements reached between Canada and the United States during the 1986–87 negotiations represent a fundamental watershed for Canadian cultural policymaking.

With successive trade negotiations and agreements Canada has concluded since 1987, both bilaterally and multilaterally, as well as technological developments that have changed how artistic works are produced and distributed to audiences, these constraints have further restricted our cultural policymaking space. The box has been made smaller and useful tools have been removed from our policy toolkit.

As we consider the range of cultural sectors that have been affected by trade agreements, it is important to recall how NAFTA was built upon and succeeded CUSFTA, and that as NAFTA was being negotiated between Canada, the United States and Mexico, the three countries were also engaged in the Uruguay Round of GATT talks. In those talks, the need for "l'exception culturelle" was front and centre. These concluded in April 1994 and resulted in the launch of the World Trade Organization on January 1, 1995. As we have already seen, the launch of the WTO and the General Agreement on Trade in Services constrained our cultural policymaking capacity. The cultural issues intersect with the negotiation, and the final form, of all these free trade agreements.

# Chapter 5
# Expansion of Free Trade and Investment Agreements

In the early 1990s, the Uruguay Round of GATT negotiations was underway and the Canada–United States Free Trade Agreement was in effect. Under Prime Minister Mulroney, Canada began to expand its bilateral and multilateral trading agreements.

## Foreign Investment Protection and Promotion Agreement

The earliest of these agreements were Foreign Investment Protection and Promotion Agreements (FIPAs). Before the end of 1995, Canada had implemented investment agreements with Poland, the Russian Federation, Argentina and Hungary. From Canada's perspective, these agreements were initially designed primarily to protect the interests of Canadian mining and other natural resource companies that operate around the world, and perhaps less significantly the interests of banks and other financial services.

The key elements of FIPAs involve requirements on each party to:

- create favourable conditions for investors

- provide National Treatment with respect to investments and returns, and the right to repatriate profits
- ensure Most-Favoured-Nation treatment for investments, and
- provide a method for investors to challenge through private arbitration any government action that may negatively impact their investment, including requirements to compensate in case of expropriation.

Before NAFTA was negotiated, the Canadian government paid no attention to the particular circumstances of the cultural industries potentially affected by these agreements, and no cultural exemptions appear in the early FIPAs. However, there was also little concern. Canadian cultural industry firms had little presence beyond markets in the United States, United Kingdom, France and several other major English- and French-speaking countries. Investors from the countries involved in our early FIPAs are unlikely to invest, other than marginally, in Canada's cultural industries, and the basic rights accorded to foreign investors contained limitations.

Most particularly, in these FIPAs the National Treatment obligation is limited. Each party is required to admit investments from the other only "to the extent possible and in accordance with its laws and regulations." There is also a provision under which either party may implement laws and regulations in connection with a) the establishment of a new business enterprise, or b) the acquisition or sale of an existing business enterprise, as long as such provisions apply equally to all foreign investors.[1]

The Canadian government approach began to change following negotiation of NAFTA's investment chapter and the election of a Liberal government in October 1993. The FIPA concluded in October 1994 with Ukraine contains a provision that exempts Canada's cultural industries and uses the NAFTA definition agreed to in 1993.

Since 1995, Canada has implemented FIPA agreements with thirty-two countries: Armenia, Barbados, Benin, Burkina Faso, Cameroon,

China, Costa Rica, Côte d'Ivoire, Croatia, Czech Republic, Ecuador, Egypt, Guinea, Hong Kong, Jordan, Kuwait, Latvia, Lebanon, Mali, Mongolia, Panama, Peru, Philippines, Romania, Senegal, Serbia, Slovak Republic, Tanzania, Thailand, Trinidad and Tobago, Uruguay and Venezuela. Here are a few notable facts about these agreements:

- Each of these agreements contains a cultural exemption.
- The majority have an exemption that covers both parties and appears either in the "General Exceptions" or "Miscellaneous Exceptions" article.
- In the case of Lebanon, the cultural exemption appears in an article entitled "General Exceptions and Exemptions."
- Like the agreement with Ukraine, a few have a Canada-specific exemption.

The agreement with the Philippines is asymmetrical. Canada has exempted its cultural industries, while the Philippines has exempted its "mass media as defined in (its) Constitution."

## Free Trade Agreements

In October 1993, Liberal Jean Chrétien was elected prime minister with a majority government. Perhaps in part because he reneged on his promise to renegotiate NAFTA, his government embarked on a campaign to develop Canada's bilateral trading relationships beyond the United States. The new government also undertook a thorough review of Canada's foreign policy and published *Canada in the World* in February 1995.[2] Canada's new foreign policy direction had three pillars:

- promoting prosperity and employment
- protecting security within a stable global framework, and
- projecting Canadian culture and values.

Thus, it is not surprising that the FIPAs concluded in 1994 and later, as well as the free trade agreements that the new Liberal government began to pursue, contain cultural exemptions.

At the first Summit of the Americas held in Miami in December 1994, government leaders from 34 of the 35 countries in the region (Cuba was not invited) agreed to establish closer trading relationships and to create a Free Trade Area of the Americas (FTAA). While the FTAA initiative, which sought to "mutlilateralize" NAFTA, was abandoned in 2004, Canada used it to open negotiations for free trade agreements with various hemispheric partners. The first of these was concluded with Chile and came into force in 1997, followed by Costa Rica (2002), Peru (2009), Colombia (2011), Panama (2013) and Honduras (2014).

Canada also expanded its negotiations outside the hemisphere, concluding the following agreements, which came into force in the year noted and remain in effect today:

- Canada–Israel FTA (1997)
- Canada–European Free Trade Association (Iceland, Liechtenstein, Norway and Switzerland) FTA (2009)
- Canada–Jordan FTA (2012)
- Canada–Ukraine FTA (2017)

In the ten free trade agreements Canada entered into between 1994 and 2014 (including NAFTA), as well as the agreement with Ukraine, the approach taken with respect to cultural industries has been to include an exemption as originally achieved with the United States in 1987, along with the definition agreed to in NAFTA.

For example, the Canada–Israel Free Trade Agreement reached in 1996 states in Article 10.5 that "Measures affecting cultural industries are exempt from the provisions of this Agreement, except as specifically provided in Article 2.1." Article 2.1 deals with tariff elimination. Interestingly, the original agreement did not define cultural industries, but in the renewed agreement signed in 2018, the Parties:

- expanded the number of Chapters from 11 to 21
- maintained the cultural exemption language, and
- included the standard Canadian cultural industries definition, without any amendment.

The Canada–European Free Trade Association Free Trade Agreement finalized in 2008 is slightly more elaborate. This agreement covers only trade in goods and focusses on tariff reductions. The exemption reads as follows:

> *Nothing in this Agreement shall be construed to apply to measures adopted or maintained by a party with respect to the cultural industries as defined in paragraph 2, except as provided in Article 10, subparagraph 2(e) of Article 26, and Article 37 of this Agreement.*

The articles mentioned function as follows:

- **Article 10** — Prohibits parties from imposing customs duties
- **Article 37** — Provides that government laws, regulations and procedures, as well as government rulings, agencies and the judiciary, must be publicly available
- **Article 26** — Establishes a joint committee between the parties that is empowered to consider a range of issues, including in 2(e) to "discuss, upon request by a party, measures with respect to cultural industries maintained or adopted under Annex J (cultural exemption)."

While the definition of cultural industries in paragraph 2 remains identical to the standard Canadian language, the preamble is changed slightly to the following: "The *expression* 'cultural industries' means persons engaged in any of the following activities" (emphasis added).[3]

Beginning with the Free Trade Agreement reached with the Republic of Korea in 2014, Canada's approach to the cultural exemption began to change. Before reviewing that agreement and other significant contemporary agreements reached subsequently, we must first review an agreement that was close to conclusion but not finalized due to broad public opposition, and then to consider how the global cultural diversity movement has influenced and helped to shape contemporary discussions in this area. We will also briefly touch on all negotiations involving Canada that remain unresolved in 2019.

## Multilateral Agreement on Investment (MAI)

The Organisation for Economic Co-operation and Development (OECD) is a Paris-based multilateral agency principally charged with collecting and disseminating a wide range of data related to the world's economy. In 1994, it had twenty-nine member countries.[4] As we have seen, the Uruguay Round of trade negotiations concluded that year brought several new agreements, including the agreement on Trade Related Investment Measures (TRIMs).

Major Western industrialized countries were dissatisfied with the modest outcome of TRIMs, and they approved negotiations for a Multilateral Agreement on Investment (MAI) at the OECD in May 1995. The idea was to reach a comprehensive agreement "with a high standard of liberalization," for investors and a robust dispute settlement system through an arbitration system that was to be global and private. While the OECD members would conclude the agreement, it would be an open agreement that other states could sign, on a negotiated basis. If it were signed by the twenty-nine Western industrialized countries, the expectation was that these parties could apply significant pressure on developing countries to conform to its provisions.

The agreement was negotiated in secret between 1995 and 1998, but in January 1997 a draft of the uncompleted negotiating text was leaked to civil society. Its circulation sparked outrage globally. Civil society groups from industrialized countries raised concerns about providing virtually unconditional rights to corporations and enabling them to sue governments when policies favouring environmental protection, labour rights or public health interfered with profits. Developing countries were equally outraged, believing the agreement would make it difficult for them to regulate foreign investors in the interests of their citizens. Campaigns against the agreement used Canada's experience as the most sued developed country in the world under NAFTA's Article 11 as a negative model.

Spearheaded by the International Forum on Globalization, a nongovernmental organization that brought together leading scholars, activists, writers and thinkers from more than twenty-five countries from the Global North and South, the draft text and a critical analysis were widely circulated to an extensive email list. This was perhaps the first use of the Internet to organize mass public opposition and protest.[5] The antiglobalization movement notably went on to actively challenge various international free trade negotiations through mass protests:

- Seattle 1999 — Protesters shut down the WTO meeting in Seattle, Washington in what was known as the "Battle of Seattle."
- Montreal 2000 — Thousands of protestors took to the streets in October to confront the G20 group of finance ministers.
- Quebec City 2001 — Large demonstrations also disrupted the Third Summit of the Americas, the centrepiece of which involved negotiations for a Free Trade Area of the Americas.

A second, more complete version of the secret text, dated May 1997, was also leaked. The agreement contained standard provisions related to National Treatment and Most-Favoured-Nation treatment, as well as prohibitions on performance requirements or restrictions on repatriation of profits. The agreement would also have applied to subnational governments, such as Canada's provinces, territories and municipalities, as well as to government monopolies and regulatory agencies. It allowed private investors to sue governments before private arbitration tribunals.

## Multilateral Agreements on Investment and Culture

While the agreement was never finalized and the text therefore contained options and specific additional recommendations from member states that had not been agreed upon, it was clear that the May 1997 MAI text would have been hugely problematic for Canadian cultural policymaking.

The draft contained no exception for cultural industries and while Canada could have taken a reservation for federal, provincial and municipal cultural policy measures, these would have been subject to the principles of Standstill and Rollback. Standstill would result from the prohibition of new or more restrictive exceptions. The agreement also explicitly stated that "Rollback is the liberalisation process by which the reduction and eventual elimination of nonconforming measures to the MAI would take place."

In a paper I prepared for the Canadian Conference of the Arts (CCA) in October 1997, I pointed out how virtually all of Canada's cultural policies would have been at risk under the MAI. Keith Kelly, CCA Executive Director, appeared before the House of Commons Standing Committee on Foreign Affairs and International Trade (Sub-Committee on International Trade, Trade Disputes and Investments) on November 20, 1997. He presented the paper and discussed the issues and recommendations. In his testimony, he noted the following:

> A few weeks ago, as part of this preoccupation of the CCA with trade issues, our board and some members of the working group (on cultural policy for the 21st century) met with Canada's chief negotiator for the MAI, Bill Dymond, to discuss the treatment of cultural issues in this proposed agreement. Mr. Dymond had an opportunity to review Mr. Neil's paper and took exception to only one sentence in the analysis. That was where Mr. Neil reflected that Canada has been relatively silent in the negotiations on the treatment of culture. He agreed substantially with all the other conclusions Mr. Neil reached.[6]

The CCA paper called for the introduction of a broad cultural exemption in the MAI. In the absence of an appropriate exemption, the most obvious policies that would have been at risk under the MAI included:

- **Foreign ownership** — Canada's prohibitions, limitations or restrictions on foreign ownership in the cultural industries would violate National Treatment obligations.
- **Funding program rules** — Rules at the federal, provincial or municipal level that restrict access to Canadian individuals and firms, even if a foreign producer is creating a Canadian-authored book or a Cancon audiovisual production, would violate National Treatment obligations.
- **Canadian content rules** — These could be in violation of National Treatment obligations, since a Cancon audiovisual work must be produced by a Canadian firm.
- **CRTC rules** — The requirement for private sector players to contribute to the production of Canadian content would violate the prohibition on performance requirements if applied to foreign services, and
- **Coproduction treaties** — These would violate Most-Favoured-Nation provisions.

Even Canada's immigration rules, which supported union-negotiated agreements and restricted the number of foreign performers and technicians allowed into Canada to work on foreign-financed film, television and performing arts productions, would have been at risk.[7]

While not attributed in the negotiating text, France did raise the cultural issue directly:

> *After an in-depth analysis of the implications of the MAI, this delegation has come to the conclusion that the basic principles of this agreement raise application problems for cultural industries (notably the printing, press and audiovisual sectors). In fact,*

*policies designed to preserve cultural and linguistic diversity may*
*not be entirely compatible with the disciplines of the agreement*
*and so could be endangered.*

The French delegation also recommended that a general exception be included in the agreement, as follows:

*Nothing in this agreement shall be construed to prevent any*
*Contracting party to take any measure to regulate investment*
*of foreign companies and the conditions of activity of these*
*companies, in the framework of policies designed to preserve and*
*promote cultural and linguistic diversity.*[8]

The Canadian cultural community once again joined the free trade battle, and participated actively in the antiglobalization movement, particularly beginning with the 1999 Battle of Seattle. Fortunately, negotiations for the MAI failed in 1999 when first France, and then other OECD member states, withdrew. An effort to introduce the MAI into the WTO at the 2003 Cancun meeting also failed.

On September 29, 1998, I appeared before a British Columbia legislative committee exploring how the proposed MAI could affect the authority of the province to implement its cultural policies and programs. Appearing with me was the distinguished Canadian actor, R.H. Thomson, who spoke on behalf of the Alliance of Canadian Cinema, Television and Radio Artists (ACTRA).[9] Mr. Thomson went on to represent ACTRA at several International Network for Cultural Diversity (INCD) meetings (see Chapter 6).

In my presentation, I reviewed the potential consequences of the MAI and argued that we needed a comprehensive cultural exemption. I outlined certain principles to guide such an exemption, arguing that it should:

1. **Include a comprehensive definition of culture** — The definition would include the cultural industries as defined in NAFTA —

book and magazine publishing, film, television, music and radio. It should also explicitly include the performing arts, visual arts, crafts and heritage, as well as new media and elements of the telecommunications sector involved in distributing cultural expressions.

2. **Be self-defining for each nation** — This would permit it to determine what constitutes a cultural measure and to change that definition as the sector evolves over time and as artists begin to create in other media.

3. **Include an appropriate dispute settlement system** — Any challenge should be referred to a panel of cultural experts empowered to determine initially if a given measure is a cultural policy or if it is a disguised trade barrier.

4. **Involve language to ensure that the exception overrides all agreement obligations** — This would ensure that cultural measures would not be subject to the principles of standstill and rollback.

When R.H. Thomson spoke, he agreed completely with my analysis of the potential worrisome effects of the MAI on our audiovisual sector policies, and he supported my submissions on an expanded definition of cultural industries. But he went on to suggest that it may be time to move beyond the approach of seeking "exemption" from trade agreements. This was a negative approach, and the sector had already been fighting a rearguard action for more than a decade. Instead, he postulated that the Committee should consider recommending the development of an international charter of cultural rights. Such a charter would not only preserve national sovereignty to protect and promote national values, identity and cultural diversity, it would establish rules appropriate for the cultural sector and would promote more balanced exchanges between world cultures. Furthermore, such a document would be equal to the trade agreements. Unfortunately, the Committee did not appear to have fully understood the power and elegance of this proposition.

## Agreements in Negotiation

### WTO Doha Development Round

The WTO Doha Round of multilateral trade negotiations launched in the Qatari capital in November 2001. The negotiations were meant to concentrate on the particular needs of developing countries, and thus the round is known as the Doha Development Round. Despite this focus, the issue of services once again appeared on the agenda since developed countries were unhappy with the degree of liberalization achieved by the WTO General Agreement on Trade in Services. After meetings in Cancun (2003) and Hong Kong (2005), and related discussions in Paris (2005), Potsdam (2007) and Geneva (2004, 2006 and 2008), the negotiations stalled. At the WTO Ministerial Meeting held in Nairobi, Kenya in December 2015, the final declaration acknowledged there were deep divisions on the Doha Round; some leading members felt it should be ended.

In 2018, U.S. President Donald Trump imposed tariffs on imported steel and aluminum, including from the closest allies of the United States (among them, Canada and the European Union), arguing that this was necessary to protect "national security." He also launched a trade war on China by imposing tariffs on many products imported into the United States from that country. These tariffs were also ostensibly justified under the national security exemption, but Mr. Trump has also stated that they support an effort to:

- redress the significant trade imbalance that exists between the United States and China, and
- respond to China's theft of U.S. companies' intellectual property and trade secrets (which U.S. companies are sometimes forced to give up to obtain permission to operate in the Chinese market).

Given the challenges of recent negotiations and Trump's aggressive antitrade actions, it is unlikely the WTO Doha Round will conclude in the foreseeable future. The Global Affairs Canada website that provides information and updates about all of Canada's agreements does not even list this as an active negotiation. The site lists only two WTO-related agreements as being in active negotiations, and these processes may also be in doubt given the U.S. position.

**WTO Trade in Services Agreement (TiSA)**
In an echo of the OECD's ill-fated Multilateral Agreement on Investment and as the Doha Round stalled, WTO members launched negotiations for a new Trade in Services Agreement (TiSA). TiSA parties are Australia, Canada, Chile, Chinese Taipei (Taiwan), Colombia, Costa Rica, the European Union, Hong Kong (China), Iceland, Israel, Japan, Liechtenstein, Mauritius, Mexico, New Zealand, Norway, Pakistan, Panama, Peru, South Korea, Switzerland, Turkey and the United States. Since the EU negotiates on behalf of its member states, a total of fifty countries are involved in the TiSA initiative. The EU, United States and Australia have been chairing the negotiations, which take place in Geneva, where the WTO is based.

The talks started formally in March 2013 and by September of that year, the parties had agreed to a basic text, based on GATS. By November 2016, twenty-one negotiation rounds had taken place. The European Union noted in July 2017, "Negotiations are now on hold and are expected to resume when the political context allows. There is no formally set deadline for ending the negotiations."[10]

As the talks are once again secret, Canada's position in TiSA talks is unknown, however, cultural services are potentially at risk in the talks. Given the treatment of culture in the Trans-Pacific Partnership Agreement that we will consider later, and the fact that TiSA talks were launched when Conservative Prime Minister Stephen Harper was in office, Canada may have been open to an approach that would capture cultural services within the parameters of the potential agreement.

**WTO Environmental Goods Agreement (EGA)**
These negotiations were launched in July 2014 by Australia, Canada,

China, Chinese Taipei, Costa Rica, the European Union, Hong Kong (China), Iceland, Israel, Japan, Liechtenstein, New Zealand, Norway, Singapore, South Korea, Switzerland, Turkey and the United States. Since the purpose is to reduce tariffs on environmental goods and sustainable technologies, the EGA will not have an impact on Canadian cultural policies. Like TiSA, the last EGA negotiating session was in December 2016.

Given the challenges of the multilateral talks associated with the WTO, there is an increasing focus on plurilateral and bilateral talks, so it is important to take stock of where Canada stands.

**Canada's bilateral and plurilateral negotiations**
As of January 2019, the Government of Canada is actively involved in discussions or negotiations with many other countries with respect to various trade and investment agreements.

Negotiations for FIPAs have been concluded, but agreements have not yet come into force, with Albania, Bahrain, Kosovo, Madagascar, Moldova, Nigeria and United Arab Emirates.

Negotiations for FIPA agreements are underway with Ghana, India, Kazakhstan, Kenya, Macedonia, Morocco, Pakistan and Tunisia.

Negotiations for free trade or economic partnership agreements are underway with the Caribbean Community, Dominican Republic, three Central American states, India, Japan, the Pacific Alliance, Mercosur and Singapore.

Exploratory discussions for free trade agreements are underway with the Association of Southeast Asian Nations (ASEAN), the Philippines and Turkey (see Chapter 12, Table 1).

# Chapter 6
# Global Cultural Diversity Movement and the UNESCO Convention

In December 1986, the United Nations Educational, Scientific and Cultural Organization (UNESCO) approved an Action Plan for a World Decade for Cultural Development, which it declared for 1988–1997. The interrelated issues for the decade were defined in terms of exploring how to:

- promote greater consideration of the cultural dimension in development, and
- stimulate creative aptitudes and cultural life in general.

This second issue was directed at encouraging member states "to . . . strengthen cultural policies and to mobilize the means to implement them." [1]

This launched UNESCO on a process through which it would examine culture, development and cultural rights, and continue to expand its consideration of cultural diversity in the postwar period. For UNESCO, the concept of cultural diversity initially related to the need to preserve local and distinct cultures and languages, often Indigenous, as well as multiculturalism and cultural pluralism within a society — these issues related to cultural rights. But in the early 1990s, UNESCO began to tackle questions of cultural diversity between nation-states, including intercultural dialogue and cultural fusion. In this later period, UNESCO identified the need for more balanced exchange of cultural goods and services between states, which implied that each state would have the capacity to create cultural goods and services that it could exchange — these issues related to economic development and trade.

As part of the World Decade for Cultural Development, UNESCO appointed the World Commission on Culture and Development, whose 1995 report *Our Creative Diversity* reflected a new approach to cultural policies. This approach moved away from merely preserving local cultures to embracing cultural development for economic and cultural reasons. The report drew a parallel between biodiversity and cultural diversity, arguing that:

> *Just as policies of biodiversity preservation are needed to*
> *guarantee the protection of natural ecosystems and the diversity of*
> *species, only adequate cultural policies can ensure the preservation*
> *of cultural diversity against the risks of a single homogenizing*
> *culture.*[2]

While supporting this statement's conclusion, I have always rejected the analogy between biodiversity and cultural diversity. Biodiversity implies that species be protected and isolated from others, to avoid contamination. Cultural diversity on the other hand implies that each culture will have the opportunity and capacity to grow and develop, and will be permitted to choose how it wishes to evolve and interact with other cultures. Interaction between cultures can be extremely positive for many reasons and can lead to collaboration, which in turn leads to new forms of art and cultural expressions.

The concluding event of the World Decade on Cultural Development emerged as a seminal moment in the global cultural diversity movement. In late March 1998, roughly 2,500 delegates attended the UNESCO Intergovernmental Conference on Cultural Policies for Development in Stockholm, Sweden. Attendees included ministers of culture, cultural officials, academics and delegates from a wide range of nongovernmental organizations and industry associations from every corner of the globe. Delegates realized they shared a deep concern about how globalization was bringing cultural homogenization, rather than cultural diversity. The values, worldviews, aesthetic tastes and cultural practices emanating from one place dominated; the sheer size and reach of global media and entertainment conglomerates marginalized any alternatives. They responded with the idea of urgently creating international networks of cultural actors to counter this tide.

At the Stockholm meeting, Canadian Heritage Minister Sheila Copps invited her culture minister counterparts to join her that June in Ottawa; many did. Meanwhile, the Canadian Conference of the Arts (CCA) — at the time Canada's leading arts advocacy organization, bringing together key players in Canada's cultural community — and the Swedish Joint Committee for Artistic and Literary Professionals (KLYS), invited cultural nongovernmental organizations, academics, activists and industry professionals to Ottawa. On June 29, 1998, more than 170 delegates from twenty-seven countries and sixty NGOs attended At Home in the World: an International Forum on Culture and Cooperation.

At those historic Ottawa meetings, the ministers launched the International Network on Cultural Policy (INCP) as a forum for them to consider and respond to a range of common concerns, including how certain cultural expressions dominated global markets, the impact of emerging digital technologies and the monopoly control of media. Since the world's first ministers, trade ministers and economic ministers each have one or more fora in which to meet and consider common issues, those present agreed that culture ministers should do likewise. From the beginning, the network agreed to monitor the negative effects of trade agreements and to work for alternative approaches both within their own governments and in various international institutions, events and meetings.

The attendees to the At Home in the World Conference unanimously called on CCA and KLYS to launch a parallel global civil society network to bring together artists, cultural producers, academics and their organizations so they could collaborate to counter the adverse effects of economic globalization on world cultures. This led to the launch in September 1999 of the International Network for Cultural Diversity (INCD), just prior to the second INCP meeting in Mexico.

INCD held its founding conference in September 2000 on the Greek Island of Santorini, and from then until 2006 it met annually in conjunction with the meetings of the culture ministers' network. This juxtaposition of meetings created an unprecedented dialogue between civil society and culture ministers, both in formal meetings and at informal social events. Meetings were held in Lucerne, Switzerland (2001), Cape Town, South Africa (2002), Opatija, Croatia (2003), Shanghai, China (2004), Dakar, Senegal (2005) and Rio de Janeiro, Brazil (2006). At its zenith, INCD brought together more than 1,500 members from seventy-six countries and attracted up to 200 delegates from every corner of the globe to its annual conferences.

Another civil society organization developed in Quebec in 1998, bringing together cultural industry professional associations representing artists, producers, publishers and others. The *Coalition pour la diversité culturelle* invited English-language colleague associations to join with it the following year and also encouraged the formation of a Coalition for Cultural Diversity in France. The concept spread, and the International Federation of Coalitions for Cultural Diversity (IFCCD) was formed.

With the election of Conservative Prime Minister Stephen Harper in January 2006, Canada's commitment to these Canadian-led initiatives waned. Core funding for the INCD was eliminated in 2006, although the network continued to operate on a more informal basis, and with funding from outside Canada, for another decade. The ministerial network, INCP, was allowed to wither by 2015. Because it has had core support from Quebec, the CCD-CDC (now the Coalition for the Diversity of Cultural Expressions — Coalition pour la diversité des expressions culturelles) and the IFCCD continue to operate.

## The Convention Concept Emerges and Gains Support

While I first heard the suggestion that we should work to achieve a new international agreement on culture from R.H. Thomson in September 1998 in Victoria, others in Canada were thinking along similar lines. Pressure for progressively higher levels of liberalization comprises a fundamental aspect of the free trade philosophy, an element that would continue to affect cultural policies both directly and indirectly, even if any particular agreement contains an exemption for culture. Furthermore, by 1999 it was clear that digital technologies and the Internet would also erode the impact of any exemption.

In February 1999, the Cultural Industries SAGIT (Sectoral Advisory Group on International Trade) issued a report calling for development of a New International Instrument on Cultural Diversity (NIICD). The SAGIT proposed that such an agreement would:

- recognize the importance of cultural diversity
- acknowledge that cultural goods and services differ significantly from other products
- acknowledge that domestic measures and policies intended to ensure access to a variety of indigenous cultural products differ significantly from other policies
- establish rules on the kind of domestic regulatory and other measures that countries can and cannot use to enhance cultural and linguistic diversity, and
- establish how trade disciplines would apply or not apply to cultural measures that meet the agreed-upon rules.[3]

The Canadian government adopted the recommendation for the

NIICD in October 1999. From this beginning, the idea of drafting a convention on cultural diversity burst onto the global scene. Here is a brief timeline of progress toward realizing this idea:

- At the first INCD meeting in Santorini, Greece in September 2000, delegates unanimously supported the proposed new instrument, and the INCD Steering Committee report to the INCP urged culture ministers to do likewise.
- At the second INCD meeting in Lucerne, Switzerland in late September 2001, INCD delegates further discussed the proposed convention, including a range of core principles and key provisions it should contain, and considered an analysis of where the convention could be negotiated and housed.
- During preparations for its third meeting in Cape Town, South Africa, INCD came to appreciate that, for the convention to have global appeal, it would also have to serve as a positive tool for developing cultural industries in the Global South. As one of my South African colleagues said to me at the time, "provisions ensuring access for local movies at the local cinema screens mean nothing unless you have your own movies to show in them."
- In early 2002, INCD put forward a draft convention authored by Stephen Shrybman, a Canadian international trade lawyer.

Meanwhile, UNESCO was continuing its work, which resulted in the November 2001 adoption of the *Universal Declaration on Cultural Diversity*. In Article 8, the declaration notes,

> *Particular attention must be paid to the diversity of the supply of creative work, to due recognition of the rights of authors and artists and to the specificity of cultural goods and services which, as vectors of identity, values and meaning, must not be treated as mere commodities or consumer goods.*

In the Action Plan, member states committed themselves to collaborating to promote the declaration and to achieve twenty objectives, the first one being:

> *Deepening the international debate on questions relating*
> *to cultural diversity, particularly in respect of its links with*
> *development and its impact on policy-making, at both national*
> *and international level;* taking forward notably consideration of
> the advisability of an international legal instrument on cultural
> diversity.[4] *(emphasis added)*

While initially skeptical of the idea, by 2002 the French government and its powerful cultural civil society sector had acknowledged the limitations of "l'exception culturelle" and had become strong supporters of the proposed convention.

All of this came together in Paris, France in February 2003. Key members of the ministerial network met there to give provisional approval to a possible draft convention, which had been developed by an INCP subcommittee. The Coalitions for Cultural Diversity held a civil society meeting at the same time, and the INCD Steering Committee met to consider further the question of where such a convention should be housed. On February 2, 2003, the opening reception of these events was held at the Elysée Palace. In his remarks to the gathering, French President Jacques Chirac turned to UNESCO Director General Koïchiro Matsuura and strongly urged him to have UNESCO take on this task. In October 2003, the UNESCO General Conference, the highest governing body, adopted a decision that "invited" the Director General to submit a draft convention at its next meeting in October 2005.

UNESCO formed an expert panel to study the idea. The initial stages were challenging for those of us deeply involved in developing the initial concept, as many of the "experts" had no idea about what the convention was designed to accomplish.

However, UNESCO successfully launched negotiations among the member states. These negotiations concluded in June 2005 when the final terms of the *Convention on the Protection and Promotion of the Diversity of Cultural Expressions* were agreed upon. At the October 2005 UNESCO General Conference, the final vote on the convention yielded 148 in favour, four abstentions and only two (United States and Israel) opposed. This was a remarkable achievement, particularly when you consider that it took UNESCO more than twenty years to develop and approve the *Convention for the Safeguarding of the Intangible Cultural Heritage* in October 2003. The speed with which it came together resulted not only from the issue's urgency, but also from the powerful global cultural diversity movements, both from civil society and governmental, that had spearheaded the drive.

At the negotiating sessions themselves, a cohesive group of important nations, including France, the European Union, Canada, Senegal, South Africa, Brazil and China, pushed the initiative forward. Civil society groups successfully worked to have a serious role in the deliberations, and their impact is seen in the final text. The convention came into force in 2007 and, within the following decade, had been ratified by 145 member states, as well as the European Union.

## Assessing the Impact of the UNESCO Convention

It is important to consider the key elements of the convention in order to understand how it intersects with trade rules and trade agreements.[5]

While the Preamble means little in law, it does take note that "the processes of globalization can both enhance interaction between cultures and challenge cultural diversity." The objectives, which are more important as they can be used to interpret the convention, include recognition of the:

- sovereign right of states to maintain, adopt and implement cultural policies
- distinctive nature of cultural activities, goods and services as vehicles of identity, values and meaning, and

- link between culture and development and the need to strengthen international cooperation to enhance the capacity of developing countries.

The Guiding Principles are significant since they establish the legal framework for the substantive rights and modest obligations found in the convention. These include:

- respect for human rights and fundamental freedoms
- sovereignty of states to adopt measures and policies
- recognition that cultural aspects of development are as important as economic aspects
- equitable access, and
- openness and balance.

The need to respect human rights and fundamental freedoms provides a strong and necessary limit on the sovereign right of states to implement policies and measures. This is confirmed in Article 5.1, the general provision respecting the scope of governmental authority.

The principle of "openness and balance" may also limit cultural policymaking. The convention provides that when states introduce measures they should "seek to promote, in an appropriate manner, openness to other cultures," and "ensure that [measures they adopt] are geared to the objectives," of the convention. The concept of "openness" is important since some feared the convention could be used to justify a closed society denying access to all foreign cultural products. The concept of "balance" in an international instrument normally prevents states from introducing a measure wildly disproportionate to the scope of the problem they are addressing, using the instrument as a justification.

Other similar elements appear elsewhere in the text:

- Article 7.1 provides that states "shall endeavour [to create] an environment which encourages individuals and social groups . . . to have access to diverse cultural expressions from within their territory as well as from other countries of the world."

• Article 2.1 provides that guaranteeing the "ability of individuals to choose cultural expressions" constitutes a fundamental principle in protecting and promoting cultural diversity.

## Scope and Definitions

**Scope** — The convention's scope is broad, applying "to the policies and measures adopted by the Parties related to the protection and promotion of the diversity of cultural expressions." Importantly, the focus does not rest exclusively on cultural policies *per se*, but on all policies "related to" protecting the diversity of cultural expressions.

**Cultural activities, goods and services** — These are defined as activities, goods and services that "embody or convey cultural expressions, irrespective of the commercial value they may have." This marks the first time that an international legal instrument recognizes the dual nature of cultural goods and services.

**Cultural policies and measures** — This definition is similarly broad, referring to "those policies and measures relating to culture . . . that are either focused on culture as such, or are designed to have a direct effect on cultural expressions . . . including on the creation, production, dissemination, distribution of and access to cultural activities, goods and services."

**Cultural expressions** — The definition, significant for the convention's operative provisions, reads: "those expressions that result from the creativity of individuals, groups and societies, and that have cultural content." Cultural content in turn "refers to the symbolic meaning, artistic dimension and cultural values that originate from or express cultural identities."

The definitions as a whole draw an effective perimeter around the convention and confirm that it is dealing with a society's creative and artistic output.

## Rights and Obligations of Parties

The heart of the convention rests with the fifteen Articles that outline the Parties' rights and obligations. The emphasis is on rights rather than obligations, and the overriding focus is on the sovereign right of states to adopt policies and measures they deem appropriate to protect and promote cultural diversity.

This operational part of the convention includes articles that address the extent of rights that Parties have at the national level, the need for information sharing, and requirements to implement educational campaigns to promote public awareness. It contains an Article that addresses the "special situations where cultural expressions . . . are at risk of extinction, under serious threat, or otherwise in need of urgent safeguarding." With only a couple of exceptions, rights are expressed in discretionary form — "Parties may" take certain actions favouring cultural diversity, rather than the obligatory form, "Parties shall."

**Article 6** explicitly lists measures that a party may employ, including:

- regulatory measures
- measures that "provide opportunities for domestic cultural activities, goods and services" within the overall market (e.g., content quotas)
- public financial assistance
- public institutions
- measures aimed at supporting artists and others involved in the creative process
- measures aimed at enhancing diversity in the media, including through public service broadcasting
- measures aimed at ensuring access for domestic cultural industries, and

- measures that promote the "free exchange and circulation" of ideas and cultural expressions and stimulate the "creative and entrepreneurial spirit."

Aside from measures restricting ownership of cultural industries firms, this list encompasses all of Canada's cultural policies.

**Articles 12 to 18** concern the promotion of international cooperation. Parties agreed on the need to:

- integrate culture in sustainable development
- cooperate on development, including through technology transfers, capacity building and financial support
- encourage collaborative arrangements, and
- assist each other where there is a "serious threat to cultural expressions."

They further agreed to increase capacity in the public sector, public institutions, the private sector, civil society and nongovernmental organizations, all of which have a role to play in fostering the diversity of cultural expressions. This cooperation is designed to "foster the emergence of a dynamic cultural sector." Once again, the tools that may be used to achieve this objective are outlined explicitly.

**Article 16** contains innovative and potentially significant commitments. It provides that developed countries

> shall facilitate *cultural exchanges with developing countries by granting, through the appropriate institutional and legal frameworks,* preferential treatment *to artists and other cultural professionals and practitioners, as well as cultural goods and services from developing countries. (emphasis added)*

This article's use of the word "shall" creates a positive obligation. As someone involved in every negotiating session, I can confirm that this was an explicit tradeoff between delegations from the Global South and the developed countries. The other articles on international cooperation provide only that Parties "shall endeavour to" do the various things being considered. Thus, they are not obligations, they only require best efforts. **Article 16** is different because it requires that developed countries provide preferential market access for cultural goods and services, as well as physical access for artists and other cultural professionals. In return for this commitment to provide preferential treatment, delegations from the Global South supported the core thrust of the convention to confirm the right of all parties to support their own artists and cultural producers.

**Article 11** also breaks new ground because it acknowledges the "fundamental role" of civil society in protecting and promoting the diversity of cultural expressions. It provides that parties "shall encourage" the active participation of civil society as they implement the convention. This is once again a positive obligation. The governing bodies of the convention have given real meaning to this commitment in their relationship with civil society representatives. Civil society groups participating in convention meetings may propose agenda items, contribute written reports to be circulated by the secretariat and have a right to speak before decisions are taken by the member states. This degree of collaboration is unique in the UN system.

## Relationship to Other Instruments

**Articles 20 and 21** outline the relationship of the convention to other international instruments. This issue was hotly debated, and the compromise solution reached at the last moment. That solution is based on the principles found in the title of the Article, of "mutual supportiveness, complementarity and non-subordination."

**Article 20** contains innovative wording that "when interpreting and applying" other treaties or "when entering into other international obligations," parties "shall take into account the relevant provisions of this Convention." This is a strong provision and the first time in international law that parties agreed to use one instrument as an interpretive tool when negotiating or applying others. It is reinforced by **Article 21**, which commits parties to work together to promote the convention's principles in other international fora.

However, all of this language is circumscribed by **Article 20.2**, which states, "Nothing in this Convention shall be interpreted as modifying rights and obligations of the Parties under any other treaties to which they are parties." While a last-minute effort was made to have this apply only to other treaties or conventions in force in 2005 and not to new agreements that would be negotiated in future, this failed to achieve a consensus.

## Convention Analysis

As envisaged by its original proponents, the convention was designed to remove trade in cultural goods and services from the trade and investment agreements. It was to serve as a legal shield against those agreements. The concept was embraced by civil society and governments in the Global South, who saw it as a powerful tool to promote cultural capacity and foster development in the creative industries. That this lofty goal was not achieved has been largely ignored in discussions, debates and analysis in the decade since the convention came into force, even though its limitation as an instrument to affect trade in cultural goods and services was observed by key players from the time the text was first agreed upon in June 2005.

**Article 25** provides for a binding dispute settlement process to address disputes that may arise between convention parties. As the convention was being negotiated it was assumed that, like trade agreements, parties would have obligations to one another and thus would need a system to settle disagreements. Examples of such obligations in trade agreement include providing National Treatment to goods and services from other parties, or to reduce tariffs by a fixed amount. If they fail to provide such treatment or to take the actions mandated, the aggrieved party can launch a dispute. If the dispute panel finds in that party's favour, the agreement requires the party to comply or authorizes retaliation if the party fails to implement the obligations and panel decision. But in the final days of negotiating the UNESCO Convention, virtually all the positive obligations between parties fell away, as the word "shall" was replaced in most articles by the words "may" or "shall endeavour to." Thus, outside only a few provisions, nothing can be disputed, and Article 25 becomes irrelevant.

As I have previously analyzed in detail, if one were to reconsider the *Canada Periodicals Case* with the convention in place and with the United States as a party to it (an unlikely hypothesis), the outcome of the dispute settlement process would be identical, and Canada's magazine support measures would have been found to violate GATT and GATS provisions. The trade panel would have a convenient way to resolve the apparent contradiction between Articles 20.1(b) and 20.2. They could confirm that although Canada does have a sovereign right to implement policies respecting magazines as cultural expressions, there is nothing in the convention that prevents Canada from agreeing to limit its sovereign right through commitments it makes under other treaties. They could thus conclude that Canada is free to support its magazines, but it must do so in a manner that is consistent with the commitments it has made to the United States under the WTO agreements. This could include subsidies, permitted under GATT, but not the tariff measure, excise tax and other efforts to limit advertising in U.S. split-run magazines.[6]

When the convention text was finalized, the Steering Committee of INCD considered the possibility of opposing it. The June 3, 2005, INCD press release stated:

> *The International Network for Cultural Diversity took a cautious approach on the final outcome of UNESCO negotiations for a new convention on cultural diversity . . . Speaking in Paris today, Garry Neil, INCD Executive Director said: "If the objective of the new Treaty is to declare the right of States to implement cultural policies and to establish a new foundation for future cooperation, the Treaty has succeeded. If the objective is to carve out cultural*

*goods and services from the trade agreements, the Treaty is*
*inadequate, at least in the short term . . . INCD played an active*
*and positive role in the process, and we appreciate the efforts of*
*negotiators to deal with very difficult issues over the past months.*
*INCD will carefully analyze the final text over the next few weeks*
*to assess its value as a tool for protecting and promoting cultural*
*diversity."*

In its press release issued at the same time, the Motion Picture Association of America also cautiously welcomed the new convention and highlighted explicitly that it did not affect trade agreements.

Over the summer, I analyzed the convention and discussed it at length with INCD members around the world. Together, we agreed that it was a significant achievement that resulted from a remarkable campaign among governments and civil society players. If this powerful alliance could be held together and continue to collaborate, the convention could be an important political tool. It confirms the right of states to take actions to support their own artists and cultural producers. It confirms in international law the dual nature of cultural activities, goods and services, as having both economic and cultural value. The convention defines the issues in a way that clarifies the challenges, and gives parties broad scope to respond to the changing technological and political environment. While it effectively remains subordinate to trade and investment agreements in the short term, it provides a focus and a forum for states to continue to work together and with civil society to achieve, in the longer term, the objective of carving out cultural goods and services from trade and investment agreements.

The convention also offers an important political tool for cultural development. By outlining a range of measures states may use to develop their domestic cultural capacity, it provides a model for those countries that do not yet have developed cultural policies. Civil society groups can use it in their advocacy work. By enunciating detailed measures that developed countries should use to support the development of cultural capacity and industries in countries of the Global South, it has established benchmarks for these countries to meet.[7]

Having no doubt undergone a similar reflection, by October 2005, the MPAA announced it was opposed to the convention and called on UNESCO not to approve it. On the other hand, INCD was fully supportive and congratulated UNESCO when the convention was adopted in this October 20 press release:

> "*The strong support for the Convention is a watershed moment in the history of the cultural diversity movement," said Garry Neil, INCD Executive Director, "and we are proud of the role INCD and other civil society groups played in reaching this moment. But there is much more to do. Civil society will continue to play an active part in the next phase of the work and we call today on all States who voted in favour to ratify the Convention, to make it as effective as possible, and to commit to supporting cultural diversity both within their own territories and globally . . ." INCD urged governments to work with each other, with civil society, intergovernmental institutions and their own artists and cultural producers to achieve the real promise of the Convention. "After all, we need to collaborate against the continuing pressure from those who want trade in cultural goods and services to be covered fully under the World Trade Organization and regional and bilateral trade treaties. We also need to ensure that developing countries have the resources they need to bring their stories, music and other artistic works to local and global audiences."*
>
> *INCD urged governments to incorporate provisions of the new Convention into their bilateral and multilateral cultural agreements. "The Convention only establishes minimum standards, and we want the richer countries of the north to make specific and concrete commitments to countries of the south to help them develop creative industries and cultural capacity. We*

*also want the richer countries to open their markets to artistic works from countries of the south," continued Mr. Neil.*

*INCD urged the world's culture ministers, organized in the International Network on Cultural Policy, to renew their commitment to this work. "Culture is significant in all dimensions of governance, including trade, security, development and human rights, and this is only beginning to be understood. The INCP must strengthen its resolve to continue, must build its membership and prepare for the next round of cultural diversity work in UNESCO, as well as the important upcoming work with finance and trade ministers, and heads of government."* [8]

While the UNESCO *Convention on the Protection and Promotion of the Diversity of Cultural Expressions* was not the magic bullet many wanted, it is an important tool in global efforts to protect cultural policymaking from trade and investment agreements. As we shall see later, if it is used creatively by its many parties, it could provide a radically different approach to these questions.

# Chapter 7
# Korea and European Union Trade Agreements

Conservative Stephen Harper became Prime Minister in February 2006 and served in that role until November 2015. During his time in office, Canada aggressively pursued bilateral free trade agreements. Negotiations were concluded with Peru, Colombia, Panama, Honduras, Jordan, the European Free Trade Association and Korea. More importantly, the Harper government launched negotiations with the European Union in 2009 and lobbied for Canada to join the ongoing negotiations for the Trans-Pacific Partnership Agreement, which it did in 2012.

Stephen Harper's conservative economic views included a classic belief in the benefits of free trade. He could also barely conceal his disdain for the arts and culture community. This was highlighted by his quip during the 2008 federal election that "ordinary people" don't care about arts funding and could not relate to people at a "rich gala all subsidized by taxpayers claiming their subsidies aren't high enough."[1]

Harper initially came into office as Prime Minister with a minority government. After he was re-elected with a majority government, Harper's colours were fully revealed with his 2012 austerity budget. It cut the budgets for culture and the arts as follows:

- Canadian Broadcasting Corporation (CBC), National Film Board (NFB) and Telefilm by 10 per cent each
- Library and Archives Canada by 8.2 per cent, and
- Department of Canadian Heritage by 7.4 per cent.

While the budget of the Canada Council for the Arts was maintained, its funding on a *per capita* basis had already fallen by 8.3 per cent since Harper's election six years earlier.[2]

Canada and the Republic of Korea had launched discussions for a free trade agreement in 2005, but an agreement was not finally initialled until March 2014 when Prime Minister Harper visited South Korean President Park Geun-hye in Seoul. It was the first Canadian free trade agreement with an Asia-Pacific country.

When terms of the deal were made public, they surprised some in the cultural community. Many had worried that Harper might jettison the cultural exemption, but the agreement with Korea went further than any other agreement. Cultural exemptions had been continued in every free trade agreement finalized during Harper's tenure as Prime Minister, but most were on a very small scale. The Canada–Korea agreement was the first to be concluded with a country that had such a large population (fifty million people) and significant economy (eleventh largest in the world). Given Prime Minister Harper's political beliefs, the only plausible explanation for this development was that the treatment of culture had not been initiated by Canada, but rather at the request of our negotiating partner, South Korea, for its own domestic reasons.

Thus, before we consider the Canada-Korea Free Trade Agreement in detail, we will look at other international contemporary developments that have had an impact on trade agreements, including those most recently concluded by Canada.

# European Union Sets a New Course on Culture and Trade

In 2000, the European Union and seventy-eight ACP countries (African, Caribbean and Pacific Group of Countries) signed the Cotonou Agreement. The agreement provided nonreciprocal trade preferences in the European market for these developing countries. Article 37 of the agreement called for negotiation of an Economic Partnership Agreement (EPA) to replace Cotonou's limited trade chapters.

In 2004, the European Union and Cariforum (The Caribbean Forum of ACP) commenced negotiations for an EPA. Cariforum members include: Antigua and Barbuda, The Bahamas, Barbados, Belize, Cuba, Dominica, Dominican Republic, Grenada, Guyana, Haiti, Jamaica, Saint Kitts and Nevis, Saint Lucia, Saint Vincent and the Grenadines, Suriname and Trinidad and Tobago.

The UNESCO Convention was approved by the General Conference in 2005 and came into force in 2007. As an economic integration organization, the European Union was entitled to join, and it ratified the convention in December 2006. As a consequence of the convention, the EU began to change how it approached issues of culture and trade.

In 2008, the EU and Cariforum concluded the terms of the new Economic Partnership Agreement. While the General Exceptions article contains a cultural exemption only for measures that are "necessary to the protection of national treasures of artistic, historic or archaeological value," the agreement contains an extensive provision on cultural cooperation.

The Cultural Cooperation Protocol cites the parties' mutual commitment to the convention and provides for implementation through collaborative actions in line with the convention's provisions, notably:[3]

- **Article 14** — Cooperation for Development
- **Article 15** — Collaborative Arrangements, and
- **Article 16** — Preferential Treatment for Developing Countries.

The protocol also recognizes "the importance of the cultural industries and the multifaceted nature of cultural goods and services as activities of cultural, economic and social value."

The operative provisions of the protocol include:

- promoting collaboration among the parties to increase exchanges of cultural activities, goods and services and to redress imbalances that have existed in such exchanges
- various obligations designed to improve the capacity of cultural industries in the Cariforum countries, such as training, cultural policy development and the transfer of technologies and knowhow
- expansion of co-production agreements in film and television, and commitments to encourage performing arts co-production activities, and
- special provisions related to writing and publishing, including support for book fairs, translation, copublishing and professional development.

By far the most significant commitment made by the European Union is a requirement for it to allow "the entry into and temporary stay in their territories of artists and other cultural professionals and practitioners from the" Cariforum countries, "for a period of up to 90 days in any 12-month period." This explicit provision includes film and television artists, actors and technicians, as well as "artists and other cultural professionals and practitioners such as visual, plastic and performing artists and instructors, composers, authors, providers of entertainment services and other similar professionals and practitioners."

The provisions related to the movement of people were meant to give real meaning to Convention Article 16, which requires preferential treatment for developing countries. This was seen as a very powerful initiative and warmly welcomed by cultural industries, not only in Cariforum countries, but throughout the Global South. Disappointingly, after more than a decade, the EU has been unable to operationalize these provisions. To understand what happened, it is necessary to know about the Schengen area. While twenty-six EU countries have abolished passport and all other types of border controls at their mutual borders and use a common visa policy, some Schengen countries (notably Norway, Switzerland and Iceland) are not part of the European Union. These countries participate in the open border arrangements, but are not party to the EU-Cariforum EPA. Meanwhile, some EU countries are not part of the Schengen area. Preliminary discussions among the Schengen countries did not result in agreement to implement the "artist visa," and more recent European developments related to security concerns and the influx of refugees across the Mediterranean Sea have prevented the initiative from moving forward.

In May 2007, the European Union and Republic of Korea commenced negotiations for a free trade agreement and concluded formal negotiations in 2009. As we have seen, Korea had reached agreement with the United States on their bilateral Free Trade Agreement in April 2007. As a precondition for negotiations with the United States, Korea had cut its cinema screen quota in half, and the Korean film and television sector had joined with trade unions and farmers to mount a significant campaign against the proposed agreement with the United States. This campaign was still underway when negotiations commenced with the EU. Given this context, it is not surprising that both the European Union and Korea wanted to negotiate a cultural protocol in their free trade agreement negotiations, similar to the one agreed with Cariforum.

When details of the EU–Korea cultural protocol were leaked, tremendous opposition to the proposal emerged in Europe, particularly from France and Wallonia (the French-speaking part of Belgium), together with French cultural professionals and the European Coalitions for Cultural Diversity.

The first criticism of the agreement arose from the fact that in the EU structure, culture is within the competence of member states and not the European Union. The EU has competence for trade matters and had been involved in developing the UNESCO Convention, alongside the member states, only because it was an instrument addressing issues of trade in cultural goods and services. European critics also objected to the fact that the protocol was negotiated and contained within a free trade agreement. This meant that it was subject to the back and forth of negotiations and susceptible to tradeoffs to obtain concessions in other economic sectors. Finally, critics objected to the fact that the protocol was based on the Cariforum EPA, which had been negotiated with a diverse collection of small developing countries, rather than addressing the issues in the context of an agreement with a developed economy that has mature cultural industries.[4]

The EU-Korea Agreement was delayed for several years after formal negotiations concluded, and during the hiatus significant changes were made to the Free Trade Agreement and to the Cultural Protocol. These made it possible for France and Wallonia to support the outcome, although lingering concerns within European cultural civil society groups persist. Some of the changes made include the following:

- The protocol was taken out of the Free Trade Agreement; it became a stand-alone agreement between the EU and Korea, subject to ratification at the national level in Europe.
- The Free Trade Agreement article on Cross-Border Trade in Services now contains an exemption for audiovisual services.
- The parties established a Committee on Cultural Cooperation, comprising senior officials. This Committee "shall exercise all functions of the Trade Committee (which otherwise oversees the FTA) as regards this Protocol, where such functions are relevant for the purposes of implementing this Protocol."
- Disputes arising from the protocol will now be dealt with under its specific dispute settlement process, in which experts on the matters addressed in the protocol will be involved. The Committee on Cultural Cooperation will oversee the arbitration process.
- The section on audiovisual coproduction has detailed rules regarding all issues, including financing and the procedures

through which films and television programs produced under its terms can be certified as "domestic" content, both in the European Union and Korea.[5]

It is clear from the agreement Korea reached with the EU that it was responding to the criticism brought by the film and television sector during negotiations with the United States. By including an audiovisual coproduction treaty as part of the agreement with the EU, Korea was expanding opportunities for its film and television production sector.

Korea also launched free trade negotiations with the People's Republic of China in May 2012 and concluded that agreement in November 2014. One practical outcome of those talks involved implementation of a film coproduction treaty. Under the treaty, coproduced films involving Korea and Chinese firms are considered domestic content in China and thus qualify for financial incentives and bypass Chinese import quotas on foreign films. This also provides a boost for the Korean film industry.

## Canada-Korea Free Trade Agreement

Understanding the history of how Canada treated culture in trade agreements during the Harper years, and with the knowledge of developments in Korea regarding its agreements with the United States, the European Union and China, it is not surprising to see how Canada and Korea covered the cultural sector in the free trade agreement that came into effect January 1, 2015.

**Article 22.6** provides that "This Agreement is not to be construed to apply to measures adopted or maintained by either party with respect to cultural industries, except as specifically provided in Articles 1.6 (Cultural Cooperation) and 2.3 (Tariff Elimination)."

**Article 22.8** provides the now standard definition of cultural industries:

*Cultural industries means persons engaged in any of the following activities:*

- the publication, distribution, or sale of books, magazines, periodicals or newspapers in print or machine readable form but not including the sole activity of printing or typesetting any of the foregoing
- the production, distribution, sale or exhibition of film or video recordings
- the production, distribution, sale or exhibition of audio or video music recordings
- the publication, distribution, or sale of music in print or machine readable form
- radio communications in which the transmissions are intended for direct reception by the general public
- radio, television and cable broadcasting undertakings, or
- satellite programming and broadcast network services

**The Cultural Cooperation Article** outlines how the Parties will collaborate to promote cultural exchanges and carry out joint initiatives. The article includes a specific commitment to negotiate an audiovisual coproduction agreement through the competent authorities of each party. While "such a future audiovisual coproduction agreement shall form an integral part of this Agreement," it is exempted from Article 23.2, which establishes how the FTA can be amended, and the dispute settlement provisions of Chapter 8 (Investment) and Chapter 21 (Dispute Settlement). A coproduction treaty has not yet been concluded between Canada and South Korea.[6]

This was the first free trade agreement reached by Canada that took a different approach to culture from the cultural exemption first negotiated in the Canada–United States Free Trade Agreement. But other different approaches would soon follow.

## Canada-European Union Comprehensive Economic and Trade Agreement (CETA)

At the European Union–Canada Summit in Berlin in June 2007, the parties agreed to conduct a joint study to consider the costs and benefits of negotiating a closer economic partnership. At the Summit in 2009, Canada and the European Union announced the launch of negotiations. A complete text was agreed to in August 2014. All of this happened with the Conservative government in power in Ottawa.

As stated in its title, CETA is certainly comprehensive. Over its thirty chapters and annexes, it covers close to 1,600 pages. Its chapters cover:

- trade in goods and services
- investment measures (including an investor-state dispute settlement system), and
- issues related to these, such as technical barriers to trade, subsidies, competition policy, temporary entry of business persons, recognition of professional qualifications, domestic regulations and regulatory cooperation.

It has specific chapters on:

- financial services
- international maritime transportation
- telecommunications
- electronic commerce
- state-owned enterprises and public monopolies
- government procurement
- intellectual property
- trade and sustainable development
- trade and the environment
- trade and labour, as well as
- a dispute settlement system.

Relevant provisions cover subnational governments, which for Canada means provinces, territories and municipalities.

## CETA and Cultural Policies

As we have seen, beginning in the late 1980s, Canada's approach to culture and trade issues had been to negotiate a broad cultural exemption in all trade and investment agreements. But this changed in our negotiations with Korea and also at the request of EU negotiators. The EU had begun to address cultural issues differently after the UNESCO Convention was negotiated and implemented. EU negotiators suggested, and the Canadians agreed, that specific cultural exemptions would be taken on a chapter-by-chapter basis. Many CETA chapters obviously have nothing to do with culture, and "the chapter on Intellectual Property actually benefits Canadian creators so it would not have made sense to exclude it."[7]

Culture occupies an important place throughout the CETA text. Indeed, right from the outset — the Preamble — the Canada–EU Agreement contains several strong and positive statements relating to cultural diversity. Following several clauses that acknowledge the fundamental importance of human rights and a shared concern about human security and democracy, the Preamble goes on to highlight the importance of cultural diversity, the right of states to implement cultural policies and support for the UNESCO Convention:

> *RECOGNISING that the provisions of this Agreement preserve*
> *the right of the Parties to regulate within their territories and*
> *the Parties' flexibility to achieve legitimate policy objectives,*
> *such as public health, safety, environment, public morals and the*
> *promotion and protection of cultural diversity*

> *AFFIRMING their commitments as parties to the UNESCO*
> *Convention on the Protection and Promotion of the Diversity*
> *of Cultural Expressions, done at Paris on 20 October 2005,*
> *and recognising that states have the right to preserve, develop*
> *and implement their cultural policies, to support their cultural*
> *industries for the purpose of strengthening the diversity of cultural*

*expressions, and to preserve their cultural identity, including
through the use of regulatory and financial support*

The chapter-specific exemptions are further supported in Article 28.9, which states:

*Parties recall the exceptions applicable to culture as set out
in the relevant provisions of Chapters Seven (Subsidies),
Eight (Investment), Nine (Cross Border Trade in Services),
Twelve (Domestic Regulation) and Nineteen (Government
Procurement).*

Interestingly, the recollection of the parties in Article 28.9 is somewhat flawed, since it does not exactly conform to the exceptions agreed upon by negotiators. In particular, *there is no exemption* in Chapter 19, and there are peripheral exemptions in other chapters.

## Culture and CETA Chapters

**Chapter 7** establishes rules and regulations regarding subsidies, and Article 7.7 explicitly states that "Nothing in this Agreement applies to subsidies or government support with respect to audiovisual services for the European Union and to cultural industries for Canada."

**Chapter 8** covers investment and provides the standard obligations for the establishment of investments, non-discriminatory treatment of investments and National Treatment and Most-Favoured-Nation treatment. Article 8.2 provides that these obligations do not apply to measures that deal with audiovisual services for the European Union and cultural industries for Canada.

**Chapter 9** covers cross-border trade in services, and Article 9.2 carves out any measure affecting audiovisual services for the European Union and cultural industries for Canada.

**Chapter 10** relaxes immigration rules to permit temporary entry and stay for qualified business persons. This could affect the union-negotiated agreements and restrictions on the number of foreign performers and technicians allowed into Canada to work on foreign-financed film, television and performing arts productions. However, the Chapter incorporates the scope from Article 9.2 of the Chapter on cross-border trade in services, and thus exempts cultural industries for Canada and audiovisual services for the EU.

**Chapter 12** covers domestic regulation, and Article 12.2 provides that the Chapter does not apply to licensing requirements and procedures, or qualification requirements and procedures relating to various sectors, including cultural industries for Canada and audiovisual services for the European Union.

**Chapter 15** covers telecommunications. Particularly in the digital era, commitments and undertakings in this chapter may have an impact on cultural policies. However, Article 15.2 provides that the Chapter does not apply to a measure by a party affecting the transmission of radio or television programming intended for reception by the public, "by any means of telecommunications, including broadcast and cable distribution."

**Chapter 18** is titled "State Enterprises, Monopolies, and Enterprises Granted Special Rights or Privileges." Article 18.4 provides rules for non-discriminatory treatment, and Article 18.5 provides that a "covered entity in its territory (must act) in accordance with commercial considerations in the purchase or sale of goods." The Chapter also provides that these two Articles are covered by the scope clauses in Articles 8.2 and Article 9.2, where cultural industries for Canada and audiovisual services for the EU are specifically exempted.

**Chapter 19** on government procurement does not contain an exception applicable to culture as CETA states in Article 28.9. However, Canada's Annex to Chapter 19 specifically covers procurement by the Canadian Radio-television and Telecommunications Commission, Copyright Board, Department of Canadian Heritage, Library and Archives Canada and the National Film Board; provincial and territorial departments of culture and cultural agencies are also included.

The Annex also covers all Crown corporations accountable to Parliament, which includes the Canadian Broadcasting Corporation, Canada Council for the Arts, National Arts Centre and various museums. In the Annex, Canada has exempted twelve matters from the provisions of Chapter 19, two of which relate to culture:

> *(h) for the acquisition, development, production or co-production of programme material by broadcasters and contracts for broadcasting time*

> *(i) by Quebec entities of works of art from local artists or to procurement by any municipality, academic institution, school board of other provinces or territories with respect to cultural industries. For the purpose of this paragraph, works of art includes specific artistic works to be integrated into a public building or a site*

Finally, CETA's Article 1.1 contains Canada's standard definition of cultural industries.

## Analysis of CETA

The treatment of culture in the Canada-Korea Free Trade Agreement represented a small shift in how Canada has treated culture in its trade and investment agreements. The broad general exemption for the cultural industries was accompanied by an article on cultural cooperation and a commitment to negotiate an audiovisual coproduction agreement between Canada and Korea. CETA represents a much more significant shift and is a completely new approach.

While negotiations were conducted in secret as always, it is clear that the European side initiated the changes we see in CETA. Canada's Conservative government had little interest in the culture file, while the European Union's negotiating position changed substantially following adoption of the UNESCO Convention.

There are some very positive elements in how CETA treats culture.

The agreement contains a strong statement of support for the UNESCO *Convention on the Protection and Promotion of the Diversity of Cultural Expressions*. The Preamble acknowledgement of the right to regulate to achieve legitimate policy objectives includes doing so with respect to the "promotion and protection of cultural diversity." This is a groundbreaking commitment. The clauses exempting culture from Chapters 7, 8, 9 and 12 are significant and clear. They sustain the right of each party to develop, implement and change a broad range of cultural policy measures.

The agreement is nevertheless far from perfect in some respects, and some of the language is unclear and subject to differing interpretations; this could lead to future challenges to cultural policymaking, on both sides of the Atlantic.

**Uncertainty of CETA language**

We have seen that the CETA language is unclear in a very important respect. While Article 28.9 recalls "the exceptions applicable to culture as set out in the relevant provisions of . . . Chapter 19 (Government Procurement)," there is no comprehensive exemption in the chapter. The exemption claimed by Canada for "broadcasters" in its annex presumably is limited to the CBC, TV Ontario and other (public) provincial broadcasters. The exemption in relation to "works of art" may be applicable only to Quebec, since visual arts are not included in the definition of cultural industries. Meanwhile Chapter 18 (State Enterprises), by reference, does exempt any cultural enterprise the government may establish or authorize to operate with special rights from certain agreement obligations.

Accordingly, one can hypothesize that, looking at the language in Chapter 18 and considering the sectors carved out in Articles 8.2 and 9.2, negotiators intended that a government agency established in the exempted cultural sector (cultural industries for Canada and audiovisual services for the EU) is free to ignore the requirement to provide non-discriminatory treatment in certain of its procurement activities.

Further, it may be that any procurement of a good or service by such an agency is not considered by Chapter 19 to be a "procurement for governmental purposes."

However, this would seem to be a very convoluted way to say that when the National Film Board commissions a film, it does not need to act strictly in accordance with "commercial considerations" and can limit its commissions to domestic producers. Presumably, as Crown corporations are specifically included in Canada's Annex to Chapter 19, the Canada Council for the Arts and the Canadian Broadcasting Corporation are covered when they procure construction or related services that have a value beyond the threshold limits, but are exempted from other procurement requirements because they are State Enterprises operating in the field of cultural industries. Presumably CBC is also covered by the exemption for broadcasters "for the acquisition, development, production or coproduction of programme material."

While it is possible to hypothesize about a potential challenge to an NFB decision (which does not enjoy the broadcaster exemption) or the Canada Council, such a challenge is likely to fail, if only because when there is ambiguity in the *language* (as there surely is here between Chapters 18, 19 and 28), then the parties' *intention* becomes a relevant consideration. Fortunately, the parties' intention to implement the UNESCO Convention, which recognizes they each have a right to implement policies favouring the diversity of cultural expressions, is crystal clear.

The error in Article 28.9 about the "exception related to culture" in Chapter 19 (Government Procurement) and the failure of the Article to reference the important indirect exemptions provided to Canadian cultural industries and European audiovisual services in Chapter 10 (Temporary Entry and Stay of Natural Persons for Business Purposes), Chapter 15 (Telecommunications) and Chapter 18 (State Enterprises, Monopolies, and Enterprises Granted Special Rights of Privileges) suggests that the issues of culture and cultural diversity were not foremost in the minds of the negotiators. Nor, it would seem, were they of much concern to those involved in "the thorough legal review" that took place between August 2014 and February 2016.[8]

**Asymmetrical exemption and limitation of definitions in CETA**

Canada and the European Union have taken different approaches to the cultural exemption. For Canada, the exemption relates to cultural industries, defined as they have been since 1992. For the EU, the exemption is for audiovisual services. It should be noted that, while the agreement contains a definition of cultural industries, there is no definition of audiovisual services. This asymmetrical treatment may bring future challenges, most particularly for the Europeans. For example, since the EU has not exempted writing and publishing while Canada has, Canadian publishers may be able to claim benefits in Europe under National Treatment rules that would not be enjoyed reciprocally by European publishers in Canada.

The French first introduced the concept of "l'exception culturelle," in the context of the Uruguay Round of GATT talks, arguing that cultural goods and services are unique and must not be treated in the same way as other goods and services. Since it was first used however, it has always been about the audiovisual sector. Since the GATT contains an exemption for cinema screen quotas, which by extension could support some other policies relating to cultural goods, French concerns have primarily focused on ensuring that *audiovisual services* are exempted from the trade and investment agreements.

Hollywood movies and television shows have been dubbed or subtitled into French for many years, and in this form they came to dominate French screens. On the other hand, France's writing and publishing industry has always been the largest French-language industry in the world and has enjoyed language protection as well as physical distance from other French-language markets. The French music industry has enjoyed similar advantages until recently, and thus the French have now begun to consider that the music sector is subsumed into audiovisual services.

As we have seen, the Canadian definition of cultural industries remains mired in the past — the term "machine-readable form," may not adequately cover digital technologies and media. Similarly, the reference to "broadcast network services," is rapidly becoming outdated.

**Exemption limited to certain chapters**
The cultural exemption applies only to certain CETA chapters, yet culture may be implicated in others.

The exemption is not contained in Chapter 2 which covers trade in goods. As we have seen, it is clear that books, magazines, film reels, CDs containing music or audiovisual programs, records, visual arts and sculptures, as well as artistic works captured in physical digital media, are considered to be goods within the meaning of trade agreements. Thus, trade rules apply to these cultural goods, unless they are exempted. This CETA Chapter is primarily concerned with duties, tariffs, import-and-export restrictions and similar matters related to the movement of goods. With the digital shift, the transfer of physical cultural goods between Canada and the EU is now limited and the provisions may not prove problematic. Canada eliminated most duties on imported cultural goods many years ago. Nevertheless, there is no reason that the cultural sectors should not have been exempted from Chapter 2.

In this connection, the Chapter 16 rules on Electronic Commerce could be more challenging, since they cover the primary way that artistic works are exchanged today. However, Article 16.7 provides that, "In the event of an inconsistency between this Chapter and another chapter of this Agreement, the other chapter prevails to the extent of the inconsistency." Thus, it is likely that the exemption for cultural industries and audiovisual services would apply in a case where an artistic work is transferred electronically between Canada and a member state of the European Union, since this would constitute a transfer of a service rather than a good. Once again, however, it would have been far better to explicitly exempt the relevant cultural sectors from Chapter 16.

## Preserving Scope for Cultural Policymaking

For the cultural sector, the agreements Canada reached with the Republic of Korea and the European Union represented a significant departure from the trade and investment agreements we had negotiated with other countries. But each of these was negotiated with a partner that shared the Canadian concern about promoting domestic artists and cultural producers and preserving the right of governments to implement cultural policies that favour them. Thus, while not perfect, each agreement retained broad scope for Canadian cultural policymaking. As Canada turned its attention to more contemporary agreements with the United States, this scope would soon come under tremendous pressure once again.

# Chapter 8
# The Trans-Pacific Partnership and Its Successor

The Comprehensive and Progressive Agreement for Trans-Pacific Partnership (CPTPP) is the successor agreement to the Trans-Pacific Partnership (TPP) Agreement and can only be understood fully by reviewing its predecessor and the political events that transpired after the TPP provisions were finalized.

TPP began life innocuously when negotiations involving the Pacific Three (New Zealand, Chile and Singapore) were launched on the sidelines of the Asia-Pacific Economic Cooperation (APEC) forum in 2002. Brunei joined the negotiations and the Pacific Four (P-4) Trans-Pacific Strategic Economic Partnership Agreement was concluded in 2005. Negotiations on financial services and investment were deferred for two years.

In early 2008, the United States announced that it would join the P-4 as its negotiators were discussing financial services and investment. The United States wanted to be involved because of the increasing economic importance of the Asia-Pacific region and the geopolitical concerns stemming from China's growing power and influence. This position was solidified with President Barack Obama's announcement of a military, economic and diplomatic "pivot" toward Asia in late 2011.

In September 2008, the parties announced that negotiations for a more comprehensive and expanded agreement would begin. Australia, Peru and Vietnam were invited to join, which they did shortly after, and a new round of negotiations started in 2009. Malaysia joined during the third round of negotiations the following year. In 2010, Canada and Mexico were admitted as observers, but there were impediments to Canada joining the talks, particularly concerning our supply management system for dairy and poultry products. Canada and Mexico formally joined the talks during the fifteenth round in December 2012. Japan became the twelfth member of the TPP club when it joined the negotiations in 2013. The final agreement was reached on October 5, 2015 during the Canadian federal election that brought the end of Prime Minister Harper's Conservative government.

While some provisions on intellectual property rights were leaked in 2012, and the entire chapter dealing with that issue was made available publicly in May 2015, the complete official text of the agreement was not released until November 2015, just months before it was signed by the twelve parties on February 4, 2016. The TPP was signed for Canada by the Liberal government of Prime Minister Justin Trudeau, which had come to power in the October 2015 election.

This history is important to understand because the agreement's architecture and many of its key provisions had been negotiated well before Canada officially joined the talks in late 2012. Equally important, the final terms of the agreement were concluded in the last days of the Conservative government led by Prime Minister Harper, meaning it was that government that made the difficult tradeoffs and hard political decisions so important to determining Canadian winners and losers.

The TPP Agreement is comprehensive. Its thirty chapters and 6,000 pages of text cover all of the matters covered in CETA, as well as other issues, including textiles and apparels, competitiveness, cooperation and capacity building, development, small and medium-sized enterprises, and transparency and anticorruption.

# Trans-Pacific Partnership Agreement and Cultural Policies

## Preamble

The TPP text contains few references to culture, cultural diversity or cultural policy. Parties acknowledge the importance of cultural diversity in the preamble, but they do so with a significant corollary: "Recognise the importance of cultural identity and diversity among and within the Parties, and that trade and investment can expand opportunities to enrich cultural identity and diversity at home and abroad."

Unlike with CETA, culture and cultural diversity are absent from the clause covering the inherent right to regulate. The parties have preserved flexibility to set legislative and regulatory priorities and "to protect legitimate public welfare objectives, such as public health, safety, the environment, the conservation of living or non-living exhaustible natural resources, the integrity and stability of the financial system, and public morals."

Culture and cultural diversity are also largely absent from the chapter governing exceptions. There is no general exception for culture or cultural diversity and only two relevant references:

- **Article 29.6** — A specific provision stating that the New Zealand government may adopt measures giving more favourable treatment to Maori, including in fulfilment of its obligations under the Treaty of Waitangi.
- **Article 29.8** — A statement that "Subject to each party's international obligations, each party may establish appropriate measures to respect, preserve and promote traditional knowledge and traditional cultural expressions."

## Protective exceptions and restrictions

To discover how Canada sought to protect its right to implement, maintain and adapt cultural policies, we need to look at each chapter of the Trans-Pacific Partnership Agreement. As we have seen in multilateral trade agreements structured on the basis of a "negative list," parties may list existing "nonconforming measures." Such measures may be continued or promptly renewed. They can only be changed however if any amendment to the nonconforming measure does not *decrease* its level of conformity.

Canada has listed certain nonconforming measures and taken a reservation against various obligations in Chapters 9 (Investment), 10 (Cross-Border Trade in Services), 15 (Government Procurement) and 17 (State-Owned Enterprises and Designated Monopolies). Here is a review of these key exceptions:

**TPP Annex II** — Canada has taken a reservation from the National Treatment and Most-Favoured-Nation obligations in Chapters 9 and 10, from Performance Requirements in Article 9.10, Senior Management and Boards of Directors rules in Article 9.11 and Local Presence rules in Article 10.6. Canada's specific reservation under the heading: *Investment and Cross-Border Trade in Services* is this:

> *Canada reserves the right to adopt or maintain any measure that affects cultural industries and that has the objective of supporting, directly or indirectly, the creation, development or accessibility of Canadian artistic expression or content, except:*
>
> *a)  discriminatory requirements on services suppliers or investors to make financial contributions for Canadian content development; and*
>
> *b)  measures restricting the access to online foreign audiovisual content.*

**TPP Annex 15-A** — Canada states that government procurement rules will not cover "Services related to culture or cultural industries," and further that government procurement rules are subject to Canada's reservations to Chapters 9 (Investment) and 10 (Cross-Border Trade in Services).

**Chapter 17** — In this chapter dealing with state-owned enterprises and designated monopolies, Canada has taken extensive reservations for the Canadian Broadcasting Corporation, Telefilm Canada and "any new, reorganised or transferee enterprise related to cultural industries." Among other things, each of these enterprises

> *may take into account factors other than commercial considerations, and may accord preferences in its purchase and sale of goods and services to Canadian products, suppliers and persons . . . [and] may provide non-commercial assistance with respect to the supply of a service from Canada to the territory of another party.*

The CBC (or any new enterprise) may also specifically:

> *originate programmes, secure programmes from within or outside Canada by purchase, exchange or otherwise and make arrangements necessary for their transmission . . . [and] provide non-commercial assistance with respect to the production and sale of a good in competition with a like good produced and sold by a covered investment in the territory of Canada and the supply of a service from Canada to the territory of another party.*

The NFB (or any new enterprise) may also specifically:

> *make loans to producers of individual Canadian productions and charge interest on those loans; and advise and assist Canadian producers in the distribution of their works and in the administrative functions of film production.*

The reservation also excludes Canada's *Broadcasting Act*, its regulations and any future amendments. The reservation includes Canada's standard definition of cultural industries.

**Electronic commerce**

There are also important considerations and some degree of cultural exception in Chapter 14 (Electronic Commerce). The key obligation is found in Article 14.4:

> No party shall accord less favourable treatment to digital products created, produced, published, contracted for, commissioned or first made available on commercial terms in the territory of another party, or to digital products of which the author, performer, producer, developer or owner is a person of another party, than it accords to other like digital products.

However, 14.4.3 provides that the Article does not apply to subsidies or grants, and Article 14.4.4 provides that the Article "shall not apply to broadcasting."

Article 14.2 (Scope and General Provisions) also limits its application in certain respects. Article 14.2.5 limits the application of certain provisions in the Chapter by providing they are

> a)  subject to the relevant provisions, exceptions and non-conforming measures of Chapter 9 (Investment), Chapter 10 (Cross-Border Trade in Services) . . . and

> b)  to be read in conjunction with any other relevant provisions in this Agreement.

While Article 14.3 prohibits imposition of customs duties on cross-border electronic transmissions, 14.3.2 provides that this

> shall not preclude a party from imposing internal taxes, fees or other charges on content transmitted electronically, provided that such taxes, fees or charges are imposed in a manner consistent with this Agreement.

### Intellectual property

There is an extensive and substantive chapter on Intellectual Property rights that was subject to much opposition in many of the twelve countries that negotiated TPP, including the United States. These included requirements to increase the term of protection for the authors and creators of the works covered. However, given the changes made when the TPP became the CPTPP and the subsequent agreement with the United States and Mexico on a renegotiated NAFTA, these will not be reviewed here.

## Analysis of TPP and Cultural Policymaking

### Preamble

While it is positive that the parties acknowledge "the importance of cultural identity and diversity among and within the Parties," the assertion that trade and investment "can expand opportunities" is on the whole simply incorrect where such trade and investment is left unregulated. Unfettered trade and investment bring cultural homogenization, where the few dominant cultures overwhelm smaller cultures — not cultural diversity.

The failure of the Canadian feature film industry offers a classic example of how this works. Despite our world-class talent pool and production capacity, Canadian English-language movies have historically struggled to achieve even a 2 per cent market share in Canadian cinemas. This is because the major U.S. studios have invested in Canada without restrictions and have controlled film distribution and exhibition since the first movies were released, free of regulations or requirements to invest some of their returns in Canadian movies. Meanwhile, this same world-class industrial structure creates Canadian television programs that tell Canadian stories and present a Canadian perspective. These programs draw large audiences at home and abroad and bring in millions of dollars annually from foreign sales. The underpinning of this success consists of robust Canadian content rules and other broadcasting regulations, as well as direct and indirect funding programs.

Compare the modest and misleading TPP language with the CETA language we reviewed in Chapter 7. Even in the agreements Canada concluded before CETA, such as with Peru, Honduras, Jordan, Panama and Peru, the language is far more robust:

> *Recognizing that states must maintain the ability to preserve,*
> *develop and implement their cultural policies for the purpose*
> *of strengthening cultural diversity, given the essential role that*
> *cultural goods and services play in the identity and diversity of*
> *societies and the lives of individuals.*

While TPP Article 29.8 on Traditional Knowledge and Traditional Cultural Expressions approaches an exemption, it is far too narrow to provide any protection for measures parties may take to support their arts and cultural industries. Typically, "traditional knowledge" and "traditional cultural expressions" refer to those that are passed along from generation to generation within First Nations' or Indigenous Peoples' communities. The World Intellectual Property Organization notes that such knowledge forms part of the culture or spiritual identity of these communities.

It is positive and appropriate to include a provision that gives parties the right to enact measures to support First Nations and Indigenous Peoples, including in their cultural expressions, but it is simply inappropriate for such a provision to be conditional on "each party's international obligations." The obligation can and should exist at a national level, in every country, even in the absence of any international obligation.

**TPP chapters**
In late 2015 and early 2016, there was an important exchange about the TPP between Professor Michael Geist, an Internet and intellectual property lawyer, and Peter S. Grant. Peter Grant is Counsel at McCarthy Tétrault LLP and an expert on communications and cultural

policy. He co-authored the book *Blockbusters and Trade Wars: Popular Culture in a Globalized World*, which focused on the interrelationship of trade law with cultural policy.[1] He was a member of the SAGIT that proposed the New International Instrument on Cultural Diversity in 1999.

Professor Geist argued that TPP represented a "major departure" from the approach taken in past trade agreements. Mr. Grant responded that this position is not "entirely wrong" because Canada's negotiating approach until 2012 was to negotiate "a broad cultural exemption to all its trade and investment treaties." At the request of EU negotiators, Canada agreed in CETA "to take specific cultural exemptions on a chapter-by-chapter basis." He argued that Canada merely used a similar approach in TPP "and carefully excluded Canadian cultural policies" from the application of relevant chapters.

On electronic commerce, Professor Geist wrote that "it is shocking to find the Canadian government locking itself into rules that restrict its ability" to impose requirements such as for foreign over-the-top (OTT) services (like Netflix) to contribute to Canadian content production, or other measures. In his response, Mr. Grant concluded that "there is nothing in the TPP to preclude Canada from imposing non-discriminatory requirements on Internet service suppliers to support Canadian content. Nor would the TPP preclude the government from imposing a tax on foreign suppliers of content over the Internet to ensure that HST revenue is collected, not avoided."[2]

Mr. Grant is Canada's leading communications lawyer who has written extensively on key related issues over many years. Thus, his conclusion that the nature of the "broadcasting" exception and the limited obligations in the Electronic Commerce Chapter would permit Canada to impose non-discriminatory requirements on foreign services or to enforce HST collection to ensure such services do not have a competitive advantage over Canadian ones is persuasive. However, Mr. Grant's general conclusion that Canada has "carefully excluded Canadian cultural policies" is incorrect.

## Why TPP Would Threaten Canada's Cultural Policies

Canada has used a reservation approach to protect culture. The mechanism used to remove Canadian cultural policies from various TPP obligations is to list existing nonconforming measures and to specifically reserve the right to implement policies related to cultural industries in TPP Chapters 9 (Investment), 10 (Cross-Border Trade in Services), 15 (Government Procurement) and 17 (State-Owned Enterprises and Designated Monopolies).

This is first of all a one-way approach. There is no mutual or multilateral understanding that Canadian cultural policy measures are exempted, particularly in the absence of supportive acknowledgement of the UNESCO *Convention on the Protection and Promotion of the Diversity of Cultural Expressions*. Once again, this is in stark contrast to the mutual, albeit asymmetrical, provisions in CETA.

A reservation also inherently provides only very weak protection. Assuming Canada's exemptions are robust enough to cover all existing measures at national, provincial, territorial and municipal levels, these may only be "continued" or promptly "renewed." If a measure is, for any reason, not achieving the policy objective, it cannot be strengthened because this would "decrease the conformity" of the measure and thus would violate the TPP.

There is also a strong assumption in TPP and in international trade law generally that all sectors should be liberalized and made to conform fully to the obligations. By its very definition, a "reservation" is an acknowledgement that a certain measure is contrary to the terms of the agreement. Canada would be under strong pressure to restrict measures implemented under the reservation and, ultimately, to remove the reservation entirely. If it were ever to do so, the sector could never be reprotected, as we saw earlier with New Zealand broadcasting.

Also, if artists in future begin to work in an entirely new medium that does not yet exist, such a medium would be covered by the TPP terms because it is a "negative list" agreement. While some may find it absurd to contemplate an entirely new medium of creative expression, remember that we could not possibly have contemplated the book, the sound recording or the movie, before the relevant technology was developed. Virtual reality is only now emerging as a technology that will have enormous implications for artists and storytelling.

Issues may also arise in future in relation to TPP chapters in which Canada has not listed any reservations. It is impossible to speculate about every possibility in an agreement this comprehensive and detailed. For example, recall that some cultural expressions, including books, magazines, periodicals and visual arts, are still circulated in a physical form. Given the *Canada Periodicals Case*, in which the WTO found that published works constitute goods and thus are subject to trade rules governing goods, the provisions of TPP Chapter 2 (National Treatment and Market Access for Goods) would apply to such goods, since there is no exemption.

## Comparing CETA and TPP

There is a significant difference between the approach taken by Canada and the EU in CETA and the approach taken in the TPP. The chapter exemptions in CETA are mutual, albeit with a different focus: cultural industries for Canada, audiovisual services for Europe. These exemptions are underpinned by very strong language in the Preamble confirming the parties' right to regulate, including for "the promotion and protection of cultural diversity" and acknowledging their mutual commitment to the UNESCO Convention. Further, CETA Article 28.9 provides additional support by highlighting the chapters subject to the exemption.

If Canada were confronted on the use of its reservation for cultural industries in TPP, it would not have any similar strong language to justify the cultural policy measure being challenged.

## Limits on Canada's Reservations

TPP also explicitly limits Canada's right to implement new policies. Specifically, in its own reservation, Canada preemptively excluded the possibility of implementing "a) discriminatory requirements on service suppliers or investors to make financial contributions for Canadian content development and b) measures restricting access to online foreign audiovisual content."

In the electronic commerce chapter, parties have certain rights to impose requirements, but these must not be more onerous for the works or goods from other TPP parties. Thus, while the CRTC may be free to impose requirements on OTT services under the *Broadcasting Act*, any such requirements would only conform with the TPP if they were to apply equally to both domestic and foreign OTT services. However, this may not be the most appropriate policy mechanism to address the particular challenge or need.

Finally, it is important to note that Canada's reservation does not just apply to "measures affecting the cultural industries," as has been the case in every agreement since the late 1980s. Under the TPP, these measures must also have "the objective of supporting, directly or indirectly, the creation, development or accessibility of Canadian artistic expression or content." While this may not appear on the surface to be a significant limit on Canada's right to implement cultural policies, it is the first time such language has been used. It is certainly possible to contemplate a challenger suggesting that a certain policy, while directed at the cultural industries, fails to meet this objective. Recall that Country Music Television argued that the CRTC decision to delist it was not a cultural policy as it had nothing to do with promoting Canadian content — it was strictly a business matter. The language is clearly far more restrictive than CETA and we will consider the implications further in Chapter 11.

## TPP – The Worst Deal Ever for Canadian Culture

From the perspective of Canadian culture, there is no question that the Trans-Pacific Partnership Agreement is the worst trade deal Canada has ever signed. Given this, it is surprising that Canada's cultural community was largely silent during the initial stages of the discussion, both during the election and afterward, a significant change from the debates about the Canada–United States Free Trade Agreement and NAFTA.

In March 2016, the Canadian Centre for Policy Alternatives published a study by Alexandre Maltais on TPP and Culture.[3] This study noted that there were

> weaker protections for culture and cultural industries in the TPP
> than in other trade treaties, including the North American Free
> Trade Agreement (NAFTA) and . . . the Comprehensive Economic
> and Trade Agreement with the European Union.

However, it would appear that the key organizations in the cultural sector had been convinced by Peter Grant's opinion published the previous month. The sector became preoccupied with other issues as the new government began to roll out many studies and possible policy initiatives.

In February 2016, the House of Commons Standing Committee on International Trade decided to launch a study of TPP. The study ultimately extended over one year, and briefs and submissions were accepted until January 31, 2017. In late December 2016, I was asked by ACTRA, with which I have been associated for more than forty years, most recently as a policy advisor, to study the Trans-Pacific Partnership Agreement and prepare a draft analysis which the union could file with the Committee. That submission was finalized and filed in late January 2017; it contained an analysis similar to that provided above. In the end, the Committee heard from 312 invited witnesses and 103 individuals at "open mike" sessions and received 199 briefs.[4] In its final report in April 2017, the Committee quoted ACTRA's brief but failed to address the substantive issues ACTRA had raised in its recommendations:

> The Alliance of Canadian Cinema, Television and Radio Artists
> also recommended that the House of Commons reject the TPP,

> *believing that ratification would "restrict Canada's right to*
> *implement the full range of cultural policies Canadians need." It*
> *suggested the following regarding possible next steps: "[i]f there is*
> *any further consideration of TPP provisions or any effort to apply*
> *the Agreement to a different group of countries, [the Alliance*
> *of Canadian Cinema, Television and Radio Artists] urges that*
> *negotiations be reopened and that Canada obtain a broad cultural*
> *exemption before agreeing to the Agreement."*[5]

Other cultural groups participating in the consultation process included SOCAN, which represents songwriters, composers and music publishers, the Canadian Federation of Musicians (CFM) and the Canadian Music Publishers Association (CMPA). CFM and CMPA appeared as witnesses, while SOCAN filed a brief. The primary focus of these presentations involved support for the copyright term extension contained in TPP.

Fortunately for Canadian culture, on the third day of his presidency in 2017, Donald Trump issued an executive order withdrawing the United States from the TPP.

## The "Comprehensive and Progressive" Agreement for Trans-Pacific Partnership (CPTPP)

Immediately after President Trump's announcement, the remaining TPP partners, led by Japan and Australia, began to discuss how to proceed without the United States, since the TPP had also been signed by the other eleven remaining partners. The initiative was initially known as the TPP-11.

In late April 2017, President Trump announced that he had decided to renegotiate the North American Free Trade Agreement rather than to terminate it. Canada and Mexico agreed it was time to "modernize" this twenty-year-old agreement. Because the NAFTA cultural exemption clause is so significant, the cultural community began to realize there were problems brewing on the trade file. The Coalition for

Cultural Diversity organized a seminar in Montreal in early June 2017 regarding NAFTA. Delegates shared concerns not only about NAFTA but also about the TPP. Since there was a growing awareness about the serious challenges the TPP would pose for Canadian cultural policy-making, the community began to raise concerns in the context of the effort to proceed with TPP-11 — without the United States.

Senior officials from the TPP-11 countries met regularly from May to October to consider how to proceed. In November 2017, leaders of twenty-one APEC countries attended a Summit in Da Nang, Vietnam. The leaders were expected to announce that they had reached an agreement-in-principle on proceeding with the trade pact. However, the announcement meeting was cancelled at the last minute, with published reports indicating that Prime Minister Justin Trudeau balked at attending. International Trade Minister François-Philippe Champagne stated that, while an agreement was close, Canada was still seeking a number of key changes, including "suspension" of provisions related to intellectual property, rules of origin for the auto sector and on "how the countries will proceed with including cultural exemptions into the treaty."[6]

Negotiations continued, and during meetings in Tokyo, Japan in January 2018, the remaining issues were resolved, including "culture and autos for Canada."[7] On March 8, 2018, ministers from all eleven countries met in Santiago, Chile, and signed what would now be known as the Comprehensive and Progressive Agreement for Trans-Pacific Partnership (CPTPP).

## How the CPTPP Deals with Cultural Issues

My first observation about the agreement overall concerns its name. It strikes me as Orwellian doublespeak to believe that you can make relatively minor changes to the TPP Agreement and suddenly transform it into something "progressive."

When the parties announced the successful conclusion of negotiations for the CPTPP, Trade Minister François-Philippe Champagne and

Canadian Heritage Minister Mélanie Joly both heralded a great victory since "Canada obtained a cultural exemption." Despite their rhetoric, this is far from accurate.

With the agreed revisions, the CPTPP becomes a new agreement that incorporates the existing TPP text by reference. Parties have agreed to "suspend" twenty-two TPP provisions, including a number of the most significant and controversial IP provisions, including the extension of the term of copyright protection. The parties may "end suspension," presumably through consensus. Canada has signed a side letter with each other party respecting culture, which is stated to be "legally binding" and "enforceable."

The CPTPP preamble includes a provision that the parties:

> *Reaffirm the importance of promoting corporate social responsibility, cultural identity and diversity, environmental protection and conservation, gender equality, indigenous rights, labour rights, inclusive trade, sustainable development and traditional knowledge, as well as the importance of preserving their right to regulate in the public interest . . .*

CPTPP Article 1 provides that the terms of the TPP "are incorporated, by reference, into and made part of this Agreement . . ." except for certain structural articles that have now become irrelevant. The Article further provides that, "In the event of any inconsistency between this Agreement and the TPP, when the latter is in force, this Agreement shall prevail to the extent of the inconsistency."

The original text of the TPP thus remains in place in all of the important areas. Recall Canada's reservation in TPP Annex II:

> *Canada reserves the right to adopt or maintain any measure that affects cultural industries and that has the objective of supporting, directly or indirectly, the creation, development or accessibility of Canadian artistic expression or content, except:*

a) *discriminatory requirements on services suppliers or investors to make financial contributions for Canadian content development, and*

b) *measures restricting the access to online foreign audiovisual content.*

Canada has obtained a number of side letters on issues it sought to address. The cultural Side Letter attempts to remove the restrictions Canada placed on its own reservation in (a) and (b) above. An identical side letter was sent by Canada to each other party and each includes a confirmation of agreement from the other government.

The most significant change between TPP and CPTPP of course is that the United States is no longer party to the agreement. This is certainly the most significant issue for Canadian cultural policymaking since it is the U.S. entertainment industry that dominates the Canadian cultural space.

## Analysis of the CPTPP and Culture

The new preamble language is obviously a positive step, but it remains an open question whether it has corrected the core problem of the TPP preamble. On the one hand, the new preamble seems to imply that the parties have a right to regulate to promote cultural diversity, although use of the words "as well as" leaves a huge doubt.

It could be argued that while each party is free to "promote" the social objectives outlined in the new preamble clause, its right "to regulate in the public interest" is restricted to the issues outlined in the original TPP text i.e. "public health, safety, the environment, the conservation of living or non-living exhaustible natural resources, the integrity and stability of the financial system and public morals." Also, since the new preamble does not challenge the TPP assumption that "trade and investment can expand opportunities" to enrich cultural diversity, one could further argue that the way to promote cultural identity and diversity as provided in the CPTPP preamble is through market forces rather than regulation, and thus there is no inconsistency. This would be supported by the fact that the TPP's right to regulate and General Exceptions, incorporated without amendment into the CPTPP, make no reference to cultural diversity.

More importantly, a preamble provision can be used only for purposes of understanding the parties' intention. If the agreement's language is clear, that language applies. If the agreement language is ambiguous, unclear or limited, the preamble may be used to understand what the parties intended with the particular provision. In the provisions of most concern to cultural policymaking, the TPP provisions are clear and unambiguous.

Like a preamble clause, a side letter similarly would be used as an interpretive tool where the text is otherwise ambiguous, unclear or limited. The cultural side letter importantly uses the word "notwithstanding" the provision of the Annex, which is direct and a clear acknowledgement that the parties have taken a new approach. It is also positive that each other government officially agrees to its terms. Thus, while the cultural exemption remains for Canada alone, each other party acknowledges that Canada has removed the limitations on its own reservation. It would be difficult for any of the other governments to challenge a Canadian measure that provides for discriminatory requirements against foreign services or measures that restrict access to online foreign audiovisual content, if these are considered necessary to achieve cultural objectives. It is important to recall however that the caveat in Canada's original reservation remains in place. To qualify under the reservation, Canada's measures must have "the objective of supporting, directly or indirectly, the creation, development or accessibility of Canadian artistic expression or content." Such a qualification explicitly contemplates the possibility that a particular measure could fall outside this caveat.

Clearly, some of the challenges posed by the original TPP remain. Canada's chapter-by-chapter reservations are limited and they are still one way. While the side letters demonstrate that each other party confirms Canada's amendment of its own reservation, parties may expect that this reservation remains subject to "standstill and rollback" provisions, since this is standard practice when dealing with reservations.

There may also be a challenge relating to definitions. In its now "suspended" limitation, Canada had agreed that it would not restrict access to "online foreign audiovisual content." In the e-commerce chapter, the exception is for "broadcasting." These are not the same thing, and this significant difference may give rise to challenging discussions in future, particularly as the technology develops.

Another factor to note in discussing culture and CPTPP is that this is the first free trade agreement Canada has entered into with Japan. This is important because the Sony Corporation is a Japanese company and thus would enjoy all of the rights available to investors under the agreement, including access to the investor-state dispute settlement system. Sony Pictures is a major Hollywood studio, Sony Interactive Entertainment a major producer of video games and Sony Music the largest music company in the world. Given the overall uncertainty of the provisions relating to culture, Canada may have difficulties in relation to cultural policies that negatively affect Sony's interests in Canada, as we will see in Chapter 11.

Finally, we must consider how new parties will be accepted into the CPTPP. From Canada's cultural perspective, the major challenge we face for English-language artists and producers is the overwhelming flow of cultural products and services we receive from our southern neighbour, since our border is largely open. In the past thirty years, the only Canadian cultural policies that have been successfully challenged or forced to be changed have resulted from pressure from or complaints by the United States.

Clearly, many Pacific countries hope the United States will reconsider its decision to withdraw and CPTPP Article 1 explicitly anticipates such a development. The use of the suspension process in areas where the United States has strong interests has also set the stage for this possibility. For the cultural sector, the critical issue will be whether or not the

United States would be prepared to agree to the side letter on culture.

The CPTPP provides that any state may join, subject to negotiating terms and conditions. The process for negotiating accession is covered in the original TPP.

- Chapter 27 establishes a Commission (Ministers or senior officials from each party).
- The Commission, in accordance with Article 30.4, "shall establish a working group" to negotiate with the party seeking to join.
- Each CPTPP party can take part in the working group.
- A decision of the working group "shall be deemed to have been taken" when all parties that are members of the group agree, or, if a party that is a member of the working group is not in agreement, "that party has not objected to the report in writing."
- The Commission itself also operates by consensus, which is defined as the absence of opposition.

In other words, the potential accession of the United States would not require the unanimous consent of all other parties, but rather would occur in the absence of an objection from any other party. This process is widely used in intergovernmental organizations because it allows tremendous pressure to be applied to a dissenting party, particularly if they are standing alone. They do not have to agree to a decision, they merely have to remove their objection. Given this structure, Canada may be isolated if the United States decides to join the CPTPP.

The Comprehensive and Progressive Agreement for Trans-Pacific Partnership (CPTPP) came into effect on December 31, 2018, with Canada as one of its founding members. The problems and challenges for Canada's cultural policymaking will inevitably begin to emerge in the years ahead.

## A New and Uncertain Approach

Most likely driven by our negotiating partners, Canada's approach to the cultural exemption in trade and investment agreements changed very dramatically in the Canada–Korea Free Trade Agreement, Canada's Comprehensive Economic and Trade Agreement with the European Union and the Comprehensive and Progressive Agreement for Trans-Pacific Partnership. The Korea agreement maintains the comprehensive cultural exemption and adds a cultural protocol. CETA uses a chapter-by-chapter mutual exemption approach which is underpinned by positive language in the introductory chapters.

CPTPP uses an unsatisfactory and incomplete chapter-by-chapter reservation approach. This basic approach and the specific language creates uncertainty and leaves open the possibility of future difficulties. Most importantly, while Canada improved the position of culture in the transition from TPP to CPTPP, many of the initial challenges remain. These include the fact that the reservation is one-way and is subject to the principles of "standstill and rollback"; inevitably, there will be pressure on Canada to liberalize trade in this sector. Finally, restrictions continue to apply in the e-commerce chapter, and the absence of an exemption in other chapters may come into play in future.

# Chapter 9
# The Contemporary Canada-United States Relationship and NAFTA 2019

## From NAFTA to NAFTA 2019

Shortly after he assumed office in early 2017, United States President Donald Trump tweeted his intention to renegotiate NAFTA — or to scrap it, or to tweak it . . . Canada and Mexico both agreed on the need to "modernize" the twenty-five-year-old trade pact. In May 2017, President Trump provided official notice to the U.S. Congress of his intention to renegotiate NAFTA.

While the negotiations were challenging, chaotic and almost derailed by the unpredictable U.S. president, Canada's Foreign Affairs Minister Chrystia Freeland and United States Trade Representative Richard Lighthizer announced on September 30, 2018, that Canada and the United States had reached agreement on how the two countries would join Mexico in a new North American agreement. The United States and Mexico had reached agreement the previous month. The United States is calling the new agreement the United States–Mexico–Canada Agreement (USMCA), Canada is calling it the Canada–United States–Mexico Agreement (CUSMA), Mexico is calling it the *Tratado México Estados Unidos Canadá* (TMEUC) and many are calling it NAFTA 2.0 or the New NAFTA.

Since the word *new* cannot survive decades, I will refer to it as NAFTA 2019.

## Cultural Issues Raised by U.S. Stakeholders

Before reviewing the agreement, we look at the cultural issues raised by key U.S. stakeholders, since this is the most contemporary list of concerns that the U.S. cultural industries have about Canada's cultural policies. As we have just seen with respect to the CPTPP, NAFTA 2019 will not be the last agreement that Canada and the United States will negotiate that will touch on these questions.

For six weeks after President Trump's notice to Congress in May 2017, the Office of the United States Trade Representative invited U.S. stakeholders to submit their views on the issues the United States should seek to renegotiate in NAFTA. There was a very strong push by the U.S. entertainment industry to reopen the cultural exemption and to include rules on electronic commerce comparable to the provisions of the original Trans-Pacific Partnership Agreement.

In its submission, the **Motion Picture Association of America** (MPAA) noted that "the U.S. film and television industry is one of the most highly competitive in the world . . . The industry . . . had a positive services trade surplus of $13.3 billion [USD] in 2015 . . . The U.S. motion picture and television industry has a $1.194 billion [USD] services trade surplus with Canada."[1] The MPAA was blunt in its assessment of NAFTA:

> Canada, much unlike Mexico and the United States, did not take
> any commitments in the NAFTA for film or television services
> and investment. Rather, Canada carved out the cultural industries
> from the scope of their NAFTA obligations (other than tariffs) via
> NAFTA Annex 2016. This means that the U.S. cultural industries,
> including the U.S. motion picture and television industry, do
> not benefit from the market opening disciplines of NAFTA with
> regard to the Canadian market, while Canadian industries have

*full access to the U.S. market. The NAFTA is the only U.S. trade*
*agreement currently in force that includes a cultural carveout.*

This assessment of Canada being "closed" and the United States being "open" ignores the fact that the U.S. film and television industry continues to dominate the Canadian marketplace, as attested to by the significant trade balance which the MPAA itself highlighted. One wonders how much more of Canada's market they could capture. The MPAA then goes on to outline its view of how the cultural sector should be treated in free trade regimes:

> *Such a [cultural] carveout is inconsistent with the principles of*
> *free and fair trade. Cultural promotion and open markets are*
> *compatible and complementary. MPAA is committed to the*
> *promotion and protection of cultural diversity and firmly believes*
> *that NAFTA parties in the modernization negotiations can*
> *effectively rely on the flexibilities built into free trade agreements,*
> *including permissible support programs, to promote their cultural*
> *interests.*

The MPAA outlines three specific priorities for the NAFTA modernization process:

- **Ensure non-discrimination in the online marketplace** — Interestingly, without specifically referencing the TPP, the MPAA states, "The Canadian government has acknowledged that imposing quotas and other discriminatory measures online is unnecessary and would limit consumer choice." The MPAA also urges that NAFTA include other key elements of the TPP electronic commerce chapter, including ensuring the free flow of data between markets and the prohibition of duties on digital products delivered by electronic commerce. These proposals are supported by several other intervenors in the process, including the Coalition of Services Industries, the Recording Industry

Association of America, the National Retail Federation, the Telecommunications Industry Association and the Entertainment Software Association.

- **Elimination of ownership restrictions on pay-television services** — Like other broadcasting services, Canada requires that they be majority Canadian-owned and -controlled. The provisions in the United States that limit foreign ownership of all broadcasting outlets to no more than 25 per cent were relaxed informally by the Federal Communications Commission (FCC) in 2013. The FCC will now permit foreign ownership beyond 25 per cent, providing that there is a public interest benefit and providing further that there is no U.S. security interest. Under this revised policy, in February 2017 the FCC approved the takeover of various U.S. broadcasters by an Australian couple. In announcing the decision, the FCC noted "that allowing this kind of foreign ownership brings new sources of capital into the U.S. broadcasting industry, and may encourage other countries to relax their ownership rules to allow investment by U.S. companies in broadcast companies serving other countries."[2]

- **Improvement of protection for intellectual property rights** — The MPAA calls for NAFTA to ensure that the term of protection is extended to the life of the author plus seventy years; to require that unauthorized recording in theatres be made a criminal offence; and to require that Internet service providers take down a site when a copyright owner demonstrates that it is being used to gain access to copyright materials without consent. Several other intervenors made similar comments about copyright.

The **National Association of Broadcasters (NAB)**called for Canada's system for retransmission of broadcasting signals to be replaced by a "consent regime." Canada's system currently permits a broadcast signal to be retransmitted in the original coverage area (as defined by the signal from terrestrial broadcasting towers) without payment or permission. Where the signal is retransmitted to a "distant" market, the Canadian retransmitter (a cable or satellite company) must pay a royalty, which is distributed to rights holders including U.S. broadcasters and program suppliers. NAB also calls for the end of "discriminatory tax treatment on advertising." This is a reference to Section 19.1 of the *Income Tax Act* which prohibits a Canadian taxpayer from deducting as a business expense any advertising they place on a U.S. border station.

In an interesting submission, the **National Football League** urged the United States to help it overturn the CRTC decision that the broadcast of the Super Bowl in Canada must use the original signal, which includes U.S. commercials. This decision was made notwithstanding the longstanding CRTC simultaneous substitution policy and the existence of a private contract between the NFL and Bell Media, the Canadian broadcaster. The CRTC decision was championed by Jean-Pierre Blais, the commission's chair from 2012 to 2017, and was apparently made because the CRTC had received 100 individual complaints in the previous decade. As a result of the CRTC decision, Canadians were able to watch the original U.S. Super Bowl telecast, together with the American commercials, in 2017, 2018 and 2019. The NFL opposed the CRTC's policy because the fee it receives from the Canadian broadcaster for the exclusive rights to broadcast the Super Bowl in Canada is far greater than the additional advertising revenues U.S. broadcasters could generate by simply adding the Canadian market for advertisers. For some advertisers, the Canadian market is irrelevant; for others it is worth only a small amount.

In its submission, the NFL went far beyond the simultaneous substitution issue:

> Canada has a long history of discriminating against U.S. copyright
> interests and has consistently appeared on the "Watch List"
> or "Priority Watch List" produced annually by the U.S. Trade
> Representative to identify countries neglecting their trade and

*intellectual property obligations ... Canada's discrimination*
*against the NFL bears similarities to two prior efforts by Canada*
*to discriminate against U.S. television programming and sports-*
*related advertising.*

The cases the NFL referenced are the CRTC decision to remove carriage of Country Music Television when it licensed a competing Canadian service, and the restrictions on Canadian advertising in *Sports Illustrated* and other split-run U.S. magazines. According to the NFL submission, "In both cases, the United States responded firmly to enforce U.S. rights under NAFTA, causing Canada to abandon both discriminatory measures." While Canada would argue that it did not abandon its measures, perhaps this hints that the CRTC decision to eliminate the rule under which it had delisted CMT was part of an agreement between the United States and Canada to resolve that dispute.

The most comprehensive assault on Canadian cultural policy measures was launched by the **Coalition of Services Industries (CSI)**, whose membership "includes major international companies from the banking, insurance, telecommunications, information technology, logistics and express delivery, audiovisual, retail and other service industries. CSI members conduct business in all 50 states and in more than 100 countries." CSI called for:

- Continuation of the negative list of "narrow" exemptions and appropriate ratchet provisions to eventually eliminate these exemptions
- Trans-Pacific Partnership Agreement provisions or better
- No cultural carveout, including for online services
- Investor protections for "all sectors"
- Fair competition by state-owned enterprises (SOEs)
- Various matters relating to copyright.[3]

The Office of the United States Trade Representative (USTR) released its objectives for the NAFTA renegotiation in July 2017:

- **Services** — The USTR announced it would seek commitments from NAFTA countries to provide "fair and open conditions for services trade," including a prohibition against discrimination or rules that restrict the number of services suppliers in the market or requirements that they first establish a local presence. Where exceptions are permitted, these should be negotiated on a negative list basis and be the narrowest possible exceptions with the least possible impact on U.S. firms.
- **Digital trade and cross-border data flows** — the USTR announced it would seek "commitments not to impose customs duties on digital products (e.g., software, music, video, e-books) . . . and ensure non-discriminatory treatment of digital products transmitted electronically and guarantee that these products will not face government-sanctioned discrimination based on the nationality or territory in which the product is produced." These provisions were all agreed to in the TPP.
- **Investment measures** — The USTR announced it would seek commitments to "establish rules that reduce or eliminate barriers to U.S. investment in all sectors in the NAFTA countries."
- **State-owned enterprises** — The USTR announced it would seek commitments to "ensure that SOEs accord non-discriminatory treatment with respect to purchase and sale of goods and services" and further to "ensure that SOEs act in accordance with commercial considerations with respect to such purchases and sales."

A significant issue for Canada in the NAFTA renegotiations was that the last trade agreement Canada and the United States had signed was the original Trans-Pacific Partnership Agreement. This was problematic because the United States assumed that this was the starting point for the NAFTA talks. As we have seen, the general trade theory is that liberalization is an objective in itself, and that all exceptions should be narrow, targeted and eventually eliminated. U.S. Commerce Secretary Wilbur Ross gave warning of the challenge when he said, "A card laid is a card played. And even though that hand [the TPP] is cancelled, when somebody has put something on the table in writing that is an agreed thing."[4]

If there were no general exception for cultural industries, a "modernized" NAFTA would have affected all cultural services, including audiovisual services, broadcasting, publishing, music and visual and performing arts. The stakes in the NAFTA talks were very high.

On June 8, 2017, representatives of the Canadian cultural sector met in the offices of the Department of Canadian Heritage in Gatineau, Quebec. We were invited there to hear from senior officials about the latest round of trade negotiations and the issues of concern to the sector. The Canadian NAFTA negotiators reported on preparations for negotiations with the United States and Mexico. In the presentation, negotiators argued that NAFTA had the weakest cultural exemption of any of Canada's trade agreements, primarily because it authorized retaliation against Canadian policies and had no provision whereby Canada could challenge U.S. retaliatory measures. I responded and pointed out that the Trans-Pacific Partnership Agreement was by far the worst agreement from the perspective of Canadian cultural policymaking. In the discussion, I urged negotiators to strengthen the NAFTA cultural exemption by making it a direct exemption from the entire agreement rather than a reference back to the CUSFTA exemption, by eliminating the notwithstanding clause and by updating the definition of cultural industries. I acknowledged that Canada's inability to challenge retaliatory measures was a problem.

## NAFTA 2019

The agreement concluded in 2018 between Canada, the United States and Mexico represents a significant update to the earlier NAFTA agreement. Over close to 2,000 pages, the agreement covers all the usual issues, including goods, investment, services, government procurement, state-owned-enterprises, telecommunications, competition policy, temporary entry, digital trade and intellectual property. It also contains a number of specific chapters, including on agriculture, rules of origin, textiles, labour, environment, small and medium-sized enterprises, and anticorruption.

There were major changes in important areas, such as revised rules of origin for automobiles, a minimum wage requirement on some autos that was designed to force wages higher in Mexico, a further opening of Canada's supply-managed dairy, egg and poultry industries and significant changes in intellectual property laws. There is a sunset clause of sixteen years, but a requirement for the parties to renegotiate the agreement's terms in six years. Importantly, the investor-state dispute settlement system was largely abolished.

## Cultural Exemption Strengthened

The cultural exemption appears in this form in NAFTA 2019: "This Agreement does not apply to a measure adopted or maintained by Canada with respect to a cultural industry, except as specifically provided in Article 2.4 (Treatment of Customs Duties) or Annex 15-D (Programming Services)." The definition of cultural industries is unchanged from the original NAFTA.

The exemption is stronger than in the original NAFTA, because it is direct and explicit rather than merely a reference back to CUSFTA. As we have seen, the previous formulation may have been limited to the much narrower scope of CUSFTA. The new formulation is clear and effectively excludes cultural industries from the agreement in its entirety. Importantly, it does not require that a policy have a "cultural purpose," as is the case with the CPTPP. In an October 2, 2018, briefing, the negotiators confirmed that the intention of the article is to exclude the cultural industries from all chapters, including Digital Trade.

As we reviewed earlier, the definition of cultural industries was written in 1987 and does not include performing arts, visual arts and crafts.

It continues to use the antiquated language "machine readable form," which may not adequately cover all contemporary technologies. The definition certainly does not include a future medium that artists will use to express themselves, so that such a medium would not be exempted and the agreement, given its top-down nature, would apply to it.

At one of the briefing sessions, negotiators were asked if they had considered expanding the definition to include digital production and distribution. The response, in effect, was that expanding the definition would be an admission that digital production and distribution is not covered by the existing language, which continues in force in many other Canadian agreements. As I will review later, my preference would be a wholesale rewrite of the definition, which would start with the artistic creation and apply regardless of the medium of production or distribution. However, the negotiators could also easily have avoided the problem of admitting limitations of existing language by using the common phrasing "for greater certainty." This language is used in many sections of NAFTA 2019 and in other trade agreements.

In what is now standard practice, the exemption does not apply to customs duties on imported goods. Canada has not agreed to reduce any duties in NAFTA 2019 and Article 2.4 states only that existing duties may be continued, reduced or eliminated but cannot be increased. As with other similar agreements, there is little here of concern to the cultural sector.

## Rights of United States and Mexico with Respect to Cultural Exemption

Article 32.6.3 is a new provision: "With respect to Canadian goods, services, and content, the United States and Mexico may adopt or maintain a measure that, were it adopted or maintained by Canada, would have been inconsistent with the Agreement but for paragraph 2 [Canada's cultural exemption]."

At best, this is obtuse language. Mexico has taken a reservation approach to preserve its cultural policies and thus this provision is not designed to cover Mexican (or American) cultural policies. Rather, it appears to provide that Mexico and the United States are free to introduce measures that specifically target, restrict or limit the importation of Canadian cultural "goods, services and content" or Canadian cultural industry investments. Examples could include prohibiting importation or entry of Canadian magazines, films and books, refusing to admit touring artists or musicians, or prohibiting a Canadian firm from acquiring a U.S. or Mexican entertainment industry firm. Recall that in responding to the Country Music Television case, the United States was considering the adoption of mirror rules that would have restricted Canadian broadcasters operating in the United States.

The agreement maintains the notwithstanding clause by providing that "a party may take a measure of equivalent commercial effect in response to an action by another party that would have been inconsistent with this Agreement but for" Canada's cultural exemption and Article 32.6.3, the mirror provision. In this contect, the mirror provision would seem to authorize retaliatory actions of any scope, providing only that they are "a measure . . . with respect to a cultural industry," in response to Canadian cultural policies.

The original notwithstanding clause stated that Parties could take "measures of equivalent commercial effect," but the change to the use of the singular "measure" is not significant.

## Dispute Settlement

NAFTA 2019 allows parties to resolve disputes if there is retaliation against a Canadian cultural policy measure. A panel may be established, but it can only make a finding about "whether an action to which another party responds is a measure adopted or maintained with respect to a cultural industry for purposes of this Article," and whether the retaliatory action is of "equivalent commercial effect."

This is also entirely new. While it is directed at the responding action, the panel would have authority to decide whether Canada's cultural policy in dispute is legitimately covered by the exemption. It is troublesome that the United States could now challenge a Canadian cultural policy, but this tradeoff may be acceptable in return for Canada being able to challenge the retaliatory measure if it exceeds the "equivalent commercial effect" limit. Canada likely would have been able to argue that threatened U.S. retaliation exceeded this limit in the Country Music Television dispute.

## Programming Services

As we have seen with other Canadian trade agreements that contain a cultural exemption, there can be cultural matters agreed to in the text itself. This is the case in NAFTA 2019 Annex 15-D, as Canada has agreed to make a number of changes to existing cultural policies.

The first of these is an agreement that Canada "shall rescind Broad-casting Regulatory Policy CRTC 2016-334 and Broadcasting Order CRTC 2016-335," the policy which eliminated the simultaneous substitution rule for the broadcast of the Super Bowl. While Canada can continue to provide for the substitution of U.S. programs shown simultaneously in Canada, it cannot discriminate against any specific program.

The simultaneous substitution rule is important to the Canadian television industry, and most of the key organizations joined Bell Media and the NFL in a legal challenge to overturn the CRTC decision. Bell Media paid the NFL millions of dollars in fees for the exclusive right to carry the Super Bowl in Canada, and it did so on the basis of the longstanding CRTC policy that a Canadian rights holder can require a cable company to substitute its signal, including the commercials of its advertisers, when it broadcasts the U.S. program simultaneously with the U.S. telecast. Under the simultaneous substitution rule, everyone in Canada watching the program will see these commercials, regardless of which station they select.

With respect to the Super Bowl, the reality today is that everyone can watch the unique American Super Bowl commercials online before the game is broadcast, so the concerns of the 100 Canadians who complained about missing the U.S. commercials are moot. It is also important to recall that a reasonable share of the commercial revenues received by Bell Media when it broadcasts the game are invested in Canadian content shows and local news. These kinds of programs of course are far rarer on Canadian television screens than are American commercials.

The second provision relates to the retransmission right that has been a focus of U.S. concern since before CUSFTA and was covered in that agreement in the late 1980s. NAFTA 2019 does not provide the full range of rights the U.S. border stations were seeking, but it does obligate Canada to expand rights in three ways:

- When the original U.S. signal is not available for free over-the-air reception, authorization for retransmission is required in all cases, whether the signal is local or distant.
- A signal that is intended for free over-the-air reception by the general public cannot be altered in any way or retransmitted at a different time than the original broadcast, without agreement of the broadcaster and the owner of the program rights.
- While Canada can retain its existing retransmission regime, a local licensee can take steps which enable them "to exploit fully the commercial value of its license." This presumably would permit a U.S. broadcaster to change the nature of its service, for example by beginning to charge for it, and thus fall outside the mandated Canadian system.

These changes to the retransmission regime are unlikely to be controversial, but once again they were made as a consequence of trade negotiations, rather than resulting from our own assessment of a cultural policy.

The third provision requires Canada to guarantee that U.S. home shopping programming services can be authorized for carriage in Canada and may negotiate affiliation agreements with Canadian cable, satellite and Internet Protocol television distributors.

## Digital Trade

When the NAFTA 2019 text was first released, there were initial commentaries about the Digital Trade chapter, since it is modelled on the TPP chapter and has a virtually identical non-discrimination clause. NAFTA 2019 reads,

> *No party shall accord less favorable treatment to digital products created, produced, published, contracted for, commissioned or first made available on commercial terms in the territory of another party, or to digital products of which the author, performer, producer, developer or owner is a person of another party, than it accords to other like digital products.*

Since the clause includes artists and cultural producers in its scope, there was a fear that it could override the exemption for cultural industries. However, since measures relating to cultural industries are exempt from the entire agreement, this chapter should be of little concern. Even though Netflix is in the data collection business, it proudly states that it is a producer and distributor of movies and television programs, so its activities would be covered by the definition of cultural industries and hence exempt from the agreement.

If there was any doubt, another NAFTA 2019 Digital Trade clause provides that "for greater certainty, a measure that affects the supply of a service delivered or performed electronically is subject to Chapter 14 (Investment), Chapter 15 (Cross-Border Trade in Services) and Chapter 17 (Financial Services), including any exception or non-conforming measure set out in this Agreement that is applicable to the obligations set out in those Chapters." Since Canada's cultural exemption applies to Chapters 14, 15 and 17, it is incorporated here. Thus, the cultural sector is doubly exempt.

## Copyright and Related Rights

Like the original TPP, NAFTA 2019 has an extensive and substantive chapter on Intellectual Property (IP) rights that will require Canada to amend a number of pieces of legislation. When discussing this area, it is critical to distinguish among the different issues covered under the IP umbrella. Issues connected with patents, trademarks, industrial designs and geographical indications relate only tangentially to culture; for example, entertainment logos may be registered trademarks, or certain filming processes may be subject to a patent. However, issues related to copyright and related rights are cultural policy matters.

Copyright protects the creator or author of an artistic work, such as the writer of a novel or script, the artist of a painting or sculpture or the composer of a musical work. Related rights (or neighbouring rights) are those rights provided to interpreters of artistic works, such as performers and musicians, or those who add value to the work, such as record producers and broadcasters. The creator/author/interpreter is provided with two types of rights, moral rights and economic rights. Moral rights are those that protect the integrity of the work and the reputation of the artist, and allow the artist to be named (or not) as the author of the work. These rights may be waived by the artist, but they cannot be transferred or exchanged for money. The suite of economic rights allows the artist to authorize certain uses of his or her work. These rights can be transferred (to a producer or publisher, for example) in exchange for money.

There are a number of copyright issues in NAFTA 2019. Most, including those related to technological protection measures (that protect the work from unauthorized use) and rights management information (that prohibit the removal of information attached to the work which identifies the work and the copyright holders), would not require major changes to Canada's *Copyright Act*. The detailed rules concerning civil and criminal remedies for tampering with digital locks and watermarks may put pressure on Canada's system to implement stronger penalties, but nonprofit libraries, archives (including museums), educational institutions and noncommercial broadcasters are specifically excluded from criminal sanctions.

With respect to the responsibility of an Internet service provider when a copyright holder advises it of an unauthorized use of a copyright-protected work, NAFTA 2019 establishes the "notice-and-takedown" system as the standard. This system requires the ISP to block access to the offending site until the site's owner can prove they have the necessary rights to distribute the material. However, Article 20.89 permits Canada to retain its "notice-and-notice" system. In this system, the ISP needs only to pass along to the subscriber a notice it receives about a copyright infringement, and to maintain records that could be used in court. While it preserves the system, the specificity of the NAFTA 2019 language may limit the ability of Canadian law to evolve in response to future developments.

In its copyright section, NAFTA 2019 establishes a National Treatment obligation for all copyright holders. There is no exception to this rule. Since some of Canada's copyright provisions are provided only to Canadians, or are extended to non-Canadians only on a reciprocal basis, these will need to change. For example, under Canada's private copying levy, importers and manufacturers of blank audio recording media are required to pay a royalty on each unit. Canadians are free to copy musical works for their own personal use because this royalty is used to compensate the composers, musicians, singers, publishers, record companies and others who create the works. While music authors and publishers may participate in the program regardless of their nationality, only Canadian performers and record companies qualify (since there is no reciprocal royalty in the United States). This will no longer be allowed under the new agreement.

The most significant change in Canada's *Copyright Act* required by NAFTA 2019 is an increase in the term of copyright protection. Canada currently provides that a work is protected for the life of the creator/ author plus fifty years after the year of their death, or fifty years from the year certain works are published or recorded. There are some exceptions that provide longer terms of protection. Like the original TPP provisions, NAFTA 2019 requires a minimum term of protection of seventy years after the year of death of the creator/author, or up to seventy-five years after the date of publication/fixation in those cases where the copyright term is not based on the life of a real person. This copyright term is becoming common worldwide and is overwhelmingly supported by Canadian artists and producers. Article 20.90 provides Canada with a two-and-a-half-year transition period for the new copyright terms to come into effect.

A potentially significant definition is found in the NAFTA 2019 section on Copyright and Related Rights. In defining "broadcasting," the article states that it does *not* include "transmission over computer networks or any transmission where the time and place of reception may be individually chosen by members of the public." While application of the definition is limited to the relevant copyright clauses, it is important to recall the TPP Electronic Commerce provisions, which are in effect in the CPTPP. Peter Grant's analysis of the TPP is that the exemption for "broadcasting" from the obligations of the Electronic Commerce chapter would authorize Canada to impose "non-discriminatory requirements on Internet service suppliers to support Canadian content . . . [or] a tax on foreign suppliers of content over the Internet." If the United States seeks to join CPTPP and somehow successfully includes the NAFTA 2019 definition of "broadcasting," Canada would clearly no longer be able to impose requirements of this kind.

As we enter 2019, the timetable for ratification of NAFTA 2019 is uncertain. Given requirements for notice and debate, the most optimistic timetable for U.S. ratification in Congress would be 2020. But congressional Democrats, who are now in the majority, have already demanded that the pact be reopened to strengthen various provisions. While I do not expect that this pressure will bring changes to the cultural provisions, this is not yet guaranteed.

## Pressure and Resistance: The Thirty-Year Pattern Continues

The events between 2017 and 2019 that led to the conclusion of a significantly expanded and updated North American Free Trade Agreement are a microcosm of the last thirty-plus years of history of the Canada–United States relationship respecting trade in cultural expressions. The powerful U.S. entertainment industry continues to seek open and unrestricted trade. It effectively wants Canada to be integrated totally into the U.S. domestic market. Canada continues to resist this pressure and struggles to maintain its right to support its own artists and cultural producers so that they can bring Canadian stories to life in every medium. Whatever the new agreement is called, the final result continues the thirty-year pattern. While NAFTA 2019 has an improved cultural exemption, various Canadian cultural policy measures have been constrained at the bargaining table. The box continues to shrink.

Before we provide an overall summary of how trade agreements have affected Canadian cultural policymaking and consider the possibility of a bold new approach, it is necessary to take a brief detour to consider how digital technologies, particularly digital distribution, affect Canadian cultural policymaking and trade.

# Chapter 10
# Canadian Cultural Policymaking in the Digital Era

As we consider the state of Canadian cultural policymaking in 2019, it is important to review how the digital shift has also had a significant impact. We have lived with digital technologies for forty years, and with the Internet for a quarter century. All contemporary trade agreements have provisions dealing with digital trade or e-commerce, and it is a critical element for cultural policymakers to consider.

In the first twenty years of the digital shift, digital technologies affected cultural expressions primarily by changing how they were produced. Increasingly sophisticated word-processing software made the job of the writer easier and simplified the role of editors. Desktop publishing made the design process easier, and digital printing reduced the time it took to publish the finished work. Musicians no longer needed prohibitively expensive equipment to record digitally perfect sounds. Increasingly, these sounds were stored not on physical media like the vinyl record, cassette or CD, but electronically.

More significantly, in the past twenty years digital technologies have also fundamentally changed how cultural expressions are distributed. The Internet is set to become the leading conduit through which creative works of all kinds are made available to consumers. Aside from traditional forms of visual arts and crafts, which are goods, all other creative works — music, books, magazines, movies, television and radio programs, games — can be digitized easily and transmitted globally. The Internet's takeover of the global communication landscape has been meteoric. In 1993, it communicated only 1 per cent of the information flowing through two-way telecommunications networks. By 2000, this had increased to 51 per cent, and by 2007 it had reached 97 per cent.[1]

As with every new medium that has emerged in the past 150 years, this newest medium creates challenges and opportunities for artists and the cultural industries. Some artists have used the Internet to gain new audiences, both at home and around the world. But a 2015 UNESCO report noted the challenges. Piracy is a serious problem in many places. Widespread and stable income flows do not yet exist in the digital world, and this will not change until the new business models are further developed and firmly established. Consumers, particularly those who have grown up in the digital age, have come to enjoy instant access to a wide range of artistic works, usually for free. The ease of copying and manipulating digital works also means artists have difficulty protecting their work against unauthorized uses. In this process, there has been an erosion of the perceived value of the creative endeavour.[2]

American author Tim Wu wrote in *The Master Switch* that every new communications technology has been seen as a free and open space that would unleash citizen creativity and connectivity, only to become closed and centralized as corporations took control. This same transition is well underway today with the Internet as Facebook, Amazon, Apple, Netflix and Alphabet (Google), together with their Chinese counterparts Baidu, Alibaba and Tencent (with its services including QQ and WeChat), are increasingly in control of the digital space.

Australian academic Professor Julianne Schultz writes about the profound cultural implications of this so-called Fang phenomenon (Facebook, Amazon, Apple, Netflix, and Google). She argues that the technology companies are making unprecedented amounts of money from the marriage of technology and culture, creating an economic imbalance:

> As a result we are seeing a massive redistribution of wealth from the cultural sector, where meaning is created, to the technology sector, which has figured out how to market, distribute, reach and make money out of it in ways the cultural industries never imagined possible . . . In the Age of Fang there are a handful of global companies shaping tastes, distributing and exploiting information we didn't even know we generated.[3]

In response to those who argue that the new technologies are making it easier for artists to find new audiences, Professor Schultz responds,

> It is true that the Internet has made a long tail of information more accessible than ever before. There is more, but most of it remains invisible. When the habits of human nature are combined with the algorithms designed to recognise patterns, it becomes inevitable that increasingly we go back to the same handful of sources. There is a long tail but it is an odd shaped tail — more like a fat sausage with a tiny sliver of the intestine it was stuffed into dangling at the end. And it is in that sliver that most of our [Australian] cultural product resides, virtually invisible to the rest of the world, and increasingly hard to find at home.

Canadian content tends to reside in that same sliver, alongside the Australian works.

With respect to artists' income, the 2015 UNESCO survey of member states and nongovernmental organizations reported that roughly one-third of artists have lost income as a consequence of the digital shift, one-third have gained income and one-third are in a neutral position, with winners and losers often dependent on artistic category. There is some evidence that artists most likely to benefit financially from the digital shift and the Internet are from the developing world. Artists in the developed world, particularly writers and musicians, are more likely to be among those who have lost income. UNESCO reported that studies of writers in the United Kingdom and Canada document a significant decline in income: "In each case, a leading cause of the decline is the rapid change in the publishing business model brought about by Internet distribution of books, both digital and physical copies."[4]

A more significant and recent report comes from Australia. Macquarie University has undertaken a comprehensive survey of artists' incomes for the Australian Council for the past thirty years. In November 2017, the sixth survey was released. *Making Art Work: An Economic Study of Professional Artists in Australia* showed that the median income received by all artists from their creative work fell 30 per cent between 2007–08 and 2014–15. The average decline in median income from all creative and arts-related revenues received by artists whose work is most likely to be moving to Internet-based distribution platforms (writers, actors, directors and musicians) fell by 39 per cent in this same period.[5] Given the consistency in the collection and analysis of this data, these findings are significant and likely reflect the reality of most artists in the developed world.

## Digital Shift and the Music Industry

The first cultural sector to be affected dramatically by Internet distribution was the music industry. The old business model was focused on the sale of physical recordings, whether pressed on vinyl or recorded on a cassette tape or compact disc. Consumers had to buy all of the songs on an album even if they were only interested in one or two tracks. The album or CD release of new works by major artists could be a significant event, causing lineups and sellouts at the local record store. The primary purpose of the musician's tour was to generate publicity that would increase sales of the albums or CDs.

This changed almost overnight with the development of the MP3 format that greatly compressed the size of the digital music file in the

mid-1990s and the launch of Napster in 1999 as a peer-to-peer file sharing service, initially embraced as a way to exchange music. While the
multinational record companies successfully asserted their copyright
interests and derailed Napster's initial effort, this was only temporary.
The launch of the iPod in 2001 and the iTunes Store in 2003 meant
that one could now legally acquire a wide array of music, one song at a
time, at a very low cost. But even that low-cost option was insufficient
for some consumers, who wanted to continue to obtain music for free
from Internet sources, particularly YouTube, which launched in 2005.
Streaming services followed soon after and Spotify was launched in
2008.

Music Canada, the trade organization that represents the interests of
the Canadian recording labels (both Canadian-owned ones and sub-
sidiaries of the major labels), provides statistics on the size of the Canadian music market. It divides the value of the market between physical
sales (primarily CDs, but also including vinyl, cassettes, etc.) and digital
sales (downloads, subscriptions, ad-supported and mobile).

In 2004, the total market was valued at $689.3 million, of which $674.3
million came from sales of physical products. Over the next six years,
physical sales declined dramatically and digital sales did not make up
the difference. In 2010, the total market was valued at only $418.7 mil-
lion, of which only $269.3 million came from the sale of physical prod-
ucts. Since 2010, sales of physical products have continued to decline
every year except 2015, while the sales of digital products fluctuated
year to year but on an upward trajectory. By 2017, the total market was
valued at $569.5 million, still 17.4 per cent lower than in 2004. Sales of
physical products were only $116.8 million, 80.9 per cent lower than
in 2004. Digital sales in 2017 were $368.9 million, more than 1,500 per
cent higher than in 2004.[6]

The rise of subscription music services like Spotify is widely seen as
the reason there have been modest market gains in the last few years.
Spotify offers a minimum free service supported by advertising revenues and a subscription-based premium service.

The Canadian trends are a reflection of broader global trends. Between 1999 and 2013, global music revenues decreased by approximately 70 per cent in real terms. In 2017, 54 per cent of the global music industry's $17.3 billion USD in revenues was from digital sales. Notably, despite three consecutive years of growth, the value of the market overall is still 68 per cent lower than the industry's 1999 peak revenues of $23.8 billion USD.[7]

For many years Canada was the world's seventh largest recorded music market. It was only in 2017 that Canada moved up the charts one place to sit behind only the United States, Japan, the United Kingdom, Germany and France. The International Federation for the Phonographic Industry (IFPI) also reports that Canadian singer Drake was the best-selling artist in the world in 2016, and he was followed by compatriots Justin Bieber in fifth place and The Weeknd in tenth spot.[8]

In 2016, the global music industry began referring to the "value gap," reflecting Professor Schultz's observation that there is "a massive redistribution of wealth from the cultural sector, where meaning is created, to the technology sector." In music, the value gap represents the anomaly that, while the amount of money consumers and advertisers are spending on streaming and downloading digital music has increased phenomenally, the amount received by those who write, compose, play, sing and produce this music has fallen seriously behind.

The Music Canada *Value Gap* report notes that the value gap has its greatest effect on those singers and musicians who are professionals but not in the top echelon of artists in Canada:

> *The reality for most artists is that the work into which they pour their passion and talent has effectively become at best a part time occupation and for many a mere hobby. Many of them have little choice but to supplement their income with other work and put whatever time and energy remains into their music.*[9]

The report provides a striking example of how this plays out in practice. Canadian cellist Zoe Keating has spoken out about the impact of the value gap on her earnings. In a July 2017 *Washington Post* article, it was reported that she had earned only $261 USD from 1.42 million views on YouTube. According to a February 2014 article in the *Guardian*, 92 per cent of Keating's 2013 income came from physical and digital sales. She earned $75,341 USD from sales of 32,806 singles and 8,365 albums. More than 2.8 million streams, by comparison, earned Keating just $6,380 USD.[10]

Music Canada argues that the value gap could be reduced in Canada by addressing three issues.

The first step is to address Canada's rules concerning Internet service providers and digital content companies such as YouTube, which were developed on the assumption that they were merely providing access to a new communications medium and were not responsible for the content, which was provided by others. Thus, they were analogous to the telephone companies, which have no responsibility for the messages transmitted. This was the basis for the CRTC's Digital Media Exemption Order.

But that of course is not true today, even if it may once have been the case. Today's tech companies deal in data, and the algorithms they use curate the flow of content. The search engines, YouTube, Facebook, Netflix, iTunes and others know exactly what we are looking for, what music we download, what news we consume and what movies we watch. They sell those data to advertisers, who can then precisely target their ads on the basis of a user's interests. They lead us to the places where we are most likely to find what we want. As a small aside, in writing this section, I used the search term "Spotify" to obtain basic information about the company and its service. I am now being bombarded with ads for Spotify whenever I turn on the Internet. Music Canada argues that Canada's policymakers should focus their attention on the effects that this lack of regulatory oversight is having on the Canadian music industry.

Commercial radio remains a major vehicle for the consumption of music. Of the 15.4 hours per week that Canadians spent listening to music, 40 per cent is "broadcast" by radio stations, either through the old terrestrial microwave towers or online. In Canada, commercial radio stations are now generally part of large media conglomerates and they remain profitable overall. According to the CRTC's 2017 Policy Monitoring Report, Canada's commercial radio stations reported $1.55 billion in revenues and a PBIT (profit before interest and tax) of 18.6 per cent.[11] Since 1997, commercial radio stations have been required to pay meaningful royalties for their use of music, but only on advertising revenues in excess of $1.25 million. The decision to set a nominal payment of $100 on the first $1.25 million was made in 1997 because there were many smaller radio station owners in the field. This has now changed dramatically, so the second step Music Canada is seeking is the elimination of this exemption.

Finally, Music Canada is seeking changes to Canada's *Copyright Act* to provide that singers, musicians and music producers receive royalties when their music is used in television programs and films. At present, only composers, songwriters and music publishers are entitled to such a payment.

## Digital Shift and Book Publishing

While less profound than the changes in the music industry, the effect of the digital shift on the book publishing industry has been significant. As with music, the most significant impact is on those who are professional, but not in the top echelon of Canadian authors.

According to Statistics Canada data, total revenues for all book publishers in Canada in 2004 were $2.0 billion. This declined to $1.9 billion in 2010 and to $1.6 billion in 2016 (the last year for which figures are available), a decline of 20 per cent. Total revenues from the sale of books in Canada were $1.4 billion in 2016, roughly similar to the level of book sales in 2004 and 2010. Of total book sales revenues in

2016, 53.8 per cent were generated by foreign firms; the rest went to Canadian-controlled companies. Other revenues include grants, sales of rights and sales of other goods and services.[12]

But a December 2018 report from a think tank of industry heavyweights highlights the challenges for Canadian-authored works. Using data reported to BookNet Canada, *More Canada* notes that the market share of Canadian-authored books has dropped from 27 per cent in 2005 to 13 per cent in 2017, while the number of Canadian titles published has increased. The 13 per cent market share in 2017 was roughly the same for both units sold and the dollar value of sales. For books published by Canadian-owned publishers, the average Canadian-authored trade book sold 343 copies in its first year of publication in 2017. For Canadian-authored books published by foreign-owned publishers, the average first-year sale was 2,251 copies.[13]

The Association of Canadian Publishers (ACP) represents the English-language Canadian firms. According to ACP, the 1992 Revised Foreign Investment Policy in Book Publishing and Distribution "is the bedrock of our domestic industry because it has succeeded in keeping the industry primarily in Canadian hands. This guarantees Canadians a steady supply of diverse books in all genres from authors across the country." Canadian-owned firms are responsible for roughly 80 per cent of all books published by Canadian authors each year, a figure that has stayed the same for more than thirty years, despite the enormous changes that have taken place in the industry over those years. Foreign-owned firms operating in Canada publish some Canadian-authored works, but these tend to be only proven best-selling authors. They continue to earn most of their revenue from importing books of their U.S. and U.K. parent companies, and are not primarily focused on investment in new Canadian content."[14]

Copyright is another significant issue for the book publishing industry. When Canada's *Copyright Act* was last amended in 2012, the provisions that allow for the "fair dealing" of copyright works were amended. Fair dealing is a statutory exception to an allegation of copyright infringement and is substantially different from the U.S. fair use doctrine. To determine if a dealing is "fair," you need to consider the nature of the work, the purpose and character of the dealing, the effect of the dealing on the value of the work and whether there are any alternatives. The purpose of the dealing must be one of the eight that are specified in the *Act*: research, private study, education, parody, satire, criticism, review and news reporting.

Education was added only in 2012. The effect of this change, and related cases determined by the Supreme Court in the same year, has been to seriously decrease copyright royalties. Access Copyright, the book industry collecting society, reported that its distribution to publishers was only $4.9 million in 2017, a decrease of 78.1 per cent from the previous year, because of the widespread use of published content by the education sector without payment.[15] While the Federal Court ruled in favour of Access Copyright in a legal case against York University in 2018, a decision now under appeal, the case is unlikely to overturn the earlier decisions completely. ACP is seeking to solve this problem through an amendment to the *Copyright Act*.

Finally, joining with l'Association nationale des éditeurs de livres (Canada's French-language book publishers) in a submission to the federal government's 2019 prebudget consultation process, ACP makes it clear that the other bedrock publishing policy is the Canada Book Fund. The fund currently provides $38.4 million of support to the industry, most of which is directed at assisting the production, marketing and distribution of Canadian-authored books by publishing firms that are Canadian-owned and -controlled. The organizations recommend that this be increased by more than 50 per cent. They also support the government's 2016 commitment to raise the budget of the Canada Council to $360 million by 2020–21.[16]

Meanwhile, the sixty-five recommendations in the *More Canada* report are far more comprehensive. Several urge financial support for independent bookstores to support marketing and author tours, and a countrywide scheme based on Quebec's highly successful system whereby public purchases of books (for schools, libraries, etc.) would be funnelled through these independent bookstores. The most interesting analysis and recommendations concern the widespread use of a U.S. inventory software system that does not allow for the identification of a Canadian-authored title. This makes it difficult for bookstores and libraries to find or track Canadian works. It also means the algorithms behind online selling would not highlight Canadian titles to Canadians looking to buy a book. The report recommends funding for a software overhaul.[17]

## Digital Shift and Magazine Publishing

The magazine publishing industry is on a different trajectory from the music and book publishing industries. In 2004, total operating revenues for Canadian magazine publishers were $1.85 billion, with $1.02 billion of that amount, or 64 per cent, coming from advertising. Total revenues increased until they reached a peak of $2.39 billion in 2008. Revenues then began to decline slowly, so that by 2010 total operating revenues for Canadian magazine publishers were $2.13 billion, which was still 15.1 per cent higher than 2004. The decline continued, and in 2015, the last year for which statistics are available, total operating revenues were only $1.62 billion, well below the 2004 level. Advertising revenues were $915 million, or 56.5 per cent of the total. The greatest decline occurred between 2013 and 2015, when advertising revenues declined by 32.6 per cent and circulation revenues by 16.6 per cent.[18]

Magazines Canada brings together the Canadian magazine publishers. The key issues for the industry as outlined in its prebudget 2018 submission was for the government to renew and strengthen the Canada Periodical Fund, which currently provides $75 million of support to Canadian publishers.[19] Like the book publishing program, most of this is directed at assisting the production, marketing and distribution of magazines, which must be published by firms that are Canadian-owned and -controlled, and must contain at least 80 per cent Canadian editorial content.

Magazines Canada also recommends expanding the "permitted" tax deductions provided in Article 19 of the *Income Tax Act*. These currently apply only to Canadian advertising placed with Canadian broadcasters, newspapers and periodicals. Magazines Canada wants these provisions to be extended to Canadian-owned digital platforms, and to make advertisements purchased by Canadian advertisers on foreign-owned platforms nondeductible, as is currently the case with advertising on U.S. border television stations. It finally also suggests imposing the same tax obligations that apply to Canadian companies on "foreign news aggregators, which publish Canadian news and sell advertising, directed to Canadians."

## Digital Shift and the Television, Film and Digital Media Industry

The situation in Canada's film, television and digital production industry is the most complicated of all.

The Canadian Media Producers Association's annual survey of film and television production in Canada, *Profile 2017*, reported record levels of activity in 2016–17 in every sector and every region. Canadian content production (including in-house broadcaster production) reached $4.6 billion, up 11.3 per cent from the previous year. Foreign location and service production reached $3.8 billion, up 42.1 per cent from the previous year.[20]

While some argue this strong level of production activity shows that regulation is no longer necessary, there are reasons to believe this is untrue.

Film and television production is a cyclical business, in Canada as elsewhere. Both Canadian content and foreign location and service production have fluctuated in the past twenty years, and there have been previous peaks, in 1997, 2003, 2008 and 2012, each of which was followed by a decline.

While our primary concern here is with Canadian content production, where Canadian storytellers can bring our perspective to the screens, it is important to consider briefly foreign service production. This work helps to support and maintain the Canadian production infrastructure. The amount of U.S. production in Canada fluctuates according to a variety of factors, including the relative value of the Canadian dollar and the production tax incentives available in Canada and many provinces to foreign producers. FilmLA, the film office of the Los Angeles area, releases an annual survey of various aspects of the 100 top-grossing films released in U.S. cinemas (recall that Canada is considered part of the domestic market and lumped into this calculation). FilmLA reports that, in 2017, twenty of these 100 movies were shot primarily in Canada. The next leading jurisdictions were the U.S. state of Georgia and the United Kingdom (fifteen each), California (ten), New York (six), Louisiana and Australia (five each) and France (three).[21]

A significant new factor may soon bring a decline in this work. In December 2017, the United States adopted an important tax reform package, including an overall reduction in the effective corporate tax rate from 29.1 per cent to 21.0 per cent. There is also a provision which allows studios to fully expense in one year the capital investment for film, television and live theatrical productions, if 75 per cent of the costs are incurred in the United States.[22] Recall how Canada's 100 per cent capital cost allowance tax incentive produced a boom in Canadian production between 1974 and 1982. The U.S. film industry is delighted with these measures, and we may see some work that would otherwise be produced in Canada relocated to the United States in the next few years.

More importantly, the boom in production in Canada is part of a global trend. While drama and scripted comedy have always been a backbone of television, the past few years have seen an arms race among the big players, which are producing a steady stream of higher-budgeted scripted content. This is led by Netflix, which is rapidly becoming the world's largest producer and purveyor of films and television programs. In 2018, 58 per cent of global bandwidth was devoted to video streaming, with Netflix alone taking up 15 per cent.[23] Other giants include

HBO, Amazon Prime Video, YouTube and Apple, and there will soon be new entrants in the field. Most significantly, in July 2018 shareholders approved the takeover of 21st Century Fox by the Walt Disney Company. When the takeover is completed in 2019, this company will be the largest independent media company in the world, with an enormous inventory and the financial capacity that may allow it to begin to challenge the growing dominance of Netflix.

In 2015, the philosopher king of U.S. television, John Landgraf, president of the drama-comedy network FX, described this phenomenon as "Peak TV." But the growth continues. In his January 2018 update, Landgraf reported that the 487 scripted originals that aired in 2017, either on cable, on traditional television or online, represented a 7 per cent increase from 2016, and an astonishing 125 per cent increase from 2010.[24]

Budgets are skyrocketing as well. In September 2017, *Variety* estimated "the typical range of the production budget for high-end cable and streaming dramas [is] $5 million–$7 million an hour, while single-camera half hours on broadcast and cable run from $1.5 million to more than $3 million . . . That's a significant increase, during just the past five years, over what had been $3 million–$4 million for cable dramas and around $1 million–$1.5 million for single-camera half hours [all figures USD]."[25]

Original scripted dramas and comedies attract sizable audiences, and the programs can be made available across a variety of platforms, including online where they can be watched whenever the viewer wants. English-language productions are increasingly accepted outside the Anglophone world. The costs of production can be amortized over a long period of time since high-quality scripted content has a long shelf-life. In 2018, Netflix announced plans to move into family entertainment, which is another programming genre with a long shelf-life. The strong historic catalogue of the Disney Company itself, which continues to get repurposed, is evidence of this fact.

But the concept of Peak TV implies that this global boom will come to an end, and that there will be a collapse after the peak. This is the likely fate of scripted programming content. FX reports that the number of scripted originals aired in 2018 was 495, only eight more than the previous year.[26] Either everyone will become fully armed, with a vast inventory of quality shows, or someone will emerge as king and will obtain that vast store of high-quality films and programs through consolidation. The global pace of production will decline, because once you have the critical mass of inventory, you need only keep this fresh with a modest number of new additions each year.

## CRTC Response to Digital Shift in Audiovisual Sector

Between 1999 and 2018, the Canadian Radio-television and Telecommunications Commission (CRTC), Canada's regulatory authority, responded to the digital shift by either declining to regulate or by backing away from important policy tools.

In one of the most shortsighted and flawed decisions in broadcasting history, the CRTC in 1999 issued its order that "exempts from regulation, without terms or conditions, all new media broadcasting undertakings that operate in whole or in part in Canada. New media broadcasting undertakings are those undertakings that provide broadcasting services delivered and accessed over the Internet."[27] This is now known as the Digital Media Exemption Order (DMEO).

The commission ruled at the time that Internet service providers were a conduit for material posted by others and thus were not broadcasters. They also found that there was already a reasonable amount of Canadian content on the Internet. I was part of the ACTRA delegation appearing at the 1998 hearings which argued that ISPs were providing access to programs as defined in the *Broadcasting Act*, for at least part of what they do, and thus that they should be subject to a new class of licence. Such a licence would recognize their status as both telecommunications common carriers under the *Telecommunications Act* and broadcasting distribution undertakings (BDUs) under the *Broadcasting Act*. I also urged that the CRTC look seriously at the role of search engines, since these were even at that time playing a major role in determining what news, information, music and audiovisual programming would be found by consumers.

The deeply flawed CRTC DMEO decision was exacerbated by two decisions of the Supreme Court. In 2004, Canada's top court found, in a case involving the payment of copyright royalties for the use of music, that Internet service providers play a "content neutral" role and thus cannot be regulated as broadcasters. In 2009, the CRTC referred to the courts the issue of whether ISPs could be required to pay a levy to support Canadian content production similar to the 5 per cent levy applied to broadcasting distribution undertakings (cable and satellite companies). In 2012, the top court ruled that when they are providing access to the Internet, ISPs have no role in the selection, origination or packaging of content and thus are not BDUs when they provide access to broadcasting services at the request of the end user.

These decisions are rooted firmly in the past. The DMEO was introduced at a time when music and audiovisual program suppliers, including Canadian broadcasters, were only beginning to explore how the Internet could be used as a vehicle to distribute cultural expressions. The "Internet" was seen as a dumb distribution technology like an old-fashioned landline telephone that was not responsible in any way for the content transmitted. This was true at least in part in 1999 and 2009, but it is certainly no longer the case. Several decades after the 1991 launch of the World Wide Web (which enabled the mass use of the increasingly globally connected computer networks), the "Internet" of today offers services and search engines that have sophisticated algorithms that are curating the content we listen to and watch. It has created most of the world's largest global corporations, several of which are valued at or near $1 trillion USD. Together, these corporations exercise enormous control over what we see, hear and read. They are shaping our tastes and our choices, and are leading us toward cultural homogenization rather than cultural diversity.

With the election of Conservative Prime Minister Stephen Harper in

2006, the CRTC began to move toward a deregulatory approach. The pace of that change accelerated when Jean-Pierre Blais was appointed CRTC chair in 2012. In his mandate letter, he was tasked with regulating "broadcasting undertaking only to the extent necessary" and ensuring "that regulation is targeted and transparent, and that alternatives to regulation are considered." The letter also provided that the commission should put the interests of the consumer first.[28] Thus, it was no surprise that during his five-year leadership, the CRTC accelerated a deregulatory approach that had begun a few years earlier.

Before 2010, the CRTC maintained strict content quotas on broadcasters. The main commercial networks were required to broadcast Canadian content for 60 per cent of the yearly schedule, and for 50 per cent during the evening hours of 6 p.m. to midnight. Well-established specialty services generally were required to have 50 per cent Cancon, while premium and newer specialty services had lower content requirements that varied according to the nature of the service. Pay television services were required to have Canadian films and television programs as a certain percentage of their inventory.

Canadian content is defined according to those who create the work. The core criteria require the producer to be Canadian and to exercise responsibility for the program. The production must achieve a minimum of 6 out of 10 points based on key creative functions being done by Canadians, and have a Canadian as at least one of either the director or screenwriter and at least one of the two lead performers. Finally, a minimum of 75 per cent of program expenses and 75 per cent of postproduction expenses must be for services provided by Canadians.

The key creative positions for live action productions are: director (2 points), screenwriter (2 points), first and second lead performers (one point each), production designer (one point), director of photography (one point), music composer (one point) and picture editor (one point).

In 2010, the CRTC began to change these rules. It formalized the concept of the Canadian programming expenditure (CPE) requirement, which obligates broadcasters to spend a certain percentage of their gross revenues on Cancon, and a policy that BDUs contribute 5 per cent of their revenues to support the production of Canadian content. It also introduced the concept of programs of national interest (PNIs), which are long-form documentaries, drama and scripted comedy and awards shows that celebrate Canadian culture. Since these are the most culturally significant programs, broadcasters are required to spend a certain percentage of their revenues on these programs, as a subset of their CPE. They also established rules to ensure that PNIs are scheduled at times when the majority of Canadians are watching television, and provided some incentives for these purposes. But the decision also reduced the requirement for broadcasters to show Cancon over the entire broadcast year from 60 per cent to 55 per cent.

In its *Let's Talk Television* policy released in 2017, the commission announced it would make further changes and eliminated some additional rules. The commission determined that there would be no review of the Digital Media Exemption Order and it further included Internet-distributed video-on-demand services under the DMEO, even if the services are also carried on BDUs. Thus, these services were to be no longer required to make financial contributions to Canadian productions, nor to ensure that they have Cancon films and programs in their inventory.

The commission increasingly focused strictly on providing funding for Cancon through its CPE/PNI and BDU requirements, along with tangible benefits packages offered to obtain CRTC approval when broadcasting services are bought and sold. Meanwhile, it has begun to reduce content quotas. By 2019, over-the-air broadcasters will have no minimum Cancon requirement over the whole year. The 50 per cent requirement during evening hours will be retained. Specialty and pay services will move from various Cancon requirement to a common 35 per cent over the broadcast day, which is generally the lowest common denominator, and there will be no evening viewing requirement.

The commission also eliminated genre protection for specialty services, and it implemented pilot programs which will move away from the 6-out-of-10-point definition of Cancon. It will now recognize as Canadian any drama based on the adaptation of a successful Canadian novel, with only three criteria: that the scriptwriter be Canadian, one lead actor be Canadian and 75 per cent of costs be paid to Canadians. These rules will also apply to Canadian dramas with a budget less than $2 million.

Like the DMEO before it, the *Let's Talk TV* approach continues to be shortsighted. The global television broadcasting industry is in the midst of fundamental changes, and Canada is no exception. The business models that built and sustained television for more than fifty years are breaking down, and Canadian broadcasters are challenged by unregulated online competitors that are gradually capturing their audiences. Canadians are increasingly consuming audiovisual content online, and advertisers are moving to these new markets. In Canada, total Internet advertising revenues surpassed television advertising revenues in 2013, and the gap will only grow ever greater in the coming years.

However, the full impact of these changes is still many years in the future, and it is appropriate for our broadcasting and other policies to evolve gradually to deal with the new reality.

According to iab.canada, of total Canadian Internet advertising revenues of $5.5 billion in 2016, 88 per cent went to Google and Facebook, while only 9 per cent was attached to videos.[29] Television advertising revenues in Canada in 2016 were $3.17 billion, which dwarfed the $500 million spent on the online videos. Even projecting to 2021, the CRTC predicts advertisers will spend three times more on television advertising than on advertising attached to online videos.

The CRTC's own research also shows that, while the viewing of linear television continues to slide, it remains a significant medium. According to the CRTC's 2017 *Communications Monitoring Report*, Canadians eighteen years of age and older spent on average 28.2 hours per week watching traditional television in 2016, only 1.4 per cent lower than in the previous year. The commission predicts a long-term steady decline:

"If current trends continue, TV viewing in the English-language market could decline by approximately 25 per cent to 40 per cent over the next 10 years."[30] And at least some of this decline will be merely changing the medium of transmission: We will watch the same programs, packaged for us by the same broadcasters, but will do so online.

The more significant challenges result from the fact that Internet broadcasters operate entirely outside the regulated system. These so-called "over-the-top" (OTT) services deliver television and film content via the Internet, without requiring users to subscribe to a traditional cable or satellite service. Broadcasters in the traditional system pay taxes and meet regulatory requirements. Netflix, Hulu and other OTT Internet giants now beginning to provide programming content, which compete in the same market for the same audiences, do not. BDUs, which provide their subscribers with access to programming from a broad range of suppliers, make contributions to Canadian productions and face other regulatory obligations. Internet service providers, which as part of what they do also provide their subscribers with access to programming from a broad range of suppliers, do not.

It is important to note that Canada's media industry BDUs, ISPs and broadcasters are increasingly integrated into media giants. The three largest players in the English-language market are Corus, Bell and Rogers. Each has become a huge vertically integrated company. Each of these companies remains profitable overall, despite challenges in their broadcasting divisions. In part, these companies have grown and developed under the protection of supportive CRTC policies and regulations, as well as other public policies and funding programs.

In the first quarter of 2018, Corus reported net income attributable to shareholders (an import metric in a market economy) of $77.7 million, and earnings per share of $0.38.[31] In the third quarter of 2017, BCE Inc. (Bell) reported net income attributable to common shareholders of $770 million, and adjusted earnings per share of $0.88.[32] In the third quarter of 2017, Rogers reported net income of $1.3 million, and basic earnings per share of $2.51.[33]

The solution to the challenges of the digital shift in the short to mid-term is not to deregulate the broadcasting system, but to impose appropriate regulations on the new players.

In response to a request from the government to consider the future of programming distribution, the CRTC conducted a public consultation process in 2017 and early 2018. In May 2018 it released its report, *Harnessing Change*. This new report signals a change of direction for the CRTC, since it indicates that the commission will look again at the possibility of regulating the Internet. It also calls for legislation to ensure that Internet service providers, including wireless service providers, and foreign streaming services provide appropriate financial support for Cancon production in television, music and films.

## Government's Response to the Digital Shift

From Confederation until the late 1960s, Conservative Prime Minister John A. Macdonald's 1879 National Policy was the centrepiece of Conservative party economic policies. High tariffs promoted Canadian industry against fierce U.S. competition, and nation-building projects like the Canadian Pacific Railway and the CBC were undertaken to unite a sparsely populated county. By the early twenty-first century, this had been rejected in favour of a political philosophy of free markets and limited government, highlighted by lower taxes and deregulation. Thus, it is no surprise that the government of Conservative Prime Minister Stephen Harper (2006–15) did little to support Canadian artists and cultural producers as they dealt with the digital shift. Funding programs were maintained (with lower resources), and these programs began to encourage the sector to adapt to digital production and distribution. But the government had no interest in considering any structural measures. Prime Minister Harper's "no iPod tax" mantra was front-and-centre in his 2011 re-election campaign, as was his "no Netflix tax" in 2015.

When Liberal Prime Minister Justin Trudeau was elected with a majority government in 2015, there was hope that the new government would respond more aggressively to the challenges of the digital shift for the music, publishing, film, television and all other cultural sectors. The government quickly promised an extensive cultural policy overhaul and Budget 2016 increased funding to the sector. But there has been little progress and only a few concrete initiatives in the government's first term, all of which have been funding announcements.

Budget 2017 was clear that the government believes in an open Internet that emphasizes freedom to innovate and to connect with others, as well as freedom of expression. The budget outlined the challenges and opportunities for the cultural and creative industries. But all it promised was more study and a new approach "that is focused on the future, and on bringing the best of Canada to the world, *rather than a protectionist stance that restricts growth and limits opportunities.*"[34] *(emphasis added)*

In September 2017 there were two important developments. In the mandate letter to Ian Scott, the new chair of the CRTC, the government announced a significant change of direction for the commission:

> *With respect to our culture and identity, the digital shift has led to an environment of seemingly infinite choice. Standing out requires Canadian content in both official languages that can compete with the best of the world and distribution strategies ensuring that quality Canadian content, in both English and French, is discovered in our country as well as around the world.* Global success will not be achieved without a diverse and strong domestic market that acts as a launch pad for homegrown talent.[35] *(emphasis added)*

The same month, Canadian Heritage Minister Mélanie Joly released Creative Canada as the government's "vision" for Canada's cultural and creative industries in a digital world. While providing a broad picture of how Canada's cultural sector is being affected by the digital shift, and outlining how the understanding of the sector should be expanded to incorporate the creative industries, the operative provisions of the report merely confirm the government's intention to study. The House of Commons is currently reviewing the *Copyright Act*. In June 2018, the government appointed an external panel of experts to lead a review of the *Broadcasting Act*, the *Telecommunications Act* and the *Radiocommunication Act*. The announcement promised a "balanced" approach "that takes into account the realities of Canadian consumers and businesses, and our artists, artisans and broadcasters without increasing the cost of services to Canadians . . . The review will also address how to best promote competition and affordability for Internet and mobile wireless."[36]

There is clearly a fundamental contradiction between the two emphasized clauses. As we have seen, a diverse and strong domestic market in Canada can only be achieved with policies that some would call protectionist. The UNESCO Convention outlines a wide range of measures governments can use to achieve this objective. The issues surrounding the digital shift are controversial and the current government is obviously divided on the best approach. Thus, it is not surprising that the deadline for these reviews will conveniently fall after the next federal election in October 2019.

The government's only announcements to date have involved additional funding. In June 2018, the government announced a new investment of $125 million over five years to implement an export strategy. In November 2018, it announced a much-needed $595 million package over five years to help Canada's news media sector. The money includes a labour-based tax credit for producing original news content, a temporary tax credit for online subscriptions and measures that allow nonprofit news organizations to obtain charitable status to facilitate fundraising.

The only other concrete policy was Minister Joly's September 2017 announcement of her deal with Netflix. In return for committing itself to investing $500 million in production in Canada over the next five years (which it was likely to have spent in any case), Netflix will be allowed to continue to operate outside the Canadian tax and regulatory system. This gives it a tremendous competitive advantage over Canadian services and even over other foreign ones which may already be registered for tax purposes in Canada.

In analyzing this agreement, it is critical to look at the numbers. Netflix revenues in Canada were estimated at $709 million in 2016.[37] With a blended GST-HST rate of 11 per cent and a 5 per cent contribution rate to a Canadian production fund, Netflix should have paid $113 million to our governments and to production funds in one year. As Netflix's revenues continue to grow over the next five years, which is virtually guaranteed given the increases in subscription fees in 2017 and 2018, so too will the amount of the government's foregone revenues. These clearly will be well in excess of the $500 million self-serving production commitment Netflix made over those same five years. Minister Joly's staff ought to have used their smartphone calculators when they sat down to negotiate with Netflix.

Finally, we must also ask what happens when the five-year agreement with Netflix expires. In this connection, we should recall the deal made by a previous Liberal government many years ago. Despite the promises made by Hollywood at the time, the 1950s Canadian Cooperation Project was a failure. Despite the commitments, production in Canada did not increase, there was no increase in Canadian content in our cinemas and there was no distribution of NFB movies in the United States. There were a few gratuitous references to Canada, or some Canadian locations or minor characters in Hollywood movies, but no substantive changes in the marketplace. And that agreement was quietly shelved in 1958. Efforts in the 1970s to reach voluntary agreements also failed.

Some commentators and government officials argue that it is impossible to force Netflix or other Internet-based foreign services to register for, collect and remit GST/HST or to meet regulatory requirements such as making a financial contribution to Canadian content production. This is a fallacious argument. Major international firms have a vested interest in demonstrating that they are good corporate citizens, as the following international examples demonstrate. Further, if they fail to cooperate, Canada's federal government could easily legislate a solution by requiring credit card companies and other payment services to deduct the appropriate amounts. Every consumer pays for their subscriptions through one of these services. The services would send the deducted amounts to the government and would remit the balance to Netflix or other Internet-based foreign services.

## While Canada Prevaricates, Other Jurisdictions Move Aggressively

Argentina, Australia, Brazil, Japan, New Zealand, South Africa, Taiwan and Russia, as well as several U.S. states, already impose sales taxes on OTT services and others who sell digital content, games and software, based on the value of sales in the appropriate geographic area. Quebec announced in March 2018 that it would do likewise. While some of these taxes have been challenged in court, all the decisions to date have upheld the right of the government to impose them. Netflix is collecting and remitting the tax in each case.

Developments in Europe have gone further than anywhere else. Germany imposed a 2.5 per cent levy on Netflix, Amazon Prime Video and other on-demand video suppliers based on their net annual turnover in the country. This levy will be used to fund domestic production. In June 2018, Netflix failed in its court challenge against the German measure. France soon followed the German lead and imposed a 2.0 per cent tax. By the end of 2018, the European Union required each of its member states to enact, by 2021, the necessary regulations to ensure that every on-demand service has at least 30 per cent European content in its library. France has already established rules to require that this content be highlighted on the relevant website. Member states will be free to raise this requirement to 40 per cent, and may include subquotas for original productions from their own countries. The twenty-eight (pre-Brexit) European Union member states will also be free to follow the German and French models of adding a small surcharge on subscription fees to support national production. Netflix has announced that it will "reluctantly" adhere to these new European rules respecting taxes, contributions to local productions and European content.

The European Parliament also passed a new copyright directive in September 2018. The directive includes measures that would require Internet platforms, such as Facebook and Google, to compensate media companies when music or news content is used on their sites. It also provides stronger copyright protections including implementation of systems to detect and block copyright material before it appears online. There are exemptions for small platforms, noncommercial online encyclopaedias and open-source software platforms. The directive is now with member states for their consideration and a final version is expected to be passed in 2019. In vowing to continue to fight against it, EDiMA, the trade association representing the online platforms in Europe, exhibited incredible chutzpah when it said EU legislators had "decided to support the filtering of the Internet to the benefit of big businesses in the music and publishing industries despite huge public outcry." EDiMA's members include the top five most valuable companies in the world on the Fortune 500 list: Apple, Amazon, Alphabet (Google), Microsoft and Facebook.[38] Two of these, Apple and Amazon, are the first two companies in the last hundred years to be valued at more than $1 trillion USD each. Europe's largest mass media companies are only a small fraction of the financial size of these technological behemoths.

## The Digital Shift, Canadian Cultural Policymaking and Trade Agreements

The digital shift is having a profound impact on all of the cultural industries. It has dramatically changed how cultural expressions are made and recorded, and how these are made available to audiences everywhere. It is increasingly clear that, if the various platforms remain unregulated, they will bring cultural homogenization. While there is room for everything, it will be increasingly difficult to find local and alternative cultural expressions, including Canadian stories, music and dance. Not enough of the resources generated by artistic works will find their way to the artists who create those works.

New strategies are needed, and only now are some jurisdictions beginning to impose requirements to pay taxes, to make space for domestic productions and to require funding support for domestic artists and cultural producers.

Canada has been reluctant to act. To date, the response of our governments has been limited to studying the problem and to providing some targeted funding for artists and cultural producers. These are insufficient to ensure a consistent supply of high-quality Canadian material in every medium.

Meanwhile, with each new trade agreement Canada enters into, our cultural policy options are further constrained. And without a new approach, we may find that funding will be the only instrument at our disposal to support the production and distribution of Canadian stories in the digital age. While funding support is important and is generally trade-compliant, it is subject to the financial health of governments and to the political whims of the moment. This is insufficient to ensure a dynamic cultural sector can survive in Canada over the next twenty-five years.

# Chapter 11
# Trade Agreements and Canadian Cultural Policymaking

We have seen how the negotiations that led to the Canada–United States Free Trade Agreement, NAFTA, the Comprehensive and Progressive Agreement for Trans-Pacific Partnership (along with its antecedent the TPP) and NAFTA 2019 have resulted in Canada making changes to important cultural policy measures that affect every sector of the cultural industries. The narrow definition of cultural industries, which has remained unchanged since 1987, and the limitations and reservations on future cultural policymaking that have been included in the agreements have constricted our policymakers ever more tightly.

Clearly, Canada's cultural policies will continue to be under pressure in future trade negotiations. Existing agreements will also continue to have an impact. But it is difficult to conclude definitively what these impacts might be. The provisions are complicated and complex. As we have seen, negotiations continue bilaterally and multilaterally. Some agreements (like CUSFTA) are bottom-up, meaning they only cover the specified sectors and activities, while other agreements (like NAFTA 2019) are top-down, meaning they cover all existing and future sectors and activities except for those specifically exempted or reserved.

The language in agreements may be ambiguous or may sustain different interpretations. Different provisions may not be entirely consistent with each other. Several different agreements that touch on the same issues and have been concluded with different groups of states may come into play.

In addition, there is little settled law to guide how the agreements are to be interpreted. There are only two relevant international cases decided by the World Trade Organization, both of which were initiated by the United States: the *Canada Periodicals Case* and *China — Measures Affecting Trading Rights and Distribution Services for Certain Publications and Audiovisual Entertainment Products* (which we will consider in Chapter 12). The United States has on only one occasion even threatened to invoke the "notwithstanding" clause that exists in CUSFTA and NAFTA and continues in NAFTA 2019. The cultural sector is dynamic and changeable, and the digital shift has had a huge impact on how cultural goods and services are produced, stored, distributed and consumed. Canada's cultural policies change constantly in response to technological changes, the state of the economy and the nation's finances, particular challenges and issues that emerge at a given time and the political leanings of the government of the day.

The original GATT exemption for cinema screen quotas and the cultural exemption in the Canada–United States Free Trade Agreement, which is improved in NAFTA 2019, are hugely important. Given the significant changes between CUSFTA and NAFTA 2019, Canada's trade negotiators should have expanded the definition to confirm that it applies regardless of the technologies used to produce, distribute and exhibit the cultural expressions, as well as to include performing arts, visual arts and crafts, since these sectors are included in NAFTA 2019 and not in CUSFTA. Given how the cultural sector has developed with the digital shift, it is unconscionable that our negotiators have failed to update the definition of the cultural industries since the Canada–United States Free Trade Agreement was first negotiated in 1987. It is essential that Canada maintain the broadest possible exemption in any other agreements we enter into with the United States.

With those caveats, one can state that each major trade agreement and each trade challenge have brought changes to important Canadian cultural policies. CUSFTA, NAFTA and NAFTA 2019 brought copyright changes. The WTO *Canada Periodicals Case* forced changes to Canadian magazine policies. The dispute around Country Music Television eventually resulted in the elimination of the policy that led to the original dispute. Deals were made around foreign ownership rules and film distribution policies, and these brought significant changes to policies and laws. CETA is ambiguous in many areas. CPTPP represents a step backward. NAFTA 2019 requires changes in broadcasting policies.

The UNESCO *Convention on the Protection and Promotion of the Diversity of Cultural Expressions* is an important tool that has not yet been sufficiently mobilized to address the trade challenges. The convention could provide a means to move away from the cultural exemption approach to one that is more proactive and dynamic. It can maintain the right of governments to support domestic artists and cultural producers and can ensure that stories from every country are told in every medium and made available to global audiences. Such an approach would be especially beneficial to Canada. We will review this more in Chapter 12.

From the beginning, trade agreements have shifted the thinking of Canada's cultural policymakers. Instead of analyzing a particular challenge and asking what would be the best policy to address it, they now also consider whether that policy would be consistent with our trade commitments. They specifically consider whether any measure being contemplated would violate a Most-Favoured-Nation commitment or would allow the United States to trigger the notwithstanding clause.

Let us consider the susceptibility of different types of potential cultural policies to the existing trade agreements.

# Grants and Funding Support

**Government programs**

Until 2011, Statistics Canada produced a report which summarized how much the federal, provincial/territorial and municipal governments spent on "culture." While it is now outdated, the report from 2009–10 offers an interesting perspective. In that year, the three levels of government in Canada spent $9.59 billion funding literary arts, performing arts, visual arts and crafts, film and video, broadcasting and sound recording. Even taking into account that this figure includes the $930 million spent that year on the Canadian Broadcasting Corporation, as well as funding of other cultural agencies and public venues, it represents a significant amount of public funding for those telling Canadian stories.[1] Overall, a good share of that money finds its way into the production, distribution and dissemination of cultural goods and services.

These funds are primarily distributed as grants to artists, producers and distributors of cultural expressions and others involved in supportive roles. Governments directly administer some of these programs. For example, the Department of Canadian Heritage lists eighteen cultural funding programs in 2019. Other grants are administered by agencies of the government such as the Canada Council for the Arts and the provincial/territorial and municipal equivalents, Telefilm Canada and its equivalents and others. Tax credit programs are an increasingly popular way to provide funding to producers. Producers must first invest in their project and spend money to create a finished work. They receive a credit which is based on eligible expenditures (most frequently labour costs, but these can include all costs incurred in Canada or the relevant province) which they can claim when they file a tax return. If the credit is greater than the total amount of tax payable, the programs typically provide a refund. While it is a far less significant component of funding programs today than previously, some government programs provide loans at special terms, or have policies which recoup their investment if and when a project becomes profitable.

Under WTO rules, it is generally permissible to subsidize domestic producers, whether they are growing crops, manufacturing products or providing services. There are some exceptions to this rule, including where the subsidy is for purposes of exporting and such exports cause injury or harm to producers in another country. It is likely not a coincidence that, when confronted with an issue, Canadian cultural policymakers increasingly favour a straightforward funding approach, since this generally will not conflict with trade commitments.

But there are many programs, including the newest federal government Cultural Export Strategy, which are targeted specifically at increasing exports of Canadian books, films, music, television programs, performing arts companies and other cultural goods and services. While the quantum of support may not result in injury or harm to producers in other countries, this threshold could be breached at some point. Since the WTO has made it clear that cultural goods, and the cultural services they contain, are subject to the rules of GATT and GATS, Canada could be susceptible to a future challenge if this were to happen.

### Mandated private sector programs

Another element to consider here is the fact that some of the funding that is made available to Canadian artists and producers comes from the private sector. The "net benefit" test applied to the takeover of Canadian firms by foreign interests may sometimes require expenditure of funds on Canadian authors, works or productions. The CRTC requires Canada's BDUs to contribute 5 per cent of their broadcasting revenues to the production of Canadian content, primarily through contributions to the Canada Media Fund (CMF). In 2017–18 this amounted to almost $200 million, more than half of CMF funds. Where a Canadian broadcaster is acquired by another company, a percentage of the value of the transaction is also contributed, as a tangible benefit, to the CMF.

In the current debate surrounding the role of Netflix and other OTT services, many argue that these services should be regulated along the lines of what is happening in Europe. The three key regulations that should be applied to the OTT services are requirements to collect and pay relevant taxes on their Canadian revenues, to contribute a percentage of their Canadian revenues to the production of Canadian content material since they are operating in a manner analogous to BDUs and to include a specified percentage of Canadian content in their inventories.

Having now negotiated an agreement with the Canadian government that provides for it to spend at least $500 million over five years on productions in Canada, Netflix may well be able to challenge any decision that would amend the negotiated agreement or continue it beyond the defined five-year term. Particularly as it has established an office in Canada, it is clear that Netflix would be an "investor" as defined in international investment agreements. It is therefore entitled to "fair and equitable treatment" and may not be subjected to performance requirements, including "to achieve a given level or percentage of domestic content."

While a challenge to any requirement to pay relevant taxes is unlikely to succeed, a challenge against the imposition of a content requirement or mandated contribution to Canadian content production could. While NAFTA 2019 has eliminated the Investor-State Dispute Settlement system, as an international company, Netflix may be able to successfully forum-shop and use another agreement (perhaps CPTPP) to mount a challenge to any decision before an independent tribunal. While the parties might then argue about whether the 1987 definition of cultural industries covers the latest generation of technologies, the adjudicators could well maintain that the investment protections apply in any case since the government would be trying to change unilaterally an agreement the investor entered into in good faith.

## Structural Measures

Structural policy measures are both the most effective ones and the ones most susceptible to trade-related challenges since they are *prima facie* in violation of fundamental principles of free trade. The U.S.

industry associations pointed this out in their 2017 submissions to the Office of the United States Trade Representative on the modernization of NAFTA.

**Ownership rules**
Canada limits or restricts foreign ownership in broadcasting, film distribution, book publishing and retailing and the magazine industry. The primary policy rationale for these limits is that Canadian firms are far more likely than non-Canadian firms to tell Canadian stories. The best illustration is the book publishing industry. Despite the numerous mergers, acquisitions, bankruptcies and other corporate changes and the digital shift, Canadian firms continue to publish roughly 80 per cent of Canadian-authored books, a figure that has been consistent since the 1980s. The other critical reason to retain ownership restrictions is because it is easier to regulate Canadian companies than it is to regulate foreign companies operating in Canada. As foreign investors, these companies have additional rights, as analyzed above concerning Netflix.

The area of most particular concern is where Canada might decide to strengthen regulations. Since 1987, Canada's film distribution policy has attempted to ensure that foreign film distribution firms operating in Canada do so only for importation and distribution activities related to proprietary products (the importer owns world rights or is a major investor). But the Hollywood majors were effectively grandfathered into the policy.

As we have seen, the Canadian Association of Film Distributors and Exporters (CAFDE), which represents the Canadian-owned film distribution firms, continues to call on the government to enforce the policy which requires independently-produced films to be distributed here by Canadian companies. While these account for roughly 15 per cent of the Canadian market, opportunities for Canadian firms, which are limited to this market, have been shrinking as foreign firms sign more distribution deals for independent films. CAFDE argues that the policy ensures funds are available to invest in new Canadian movies.

Acting on CAFDE's request would require the government to change the 1987 policy. Sony Corporation, which was one of the companies cited by CAFDE as acting contrary to the policy, is a Japanese company. If the policy were changed, Sony could launch an action under CPTPP's Investor-State Dispute Settlement system arguing that this change would restrict its activities in Canada and be detrimental to its profits. Film importation and distribution is clearly included in Canada's CPTPP cultural reservation. However, Sony would point out that it was grandfathered (along with the other major film studios) from the limitations imposed on non-Canadian distributors by the 1987 policy. Any change that would now restrict its operations in Canada would be unreasonable and unfair. As we have seen, where a reservation approach has been taken to preserve a nonconforming measure, that policy can never be strengthened in future, because that would make it less "trade compliant." Sony would also argue that there is no "cultural purpose" for the change, as required under Canada's CPTPP cultural exemption, since there is nothing in the 1987 policy that obligates Canadian distributors to invest in new Canadian movies. This would be a very strong case.

Were Canada ever to remove entirely its ownership restrictions in film, broadcasting and publishing, foreign firms entering into or expanding in Canada would be entitled to National Treatment. This could mean, for example, that Canada would likely need to open its funding programs to these companies when they are producing Canadian content. Further, all of Canada's policies relating to them would be effectively frozen. They could be made less stringent, but they could never be made stronger. While a foreign-owned media company could still be required to abide by Canadian content rules, these rules could never be strengthened.

### Content quotas

As we have seen, content quotas are the most important mechanism to develop and sustain a cultural industry. We created a music industry and we succeed in television because we have broadcast quotas. We do not succeed in films because we do not have cinema quotas. It is thus worrisome that the CRTC has begun to shift away from exhibition requirements in favour of funding mechanisms, using the digital shift as the rationale.

With respect to trade agreement issues, there are now at least two areas where Canada would be precluded from introducing such quotas.

Before the WTO decision in the *Canada Periodicals Case*, there had been discussion about the possibility of introducing quotas on newsstands to guarantee space for Canadian publications. Ontario had particularly considered such a move. However, the WTO decision precludes this policy approach. As newsstand sales continue to decline in favour of online consumption, this may no longer be a relevant policy option in any case.

In the 1980s, there had also been consideration of introducing requirements for theatres to produce a certain number of works by Canadian playwrights. Canadian theatre companies could be required to accept such quotas as a condition of receiving government grants. Toronto is the world's third largest English-language theatre market and it is possible that foreign investors could expand into this market in the future. Were this to happen, Ontario would be unable to introduce such a requirement. The performing arts are covered fully by NAFTA 2019, since they are outside the definition of the cultural industries exempted from the agreement.

**Protecting the integrity of the Canadian market**
As we have seen, Canada has adopted a range of policies which seek to protect the integrity of the Canadian markets. The CRTC simultaneous substitution rule ensures that a Canadian rights holder can fully exploit their investment. Provisions in the *Copyright Act* require bookstores and institutional buyers bringing books into Canada to obtain foreign-published works from the Canadian distributor holding such rights. Section 19 of the *Income Tax Act* provides a disincentive for Canadians

to advertise on U.S. border television stations or in U.S. magazines by refusing to accept such spending as an eligible business expense.

The CRTC unilaterally took the first step toward eliminating the simultaneous substitution rule in its decision to allow U.S. signals to be shown to Canadian viewers during the Super Bowl. As noted in Chapter 9, the trade issue involved was turned on its head, since the U.S. interests effectively used the NAFTA renegotiation process to force the CRTC to maintain its own rule.

Perhaps the most interesting trade and cultural policy issues concern those affecting advertising. This analysis starts from an understanding that advertising is a covered service under both CUSFTA and NAFTA 2019.

U.S. broadcasters and magazine publishers continue to object to Section 19.1 of the *Income Tax Act*. Since this provision prevents a Canadian business from counting as an eligible business expense any advertising it purchases on a U.S. border station or in a split-run magazine, it makes it cheaper for the business to advertise on Canadian television or in Canadian magazines. It is perhaps surprising that no U.S. border station or magazine challenged these rules under the original NAFTA Article 11 Investor-State Dispute Settlement (ISDS) process. It is likely that the U.S. border station or magazine would be considered an "investor" under NAFTA since it is providing a good and/or a service to Canadians across the border. This would then lead to an interesting argument about whether the advertising content, because it is contained in a good or service covered by the cultural exemption, would itself be covered by that exemption. I suggest that, given the ambiguity, an investment panel would likely rule that the clear intent of the parties was to include all services related to advertising within the agreement, so that the cultural exemption would not apply. Fortunately, NAFTA 2019 eliminates ISDS.

Many players in the cultural sector have urged the government to expand the provisions of Section 19.1 to advertising placed online by Canadian businesses. Were this change to be made, it is very likely that the Canadian provisions would be challenged since the major U.S technology companies have considerable resources at their disposal to take on such a case, and the hypothetical consideration would become very real. Importantly, unlike border stations and magazines that are fixed in place (and thus limited to seeking a remedy under NAFTA 2019), technology companies may be able to use a different Canadian agreement to access ISDS rights (CETA or CPTPP, for example). If CPTPP became the forum for considering the dispute, Canada would be required to prove the cultural purpose of such a tax measure.

**Copyright**

As we have seen, the copyright issues are complex. There is a powerful lobby in Canada which believes that copyright protections unfairly limit the right of Canadians to use creative materials. Under Conservative Prime Minister Stephen Harper, the *Copyright Act* was changed to expand fair dealing and to provide for a user-generated content exception. Canada is the only country in the world to have a "mash-up" provision which, under certain conditions, allows people to use copyright content in new works without permission or payment. Adding education as a fair dealing purpose has substantially reduced the royalty payments being made to Canadian writers and publishers when works are used in schools. Canada's copyright rules are more user-friendly than the rules in most of the Western world. The term of protection in Europe and the United States is generally seventy years, whereas in Canada it has been only fifty years. Europe and the United States have notice-and-takedown provisions when copyright material is used without authorization online, while Canada has a weaker notice-and-notice provision. NAFTA 2019 will force changes to the term of protection by 2021.

The cultural community overwhelmingly supports stronger copyright provisions. The primary organizations continue to work for copyright reform in the context of the government's 2019 study of the *Act*. Thus, on the issue of how copyright is dealt with in trade agreements, most of the community supports the stronger provisions to which Canada has agreed, including in CETA, the original Trans-Pacific Partnership Agreement and NAFTA 2019. However, most of these same players would agree that it would be far better for Canada to make these decisions outside the context of trade negotiations.

## Public Cultural Agencies

Canadian governments at all levels have established a broad range of public cultural agencies and institutions. The leading national examples of organizations that are involved in the production, distribution and dissemination of cultural expressions are the Canada Council for the Arts, the Canadian Broadcasting Corporation, the National Arts Centre, the National Film Board, the Canadian Radio-television and Telecommunications Commission, Telefilm Canada and the Canada Media Fund. There are myriad others.

More recent multilateral trade negotiations have begun to consider the role of state-owned enterprises, and bilateral agreements frequently cover government procurement. If the agreements begin to cover cultural agencies, this would be a worrisome trend, given their profound social and cultural importance. Let us consider these issues by looking at the Canadian Broadcasting Corporation.

The CBC is an important source of news, information and entertainment, written and produced with a primary focus on the needs of Canadians. It is completely inappropriate for its activities to be limited in any way by trade rules and it certainly should not be required to ensure it "acts in accordance with commercial considerations with respect to purchases and sales."

Established by the *Broadcasting Act*, the CBC has a broad mandate. The corporation should have a "wide range of programming that informs, enlightens and entertains," and it should make these available "by the most appropriate and efficient means and as resources become available for the purpose." Like all public service broadcasters, the CBC must have a strong presence on the Internet, since this is where many people today look for their news and entertainment. The December 2018 launch of CBC's GEM on-demand streaming service, which already provides more than 4,000 hours of programming, is the corporation's latest move to stay relevant in the digital age.

Once again, there are two aspects to this discussion. The greatest challenge for the CBC at the moment does not come from pressure from other countries' trade negotiators, but rather from internal debate about the corporation's size, scope and future. Some people believe that there is no need for Canada to have a public service broadcaster and would like to see the CBC abolished or privatized. Others believe it should be commercial-free and receive additional resources to compensate for the lost revenues. If any actions are taken to reduce the size and scope of the CBC, it may be difficult under trade rules to reverse that trend, even if the public view changes.

The CBC is also confronted with pressures on its budget. Liberal governments of the 1990s began to constrain the budget, and Conservative Prime Minister Stephen Harper followed suit. The 2012 budget began to reduce government appropriations for the CBC, as a result of which the corporation developed a $115 million deficit reduction plan in 2014. Liberal Prime Minister Justin Trudeau began to reverse this trend in the 2016 budget but, on an inflation-adjusted basis, the CBC's budget remains far smaller than it was in the 1990s.

The trade issues for cultural agencies and institutions are straightforward. Regardless of what Canada does in respect of the general trend to include state-owned enterprises in trade agreements, it is inappropriate to include cultural agencies in any way, since their entire raison d'être is cultural, even if they may at times operate in a commercial sphere.

## Voluntary Measures

As we have seen particularly with the 2017 Netflix deal and the 1950s Canada Cooperation Project, voluntary agreements with major multinational firms do not translate into effective cultural policy.

But there is one place where it would be entirely appropriate for our government to negotiate with foreign multinational firms and seek their cooperation. When I appeared on the ACTRA delegation in the 1998 CRTC process that resulted in the Digital Media Exemption Order, I urged the commission to consider seriously the role of Internet search engines. Even at that time, it was obvious that search engines would become the key to finding cultural expressions on the Internet. Few people today remember that in those days, when you entered a search term, Google would ask whether you wanted to limit your search to Canadian websites. Shortly after, it ceased to do this because its algorithms had become more sophisticated. But surely it is reasonable today to request that search engines operating in Canada, which provide a service to Canadians and sell advertising here, adjust their algorithms to ensure that Canadians are offered at least some Canadian choices when they are searching for artistic content. While it is neither possible nor appropriate to interfere in the final selection made by Canadian consumers, they should have a real choice available to them. As good corporate citizens, Google, Bing, Yahoo and the others are likely to agree, since the change would be both reasonable and rational. The government may be able to consider a regulatory constraint on search engines that fail to comply. For example, the *Income Tax Act* could be amended to discourage Canadians from advertising on search engines that don't offer a Canadian option. Since this provision would apply to all search engines regardless of nationality, it might survive a trade challenge.

# Chapter 12
# A New Approach to Culture and Trade

The leading advocates for the development and implementation of what is now the UNESCO *Convention on the Protection and Promotion of the Diversity of Cultural Expressions* believed that it would be a tool to remove culture from trade and investment agreements. Toward this goal, the convention was modelled on the Multilateral Environmental Agreements (MEAs).

The Montreal *Protocol on Substances that Deplete the Ozone Layer* is widely seen as the most effective MEA in history. By 1985, scientists had discovered that the ozone layer was seriously depleted over the South Pole and it was generally acknowledged that the use of chlorofluorocarbons (CFCs) was responsible. These were widely used in aerosol sprays, solvents and refrigerants. The destruction of the stratosphere's ozone layer, which absorbs most of the sun's deadly ultraviolet radiation, poses a huge risk to human and plant health. Twenty countries agreed to a framework for negotiating regulations on ozone-depleting substances, and these negotiations concluded in August 1987 with the agreement on the Montreal Protocol. Over the past thirty years, the protocol has achieved its objective.

Most significantly for our purposes, while the protocol was nego-tiated by environmental and health experts, it contains measures that affect trade. To encourage countries to join the protocol, and to prevent companies that manufacture or use CFCs from shifting operations to nonparty countries, the protocol restricts trade in CFCs and related products with nonparties. The protocol also has provisions that restrict all trade in certain controlled substances. Finally, it contains provisions for financial assistance and transfer of technology to help developing countries meet their obligations under the protocol. The World Trade Organization understands that questions arise about whether measures under an MEA are compatible with WTO rules. WTO notes specifically that if a multilateral agreement

> authorize[s] trade in a specific product between its parties, but ban[s] trade in the same product with countries that have not signed the agreement . . . this could be found to be incompatible with WTO's non-discrimination principle known as "most favoured nation treatment," which requires countries to grant equivalent treatment to the same (or "like") products imported from any WTO member country.

The WTO notes that, of the more than 250 MEAs in place in the early twenty-first century, roughly twenty contain measures that affect trade.[1]

There has not been a definitive ruling that tackles this conflict, and talks to clarify the relationship between the MEAs and trade agreements are stalled along with the rest of the Doha Round. But the reality is that trade officials defer to the environmental and health experts. Many trade agreements have a right-to-regulate clause that includes matters of human health and environmental protection. If there were any formal challenges, environmental commitments would take precedence over trade commitments, unless the environ-mental measures were patently trade barriers in disguise. At the very least, the obligations in each agreement would be considered to be equal.

As we have seen, the language of the UNESCO Convention is not as robust as the MEAs when dealing with trade agreements. The articles that address the convention's relationship to other international instruments are ambiguous. There is a statement of "complementarity" between the convention and other instruments, and a commitment by parties to work together in other international fora to promote the principles and objectives of the convention. There is also an innovative provision that parties will use the convention as an interpretive tool if they are adjudicating disputes under other international instruments. But Article 20.2 is clear: "Nothing in this Convention shall be interpreted as modifying rights and obligations Parties have to each other under any other treaties to which they are a party." This means that their commitments under trade agreements, whether those were in place before the convention was adopted or subsequently, trump their commitments under the UNESCO Convention.

But there is nothing in the convention preventing parties to it from entering into agreements with one another that would give priority to their convention commitments over their trade commitments where they are dealing with cultural expressions. Embracing their mutual commitments to the convention would then provide a basis for a new approach to the issues of culture and trade.

## Maintain the Cultural Exemption with the United States

While 145 states plus the European Union are parties to the UNESCO Convention, some countries are not. For comparison, the WTO currently has 164 members, and there are 197 signatories to the Montreal Protocol. For Canadian cultural policymaking, the United States is the most important nonadherent to the UNESCO Convention.

Without a mutual commitment to the convention, it is essential for Canada to retain the cultural exemption in every trade or investment agreement we reach with the United States. This is also the best tack when it comes to any other nonsignatory to the UNESCO Convention.

**The definition of the cultural industries should be modernized**
Perhaps the most important issue with respect to the cultural exemption is to ensure that all sectors and all current and future media used for the production or distribution of artistic expressions are included. To achieve this, the definition of what is covered needs to be updated and rewritten. A contemporary definition would put the artist and creative expression at its heart, and the UNESCO Convention could be the primary guide. The convention defines "cultural expressions" as "those expressions that result from the creativity of individuals, groups and societies, and that have cultural content." In turn, "cultural content refers to the symbolic meaning, artistic dimension and cultural values that originate from or express cultural identities." The convention also defines "cultural goods and services" as those that "embody or convey cultural expressions"; these may have both a cultural and commercial value. The precise form of their medium of production or dissemination is irrelevant to their existence as cultural expressions.

Thus, a progressive and up-to-date integrated cultural exemption and definition that would serve well into the future could read as follows:

> *Cultural expressions, including cultural goods and services,*
> *regardless of their medium of production or dissemination, and*
> *all persons involved at any stage in their creation, production,*
> *dissemination or preservation, are exempt from this Agreement.*
> *Cultural expressions result from the creativity of individuals,*
> *groups and societies and have cultural content. Cultural content is*
> *the symbolic meaning, artistic dimension and cultural values that*
> *originate from or express cultural identities.*

## CPTPP and TPP revisited

Having negotiated changes and additional provisions to the Trans-Pacific Partnership Agreement, and having successfully driven the renaming, Canada's Liberal government of Prime Minister Justin Trudeau fully endorsed the CPTPP and it came into effect on December 31, 2018. As the second element in our contemporary relationship with the United States, Canada must prepare for the strong likelihood that the U.S. will seek to join CPTPP. While this is highly unlikely to happen under the presidency of Donald Trump, it is virtually inevitable that the next president, whether a Democrat or a Republican, will take such a step.

As reviewed in Chapter 8, Canada has signed side letters with all other parties to the CPTPP that strengthen the reservations in the original TPP allowing Canada to support its cultural industries. The TPP reservations were constrained by certain limitations that are now revoked by the side letters. In addition, various provisions in the TPP chapter on intellectual property rights have been suspended by the parties.

Now that Canada has successfully continued (and strengthened) the cultural exemption in NAFTA 2019, and even without a contemporary definition or elimination of the notwithstanding clause, we are in a strong position to go a step further with respect to the United States than we achieved with other CPTPP partners. Given that the last agreement negotiated between the parties is NAFTA 2019, Canada could insist that the side letter for cultural industries with the United States mirror the language in NAFTA 2019. With the necessary foresight and strong political will, Canada could indicate that it would withhold its agreement to the U.S. joining the CPTPP without such a side letter. Since the United States will also seek to restore the TPP intellectual property rights provisions, Canada would have a bargaining chip to bring to the table.

## Moving Beyond the Cultural Exemption

Canada is currently negotiating or preparing to negotiate trade and investment agreements with a range of countries other than the United States. Most importantly, we should consider the states with which we are currently negotiating free trade or economic partnership agreements, since these create a more comprehensive relationship than do agreements that merely protect investor rights.

Among the states with which Canada is involved in ongoing negotiations are fifteen states in the Caribbean Community, three Central American states and the member states (four each) of two South American groupings, Mercosur and the Pacific Alliance. Canada is also negotiating with India and hoping to do so with China. Exploratory talks have commenced with the Association of Southeast Asian Nations (ASEAN). Most of the states involved in these negotiations or potential talks are parties to the UNESCO Convention (Table 1). The outlier is ASEAN, which has ten member countries. Only four ASEAN countries — Cambodia, Indonesia, Laos and Vietnam — are signatories to the convention. Brunei, Malaysia, Myanmar, Philippines, Singapore and Thailand are not signatories.

## Convention Provisions Can Guide the Cultural Relationship Between Two Member States: The Example of China

Perhaps the best way of illustrating what a new approach to culture would look like is to consider the possibility of such an approach with respect to China, which has the second largest economy in the world based on nominal GDP.

Canada and China have historically enjoyed a positive relationship. In 1970, Canada became one of the first Western countries to recognize the government of the People's Republic of China, and Prime Minister Pierre Trudeau, who travelled there in 1973, was among the first major Western leaders to visit.

As we have seen, Canada and China entered into a film coproduction

**Table 1: States with which Canada is negotiating: Are they signatories to the UNESCO Convention?**

| GROUP OR STATE | SIGNATORIES | NONSIGNATORIES |
|---|---|---|
| Caribbean states | Antigua and Barbuda, Bahamas, Barbados, Belize, Dominica, Grenada, Guyana, Haiti, Jamaica, Saint Kitts and Nevis, Saint Lucia, Saint Vincent and the Grenadines, Trinidad and Tobago | Montserrat, Suriname |
| Central American states | El Salvador, Guatemala, Nicaragua | |
| Pacific Alliance | Chile, Colombia, Mexico, Peru | |
| Mercosur | Argentina, Brazil, Paraguay, Uruguay | |
| India | Yes | |
| China | Yes | |

treaty in 1987, in large measure to facilitate the production of *Bethune: The Making of a Hero*, which at the time of its release in 1990 was the most expensive Canadian movie ever made and one of the first major Western movies to be shot in China. Unfortunately, overall there has been little production under the treaty in its thirty-year history. Since 2005, only six movies have been produced under its terms. Perhaps as a consequence, when Prime Minister Justin Trudeau went to China in 2016 and met with President Xi Jinping and Premier Li Keqiang, the countries signed a refreshed coproduction treaty that came into effect on May 1, 2017.

There is also a large Chinese diaspora in Canada. According to the 2011 census, the Chinese Canadian population was 1.3 million people, or roughly 4 per cent of Canada's overall population. The numbers will continue to grow since China has supplied the largest number of immigrants to Canada since 2000, averaging 15 per cent of all immigrants each year. Statistics Canada projects that, by 2031, the Chinese Canadian population will reach between 2.4 and 3.0 million, constituting approximately 6 per cent of the Canadian population. This brings significant connections on many different levels between the two countries.

There have been some recent hiccups in the relationship. The first occurred when Prime Minister Trudeau visited China in December 2017 on a trip Canadian officials touted as leading up to an announcement of the formal launch of trade talks. However, Trudeau's insistence on a "progressive" agreement that would include provisions on labour standards and gender rights puzzled the Chinese. From the point of view of the Asian giant, a tiny nation with a comparatively insignificant economy was seeking to address China's domestic concerns.

The second hiccup was the December 2018 detention in Vancouver of Huawei chief financial officer Meng Wanzhou. She was arrested at the request of the United States, which alleged she helped Huawei circumvent U.S. sanctions on Iran. Huawei is a significant Chinese company that is key to China's ambitious plan to dominate cutting-edge technologies such as advanced microchips, 5G wireless telecommunications networks, aerospace, medical devices, artificial intelligence and electric cars by 2025.

Despite these hiccups, it is highly likely that Canada and China will launch trade talks in the foreseeable future.

Canada and China were both active participants in the negotiation of the UNESCO Convention and were strongly supportive of its implementation. In November 2005 Canada was the first state to accept the convention, while China became the forty-fourth party when it ratified the convention fourteen months later. In Canada's trade negotiations with China, shared support for the convention can lay the foundation for a more robust cultural relationship. The following could be the key elements of this new relationship:

**1. Confirm that Canada and China each has the absolute right to support its own artists and cultural producers**
One of the key objectives of the UNESCO Convention is "to reaffirm the sovereign rights of States to maintain, adopt and implement policies and measures that they deem appropriate for the protection and promotion of the diversity of cultural expressions on their territories." Article 6 outlines the range of measures a party may take to achieve the objective, including: regulatory measures; content quotas and other measures aimed at ensuring access for domestic cultural industries; public financial assistance; public institutions; measures aimed at supporting artists and others involved in the creative process; measures aimed at enhancing diversity in the media, including through public service broadcasting; and measures that promote the free exchange and circulation of ideas and cultural expressions and that stimulate the "creative and entrepreneurial spirit."

As we have seen, the scope of the convention is broad because it includes policies and measures that are "related to" the protection and promotion of the diversity of cultural expressions and not just to "cultural" policies. The convention definitions reinforce the broad scope of cultural policymaking.

Overall, by confirming support for the convention, Canada and China will acknowledge that they each have the right to support their own artists and cultural producers in every sector and medium, and however the works may be distributed to consumers. They should also ensure that any dispute about the cultural provisions of whatever trade agreement they reach would be dealt with under the convention's dispute settlement system rather than the system contained in the trade agreement.

This should effectively mitigate concerns similar to those expressed by the European cultural sector when the EU negotiated its cultural protocol with South Korea — that is, the possibility that specific cultural tradeoffs might be negotiated as part of overall trade discussions. This approach also reflects a positive understanding of the broad scope of cultural policymaking and is not limited to current media. Thus, it provides far more protection for Canada than even the most comprehensive exemption Canada has negotiated in any existing trade agreement.

**2. Develop more bilateral cultural cooperation agreements in every medium**

The convention also encourages parties to develop cultural exchanges and international cooperation to promote cultural development. The goal is to provide greater access to diverse cultural expressions in each of the partner countries. One of the objectives of the convention is "to encourage dialogue among cultures with a view to ensuring wider and balanced cultural exchanges." The convention provides that when states adopt measures to support the diversity of cultural expressions, they should respect the convention principle of "openness and balance" and promote openness to other cultures.

Using all these objectives and provisions, there are a number of initiatives which Canada and China could take. Let us look at two of the most obvious ones.

The first would be to expand the film coproduction treaty to include other media, particularly television and video games. It is important to note that, while China has film coproduction treaties with Australia, Belgium, Canada, Estonia, France, India, Italy, Netherlands, New Zealand, Singapore, South Korea, Spain and the United Kingdom, it has only one television coproduction treaty. China and New Zealand entered into a television coproduction treaty in 2014. It provides a considerable advantage to New Zealand shows produced under the treaty's provisions, since they are considered domestic content in China's huge and growing broadcast market, in which foreign productions are severely restricted. Interestingly, one of the major beneficiaries of this treaty is NHNZ, which makes "ground-breaking factual television about people, nature, adventure, history and science for global broadcasters." NHNZ operates from Dunedin, New Zealand, and Beijing, China, and is wholly owned by Toronto's Blue Ant media.[2]

Expanding the coproduction relationship to include television became even more important in October 2018 when China's National Radio and Television Administration (NRTA) established harsh new rules which prevent non-Chinese content from being shown in prime time and restrict it overall to 30 per cent of total air time, including both traditional broadcasting and online streaming. The use of foreign talent and other professionals will be capped at no more than one-fifth of total staff on a Chinese TV drama. According to industry sources, this is all part of a broad crackdown on the content industry.[3]

The second obvious initiative would be to create more opportunities for Canadian musicians, other artists and performing arts companies to tour China, and for Chinese musicians and performing arts companies to tour Canada. This form of cultural exchange is extremely positive and, for the Canadians involved, potentially lucrative.

### 3. Negotiate provisions for China to import Canadian feature films

In 2001, China joined the WTO. In 2007, the United States launched a WTO complaint against Chinese import regulations that limit how many foreign films and books can be imported into the country and require that importation be done in partnership with a Chinese codistributor, effectively a state-owned enterprise. In 2009, the WTO issued its ruling in *China — Measures Affecting Trading Rights and Distribution Services for Certain Publications and Audiovisual Entertainment Products*. While China cited the UNESCO Convention in support of its measures, inevitably the dispute panel rejected this argument since the United States is not a party to the convention. The WTO ruled in favour of key parts of the U.S. complaint. While China can continue to restrict imports to protect "public morals" and can continue to control release dates, it was required to take steps to open its market.

After the WTO decision, China and the United States negotiated an agreement under which China agreed to import thirty-four feature films each year (fourteen in Imax or 3D format and twenty others) and also agreed to provide 25 per cent of the gross box office receipts from the exhibition of those movies to the U.S. producer/distributor. The percentage of revenues returned to the U.S. partner is very small by international standards.

In the years following implementation of this agreement, the Chinese theatrical market has grown substantially, from $2 billion USD in 2011 to $8.6 billion USD in 2017. Even though earlier rapid growth rates slowed markedly after May 2016, there was still a 4 per cent growth in box office receipts and continued expansion of the market with 10,000 new screens being opened in 2016. China's limitation on imports was designed to ensure that roughly 60 per cent of box office receipts are earned by Chinese films (including coproductions). This target was not reached in 2016.[4] Perhaps in an effort to kickstart the slumping market overall, China informally imported four additional Hollywood films in 2016.

According to recent reports, China is looking to slow down the massive amounts of money leaving the country in recent years in several sectors, including investments in the film industry.[5] In January 2017, Paramount Pictures announced a deal to source $1 billion USD to finance upcoming films from two Chinese firms, but this deal fell apart within the next year. This appears to be part of the same crackdown as NRTA's limits on foreign television content. The film crackdown includes aggressive caps on celebrity pay (no more than 40 per cent of production costs) and investigations into tax evasion in the industry that led to the mysterious four-month disappearance of China's biggest female star, Fan Bingbing, in the summer of 2018.[6]

The agreement on importation of Hollywood movies was set to expire in 2017 and talks began on a renewal early that year, with the U.S. objective being not only to increase the number of movies but also to increase the share of Chinese box office receipts that are returned to the U.S. partner. However, the talks stalled as they became intertwined in the broader trade war launched by U.S. President Donald Trump when he imposed tariffs on a range of Chinese imports. In May 2018, Reuters reported that "negotiations to raise a Chinese quota on imported films and boost the share that overseas producers get of box office takings are now being discussed within the broader framework of a U.S.-China trade stand-off, four industry sources said." Importantly, the report went on to state: "'It wouldn't really hit the domestic movie business much whether we bring in more foreign movies or not,' said Yu Jianhong, vice president of Beijing Film Academy. 'This should be something both parties can agree on.'"[7]

Given all these developments, Canada would be well positioned to negotiate an agreement for the Canadian film industry similar to what China has agreed to with the United States. The specific number of Canadian feature films to be imported annually for theatrical release would be negotiated by the parties. Canada could also seek either a higher percentage of the gross box office receipts to be received by the Canadian producer/distributor or propose a Most-Favoured-Nation provision that would ensure Canadian companies are treated the same as Hollywood companies.

### 4. Collaborate under other relevant provisions of the convention

The convention can provide other opportunities for collaboration. Canada and China could agree to collaborate to "promote the objectives and principles of this Convention in other international forums," as provided in Article 21. This could include working together in the WTO to ensure future multilateral trade agreements exclude creative expressions in all media.

Canada and China could promote collaboration between our respective "civil society, non-governmental organizations and the private sector," as provided in Articles 11 and 12. And while this would be extremely delicate, Canada could propose collaboration to protect forms of cultural expression that "are at risk of extinction, under serious threat, or otherwise in need of urgent safeguarding," as provided in Articles 8 and 17.

## A Potential Turning Point

In the short term, China is the most obvious potential partner for such opportunities. However, using the convention as the basis of a trading relationship could work with other countries and regions as well.

Taking such a new approach could be a fundamental turning point in the way that cultural goods and services are treated in trade and investment agreements. While it would obviously benefit cultural industries, people everywhere would have access to an ever broader and richer diversity of cultural expressions. This would be a very good thing.

# Acknowledgements

Thank you to all my family, friends and colleagues who encouraged me to write this book and supported me as I did. A special thank you and much love to my children, Christopher Craig-Neil and Amy Craig-Neil. I've finally managed to bring together in one place all the issues you've had to listen to me talk about for so many years!

# Notes

## Chapter 1

1.  UNESCO, "Learning to Live Together," retrieved from http://www.unesco.org/new/en/social-and-human-sciences/themes/international-migration/glossary/cultural-diversity/

2.  UNESCO *Convention on the Protection and Promotion of the Diversity of Cultural Expressions* (UNESCO 2005 Convention), retrieved from https://en.unesco.org/creativity/convention/texts, p. 7.

3.  Jo Marchant, "A Journey to the Oldest Cave Paintings in the World," *Smithsonian Magazine*, January 2016, retrieved from https://www.smithsonianmag.com/history/journey-oldest-cave-paintings-world-180957685/

4.  Michael Greshko, "World's Oldest Cave Art Found," *National Geographic*, February 2018, retrieved from https://news.nationalgeographic.com/2018/02/neanderthals-cave-art-humans-evolution-science/

5.  Motion Picture Association of America, *2017 Theatrical Home Entertainment Market Environment (THEME) Report,* April 2018, retrieved from https://www.mpaa.org/research-docs/2017-theatrical-home-entertainment-market-environment-theme-report/

6.  Stephen Follows, "How Important Is International Box Office to Hollywood?" *Stephen Follows Film Data and Education*, May 2017, retrieved from https://stephenfollows.com/important-international-box-office-hollywood/

7.  Canadian Media Producers Association, *Profile 2017*, retrieved from https://cmpa.ca/profile/

8.  "History of Broadcasting in Canada," *Wikipedia*, last edited January 29, 2019, retrieved from https://en.wikipedia.org/wiki/History_of_broadcasting_in_Canada

9.  Ted Magder, Piers Handling and Peter Morris, "History of the Canadian Film Industry," *Canadian Encyclopedia*, last updated February 22, 2017, retrieved from https://www.thecanadianencyclopedia.ca/en/article/the-history-of-film-in-canada/

10. J.D.M. Stewart and Helmut Kallman, "Massey Commission," *Canadian Encyclopedia*, last updated July 29, 2016, retrieved from https://www.thecanadianencyclopedia.ca/en/article/massey-commission-emc/

11. CRTC Broadcasting Regulatory Policy CRTC 2015-96, retrieved from https://crtc.gc.ca/eng/archive/2015/2015-96.htm

12. Elaine Dewar, "How Canada Sold Out Its Publishing Industry," *The Walrus*, June 2017, retrieved from https://thewalrus.ca/no-one-blinked/

# Chapter 2

1.  Christina D. Romer and Richard H. Pells, "Great Depression," *Encyclopedia Britannica*, last updated January 10, 2019, retrieved from https://www.britannica.com/event/Great-Depression

2.  WTO General Agreement on Tariffs and Trade, retrieved from https://www.wto.org/English/docs_e/legal_e/prewto_legal_e.htm

3.  All versions of GATT can be found here: https://www.wto.org/English/docs_e/legal_e/legal_e.htm#gatt47

4.  *Quota Laws on Foreign and Domestic Films by Nation*, retrieved from https://www.timetoast.com/timelines/quota-laws-on-foreign-and-domestic-films-by-nation

5.  "Cinema of Europe," *Wikipedia*, last edited January 6, 2019, retrieved from https://en.wikipedia.org/wiki/Cinema_of_Europe

6.  Ted Magder, Piers Handling and Peter Morris, "History of the Canadian Film Industry," *Canadian Encyclopedia*, last updated February 22, 2017, retrieved from https://www.thecanadianencyclopedia.ca/en/article/the-history-of-film-in-canada/

7.  UNESCO *Convention on the Protection and Promotion of the Diversity of Cultural Expressions* (UNESCO 2005 Convention), retrieved from https://en.unesco.org/creativity/convention/texts

8.  World Trade Organization, General Agreement on Trade in Services, retrieved from https://www.wto.org/english/tratop_e/serv_e/gatsintr_e.htm

# Chapter 3

1.  "Minister Joly Announces Creative Canada: A Vision for Canada's Creative Industries in the Digital Age," Department of Canadian Heritage News Release, September 28, 2017, retrieved from https://www.canada.ca/en/canadian-heritage/news/2017/09/minister_joly_announcescreativecanadaavisionforcanadascreativein.html

2.  Conference Board of Canada, *Valuing Culture*, August 2008, retrieved from https://www.creativecity.ca/database/files/library/valuingculture.pdf

3.  Motion Picture Association of America, *What Is the Economic Value of the ARTS?* January 2015, retrieved from https://www.mpaa.org/press/nea/

4.  Copyright Alliance, *Negotiating Objectives Regarding Modernization of NAFTA*, Washington, June 12, 2017 retrieved from https://copyrightalliance.org/policy/agency-filings/

5.  Norman Hillmer, "A Border People," *Canada World View*, Winter 2005, retrieved from

http://publications.gc.ca/collections/collection_2011/aecic-faitc/E12-15-24-2005-eng.pdf

6.    Alan W. Dowd and Fred McMahon, "Trashing NAFTA: Protection or Prosperity," *American Thinker*, February 2017, retrieved from https://www.americanthinker.com/articles/2017/02/trashing_nafta_protection_or_prosperity.html #ixzz5KhyrCKJi

7.    Frank Stone, "The Framework and Process of Canada–United States Trade Liberalization," *Canada–United States Law Journal*, Vol. 10, Art. 36, January 1988, retrieved from https://scholarlycommons.law.case.edu/cgi/viewcontent.cgi?article=1828&context=cuslj

8.    Council of Canadians, press release, 1985, retrieved from https://canadians.org/media/other/1985/index.html

9.    See 60th Anniversary Edition at http://www.actra.ca/our-union/our-history/

10. Reported in *National Post*, retrieved from https://www.pressreader.com/canada/national-post-latest-edition/20051029/281831459130196

11.   Scott Sinclair, *Canada's Track Record Under NAFTA Chapter 11*, Canadian Centre for Policy Alternatives, Ottawa, January 2018, retrieved from https://www.policyalternatives.ca/nafta2018

# A Digression

1.    Gareth Shute, "Does Local Radio Actually Play Any Local Music?" *The Spinoff*, April 2018, retrieved from https://thespinoff.co.nz/music/08-05-2018/does-local-radio-actually-play-any-local-music/

2.    StatsNZ, *Local Content Programming on New Zealand Television*, retrieved from http://archive.stats.govt.nz/browse_for_stats/snapshots-of-nz/nz-social-indicators/Home/Culture20and%20identity20identity and identity/local-content-nz-tv.aspx

3.    Patrick Frater and Darcy Paquet, "Korea Slashes Local Pic Quota," *Variety*, January 25, 2006, retrieved from https://variety.com/2006/film/asia/korea-slashes-local-pic-quota-1117936888/

4.    European Centre for International Political Economy, *The Effect of Screen Quotas and Subsidy Regime on Cultural Industry: A Case Study of French and Korean Film Industries*, January 2016, retrieved from http://ecipe.org/publications/the-effect-of-screen-quotas-and-subsidy-regime-on-cultural-industry-a-case-study-of-french-and-korean-film-industries/

# Chapter 4

1.    Pamela Cuthbert, Peter Morris and Anna Zuschlag, "Film Distribution in Canada," *Canadian Encyclopedia*, last edited February 21, 2017, retrieved from https://www.

thecanadianencyclopedia.ca/en/article/film-distribution-in-canada/

2.  *House of Commons Debates*, 33rd Parliament, 2nd Session, Vol. 8, p. 831, retrieved from http://parl.canadiana.ca/view/oop.debates_HOC3302_08/1?r=0&s=2

3.  Investment Canada policy on foreign investment in the Canadian film distribution sector, retrieved from https://www.canada.ca/en/canadian-heritage/services/film-video-policies/investment-canadian-film-distribution.html

4.  Richard Rapkowski (Canadian Association of Film Distributors and Exporters) at the Canadian Heritage Committee, retrieved from https://openparliament.ca/committees/canadian-heritage/41-2/36/richard-rapkowski-1/only/

5.  Canadian Media Producers Association, *Profile 2017*, retrieved from https://cmpa.ca/profile/

6.  For a contemporary analysis of these developments in book publishing see Roy MacSkimming, *Net Benefit: Canada's Policy on Foreign Investment in the Book Industry* (Toronto: Association of Canadian Publishers, 2017), retrieved from https://publishers.ca/wp-content/uploads/2018/06/ACPreportForeignInvestmentPolicyWeb.pdf

7.  Christopher S. Wren, "G. & W., in Canada Deal, Will Keep Prentice Unit," *New York Times*, March 13, 1986, retrieved from https://www.nytimes.com/1986/03/13/business/g-w-in-canada-deal-will-keep-prentice-unit.html

8.  MacSkimming, *Net Benefit*.

9.  Author's personal collection.

10.  Author's personal collection.

11.  Nancy A. Lyzaniwski, *Culture and Trade: An Analysis of Four Culture/Trade Disputes under NAFTA and the WTO* (Master's Thesis, University of Guelph, 2000), pp. 53–68, retrieved from www.collectionscanada.gc.ca/obj/s4/f2/dsk2/ftp03/MQ51078.pdf,

12.  Author's personal collection.

13.  Telefilm Canada, *International Treaties and Memorandums of Understanding*, retrieved from https://telefilm.ca/en/coproduction/international-treaties

14.  Canada's GATS exemption, retrieved from https://docs.wto.org/

15.  Keith Acheson and Christopher Maule, *Much Ado about Culture: North American Trade Disputes* (Ann Arbor: University of Michigan Press, 1999), pp. 188–91, retrieved from https://books.google.ca/

16.  Lyzaniwski, *Culture and Trade*.

17.  Garry Neil, "The Convention as a Response to the Cultural Challenges of Globalisation," in Nina Obuljen and Joost Smiers, eds., *UNESCO's Convention on the Protection and Promotion of the Diversity of Cultural Expressions: Making it Work* (Zagreb, Croatia:

Institute for International Relations, 2006), pp. 41–70, retrieved from https://www.culturelink.org/publics/joint/diversity01/index.html

## Chapter 5

1. All of Canada's trade agreements, whether in force, in negotiation or suspended, can be found here: https://www.international.gc.ca/trade-commerce/trade-agreements-accords-commerciaux/agr-acc/index.aspx?lang=eng. This language is identical in each agreement, see for example Poland, the first one that came into effect, in 1990.

2. Author's personal collection

3. Canada–European Free Trade Association Agreement available at http://international.gc.ca/trade-commerce/trade-agreements-accords-commerciaux/agr-acc/european-association-europeenne/fta-ale/index.aspx?lang=eng

4. Australia, Austria, Belgium, Canada, Czech Republic, Denmark, Finland, France, Germany, Greece, Hungary, Iceland, Ireland, Italy, Japan, Korea, Luxembourg, Mexico, Netherlands, New Zealand, Norway, Poland, Portugal, Spain, Sweden, Switzerland, Turkey, the United Kingdom and the United States.

5. "Multilateral Agreement on Investment," *Wikipedia*, last updated December 12, 2018, retrieved from https://en.wikipedia.org/wiki/Multilateral_Agreement_on_Investment

6. House of Commons, Subcommittee on International Trade, November 20, 1997, retrieved from http://www.ourcommons.ca/DocumentViewer/en/36-1/SINT/meeting-7/evidence

7. Garry Neil, "The MAI and Culture," in Andrew Jackson and Matthew Sager, eds. *Dismantling Democracy* (Toronto: James Lorimer and Co., 1998), pp. 138–59.

8. Subsequent to the public outrage, the OECD published various drafts of the negotiating text, found here: https://www.oecd.org/daf/mai/htm/2.htm. The commentary of France about cultural industries is found at page 166 of the May 1997 draft.

9. Summary of testimony and original citation is here: http://www.equalityrights.org/ngoun98/maiun.htm

10. Trade in Services Agreement (TiSA) from the European Commission available at http://ec.europa.eu/trade/policy/in-focus/tisa/

## Chapter 6

1. UNESCO, *World Decade for Cultural Development 1988–1997: Plan of Action*, available at https://unesdoc.unesco.org/ark:/48223/pf0000085291

2.  Quoted in Nina Obuljen, "From Our Creative Diversity to the Convention on Cultural Diversity: Introduction to the Debate," in Nina Obuljen and Joost Smiers, eds., *UNESCO's Convention on the Protection and Promotion of the Diversity of Cultural Expressions: Making it Work* (Zagreb, Croatia: Institute for International Relations, 2006), pp. 17–38, retrieved from https://www.culturelink.org/publics/joint/diversity01/index.html

3.  *Canadian Culture in a Global World: New Strategies for Culture and Trade*, SAGIT Report, February 1999, retrieved from https://www.international.gc.ca/trade-agreements-accords-commerciaux/topics-domaines/ip-pi/canculture.aspx?lang=en

4.  UNESCO, *Universal Declaration on Cultural Diversity*, November 2001, retrieved from http://portal.unesco.org/en/ev.php-URL_ID=13179&URL_DO=DO_TOPIC&URL_SECTION=201.html

5.  Garry Neil, "The Convention as a Response to the Cultural Challenges of Globalisation," in Nina Obuljen and Joost Smiers, eds., *UNESCO's Convention on the Protection and Promotion of the Diversity of Cultural Expressions: Making it Work* (Zagreb, Croatia: Institute for International Relations, 2006), pp. 41–70, retrieved from https://www.culturelink.org/publics/joint/diversity01/index.html

6.  Ibid.

7.  Garry Neil, "Conclusions: Perspectives and Challenges for the Convention," in Sabine von Schorlemer and Peter-Tobias Stoll, eds., *The UNESCO Convention on the Protection and Promotion of the Diversity of Cultural Expressions: Explanatory Notes* (Heidelberg, Germany: Springer, 2012), pp. 739–50.

8.  Author's personal collection.

# Chapter 7

1.  Bruce Campion-Smith, "Arts Uproar? Ordinary Folks Just Don't Care, Says Harper," *Toronto Star*, September 24, 2008

2.  Rob Maguire, "Canada's Federal Election: Who Should Get the Art Vote?" *Canadian Art*, October 15, 2015, retrieved from https://canadianart.ca/features/who-should-get-the-art-vote/

3.  Organization of American States, Foreign Trade Information System, *CARIFORUM–European Union*, retrieved from http://www.sice.oas.org/TPD/CAR_EU/CAR_EU_e.asp

4.  Jan Loisen and Ferdi De Ville, "The EU-Korea Protocol on Cultural Cooperation: Toward Cultural Diversity or Cultural Deficit?, *International Journal of Communications*, Vol. 5 (2011), retrieved from http://ijoc.org/index.php/ijoc/article/view/882

5.   "Protocol on Cultural Cooperation," *Official Journal of the European Union*, L 127/1418–22, May 14, 2011, retrieved from https://eeas.europa.eu/sites/eeas/files/protocol_on_eu-rok_cultural_cooperation.pdf

6.   *Canada–Korea Free Trade Agreement*, retrieved from http://international.gc.ca/trade-commerce/trade-agreements-accords-commerciaux/agr-acc/korea-coree/fta-ale/index.aspx?lang=eng

7.   Peter Grant, "Does the TPP Protect Canadian Cultural Policy?" *Barry Sookman*, February 7, 2016, retrieved from http://www.barrysookman.com/2016/02/07/does-the-tpp-protect-canadian-cultural-policy/

8.   *Chronology of Events and Key Milestones* (CETA), retrieved from http://www.international.gc.ca/trade-commerce/trade-agreements-accords-commerciaux/agr-acc/ceta-aecg/chronology-chronologie.aspx?lang=eng

# Chapter 8

1.   Vancouver, Douglas & McIntyre, 2004.

2.   Peter Grant, "Does the TPP Protect Canadian Cultural Policy?", *Barry Sookman*, February 7, 2016, retrieved from http://www.barrysookman.com/2016/02/07/does-the-tpp-protect-canadian-cultural-policy/

3.   Alexandre Maltais, *The TPP and Cultural Diversity* (Ottawa: Canadian Centre for Policy Alternatives, 2016), retrieved from https://www.policyalternatives.ca/publications/reports/tpp-and-cultural-diversity

4.   ACTRA Submission on TPP to the Standing Committee on International Trade, January 2017, retrieved from http://www.actra.ca/advocacy/federal-government/

5.   House of Commons Standing Committee on International Trade (CIIT) Report on TPP, retrieved from http://www.ourcommons.ca/DocumentViewer/en/42-1/CIIT/report-6/page-60#14

6.   Andy Blatchford, "Trans-Pacific Partnership Inches Closer to Reality after Vietnam Talks," *Maclean's*, November 10, 2017, retrieved from https://www.macleans.ca/news/trans-pacific-partnership-inches-closer-to-reality-after-vietnam-talks/

7.   Canada, *Comprehensive and Progressive Agreement for Trans-Pacific Partnership (CPTPP) — Backgrounder*, retrieved from http://international.gc.ca/trade-commerce/trade-agreements-accords-commerciaux/agr-acc/cptpp-ptpgp/backgrounder-document_information.aspx?lang=eng

# Chapter 9

1.  Motion Picture Association of America, *MPAA Comments to the USTR on NAFTA Modernization*, June 2017, retrieved from https://www.mpaa.org/policy-statement/mpaa-comments-to-the-ustr-on-nafta-modernization/

2.  David Oxenford, "FCC Approves For the First Time 100% Foreign Ownership of US Broadcast Stations," *Broadcast Law Blog*, February 24, 2017, retrieved from https://www.broadcastlawblog.com/2017/02/articles/fcc-approves-for-the-first-time-100-foreign-ownership-of-us-broadcast-stations/

3.  Coalition of Services Industries, *Submission to the USTR on the Modernization of NAFTA*, June 2017, retrieved from https://servicescoalition.org/resources/

4.  "Wilbur Ross Says TPP Could Form 'Starting Point' for U.S. on Revamped NAFTA Talks," Bloomberg News in *National Post*, May 3, 2017, retrieved from http://business.financialpost.com/news/economy/wilbur-ross-says-1-could-form-starting-point-for-u-s-on-revamped-nafta-talks/wcm/3a904185-fa8f-4159-b666-4f0659af5076

# Chapter 10

1.  "History of the Internet," *Wikipedia*, subheading "World Wide Web and Introduction of Browsers," last updated February 7, 2019, retrieved from: https://en.wikipedia.org/wiki/History_of_the_Internet

2.  Garry Neil, *Full Analytic Report (2015) on the Implementation of the UNESCO 1980 Recommendation Concerning the Status of the Artist*, retrieved from http://en.unesco.org/creativity/sites/creativity/files/analytic-report_g-neil_sept2015.pdf

3.  Julianne Schultz, "Australia Must Act Now to Preserve Its Culture in the Face of Global Tech Giants," *The Conversation*, May 2, 2016, retrieved from http://theconversation.com/australia-must-act-now-to-preserve-its-culture-in-the-face-of-global-tech-giants-58724

4.  Neil, *Full Analytic Report*.

5.  David Throsby and Katya Petetskaya, *Making Art Work: An Economic Study of Professional Artists in Australia* (Sydney, Australia: Macquarie University, 2017), retrieved from http://www.australiacouncil.gov.au/workspace/uploads/files/making-art-work-throsby-report-5a05106d0bb69.pdf

6.  Music Canada, *Statistics*, retrieved from https://musiccanada.com/resources/statistics/

7.  IFPI, *IFPI Global Music Report 2018* (April 2018), retrieved from https://www.ifpi.org/news/IFPI-GLOBAL-MUSIC-REPORT-2018

8.   Music Canada, *Canadian Music Blog*, retrieved from https://musiccanada.wordpress.com/2017/04/26/canada-now-worlds-6th-largest-recorded-music-market/

9.   Music Canada, *The Value Gap: Its Origins, Impacts and a Made-in-Canada Approach*, retrieved from https://musiccanada.com/resources/research/the-value-gap-report/

10.  Ibid., p. 26.

11.  Canadian Radio-television and Telecommunications Commission, *Communications Monitoring Report 2017: Broadcasting Sector Overview*, retrieved from https://crtc.gc.ca/eng/publications/reports/policymonitoring/2017/cmr4.htm

12.  Statistics Canada, "Book Publishing Industry 2016," *The Daily*, March 23, 2018.

13.  *More Canada: Increasing Canadians' Awareness and Reading of Canadian Books*, September 2018, retrieved from http://www.formac.ca/canadianforum/wp-content/uploads/2018/12/More-Canada-Report-Release-date-13-Dec-2018.pdf

14.  Association of Canadian Publishers, *Canadian Ownership*, retrieved from https://publishers.ca/canadian-ownership/

15.  Access Copyright, *Annual Report 2017*, retrieved from http://www.accesscopyright.ca/annualreport2017

16.  Association of Canadian Publishers, *2019 Pre-Budget Submission to the Standing Committee on Finance*, retrieved from https://publishers.ca/government-briefs-and-submissions/

17.  *More Canada*.

18.  Ontario Media Development Corporation, *Magazine Industry Profile*, retrieved from http://www.omdc.on.ca/collaboration/research_and_industry_information/industry_profiles/Magazine_ Industry_Profile.htm

19.  Magazines Canada, *Federal Pre-Budget Submission 2017*, retrieved from https://magazinescanada.ca/pdf/federal-pre-budget-submission-2017/

20.  Canadian Media Producers Association, *Profile 2017*, retrieved from https://cmpa.ca/profile/

21.  Dominic Patten, "Great White North, Action: Canada Tops Feature Film Location for 1st Time, Says FilmLA," *Deadline Hollywood*, August 2018, retrieved from https://deadline.com/2018/08/hollywood-production-2017-canada-top-movie-location-first-time-1202442606/

22.  Dawn Chmielewski and Dade Hayes, "Media Companies Could Reap Billions from Tax Overhaul," *Deadline Hollywood*, December 2017, retrieved from http://deadline.com/2017/12/tax-overhaul-hollywood-windfall-1202230059/

23.  Cam Cullen, *Sandvine Releases 2018 Global Internet Phenomena Report*, Sandvine press release, October 2, 2018, retrieved from https://www.sandvine.com/press-releases/

sandvine-releases-2018-global-Internet-phenomena-report

24. Joe Otterson, "487 Scripted Series Aired in 2017, FX Chief John Landgraf Says," *Variety*, January 5, 2018, retrieved from variety.com/2018/tv/news/2017-scripted-tv-series-fx-john-landgraf-1202653856/

25. Maureen Ryan and Cynthia Littleton, "TV Series Budgets Hit the Breaking Point as Costs Skyrocket in Peak TV Era," *Variety*, September 26, 2017, retrieved from https://variety.com/2017/tv/news/tv-series-budgets-costs-rising-peak-tv-1202570158/

26. *Variety*, December 13, 2018

27. Canadian Radio-television and Telecommunications Commission, *Exemption Order for New Media Broadcasting Undertakings*, December 17, 1999, retrieved from https://crtc.gc.ca/eng/archive/1999/pb99-197.htm

28. Minister of Canadian Heritage and Official Languages, Jean-Pierre Blais Mandate Letter, June 18, 2012, retrieved from https://www.slideshare.net/friendscb/jeanpierre-blais-mandate-letter-from-james-moore

29. IAB Canada, IAB Canada 2016 Actual +2017 Estimated Canadian Internet Advertising Revenue Survey, June 29, 2017, retrieved from http://iabcanada.com/content/uploads/2017/07/IABCanadaRevenueSurveyFinal2017.pdf

30. Canadian Radio-television and Telecommunications Commission, Communications Monitoring Report 2017, retrieved from Communications Monitoring Report 2017

31. Corus Report on First Quarter 2018, retrieved from https://www.corusent.com/

32. BCE Report on Third Quarter 2017, retrieved from www.bce.ca/investors/

33. Rogers Communications Report on Third Quarter 2017, retrieved from Rogers Communications Reports Third Quarter 2017 Results

34. Federal Budget 2017, retrieved from https://www.budget.gc.ca/2017/docs/download-telecharger/index-en.html, p. 108.

35. Canadian Heritage, Ian Scott Mandate Letter, September 28, 2017, retrieved from https://www.canada.ca/en/canadian-heritage/news/2017/09/new_crtc_chair_sleadershipwillhelpshapethefutureofcanadascommuni.html

36. Canadian Heritage, *Government Launches Review of Broadcasting-Telecommunications Acts*, press release, June 5, 2018, retrieved from https://www.canada.ca/en/canadian-heritage/news/2018/06/government-of-canada-launches-review-of-telecommunications-and-broadcasting-acts.html

37. CMPA, *Profile 2017*, p. 21.

38. Lucinda Shen, "Here Are the Fortune 500's 10 Most Valuable Companies," *Fortune*,

May, 21, 2018, retrieved from http://fortune.com/2018/05/21/fortune-500-most-valuable-companies-2018/

## Chapter 11

1. Statistics Canada, *Government Expenditures on Culture: Data Tables 2009/2010*, retrieved from https://www150.statcan.gc.ca/n1/pub/87f0001x/2012001/part-partie1-eng.htm

## Chapter 12

1. World Trade Organization, *The Doha Mandate on Multilateral Environmental Agreements*, 2018, retrieved from https://www.wto.org/english/tratop_e/envir_e/envir_neg_mea_e.htm

2. Blue Ant Media information, retrieved from https://blueantmedia.com/content/production-houses/

3. Scott Roxborough, "In China, Western TV Production Go Co-Production Route," *Hollywood Reporter*, October 18, 2018, retrieved from https://www.hollywoodreporter.com/news/china-western-tv-companies-go-production-route-1152752

4. Patrick Frater, "U.S. and China Struggle over Film Quotas," *Variety*, February 9, 2017. retrieved from https://variety.com/2017/biz/asia/u-s-and-china-struggle-over-film-quotas-1201979720/

5. Etan Vlessing, "Chinese Attempts to Curb Capital Spending Abroad," *Hollywood Reporter*, February 13, 2017.

6. Shannon Liao, "The Fan Bingbing Saga Shows China's Willingness to Control Overly Wealthy Celebrities," *The Verge*, October 23, 2018, retrieved from https://www.theverge.com/2018/10/23/17991988/fan-bingbing-disappearance-reappearance-china-tax-evasion-social-media

7. Pei Li and Michael Martina, "Hollywood's China Dreams Get Tangled in Trade Talks," Reuters, May 20, 2018, retrieved from https://www.reuters.com/article/usa-trade-china-movies/rpt-hollywoods-china-dreams-get-tangled-in-trade-talks-idUSL3N1SR05P

# Index

MARQUIS

Québec, Canada